THE HASIDEANS AND THE ORIGIN OF PHARISAISM

SOCIETY OF BIBLICAL LITERATURE
SEPTUAGINT AND COGNATE STUDIES SERIES

Edited by
Claude E. Cox

Number 24

THE HASIDEANS AND THE ORIGIN OF PHARISAISM
A Study in 1 and 2 Maccabees

John Kampen

THE HASIDEANS AND THE ORIGIN OF PHARISAISM
A Study in 1 and 2 Maccabees

John Kampen

Scholars Press
Atlanta, Georgia

THE HASIDEANS AND THE ORIGIN OF PHARISAISM
A Study in 1 and 2 Maccabees

John Kampen

Library of Congress Cataloging-in-Publication Data

Kampen, John.
The Hasideans and the origin of Pharisaism.

(Septuagint and cognate studies ; no. 24)
Originally presented as the author's thesis (doctoral--Hebrew Union College-Jewish Institute of Religion).
Bibliography: p.
1. Hasideans. 2. Pharisees. 3. Bible. O.T. Apocrypha. Maccabees, 1st--Criticism, interpretation, etc. 4. Bible. O.T. Apocrypha. Maccabees, 2nd--Criticism, interpretation, etc. I. Title. II. Series: Septuagint and cognate studies series ; no. 24.
BM175.H36K36 1989 296.8'12 88-31120
ISBN 1-55540-284-4
ISBN 1-55540-285-2 (pbk.)

Printed in the United States of America
on acid-free paper

TABLE OF CONTENTS

ACKNOWLEDGMENTS

This monograph began as a doctoral dissertation written for presentation to the faculty of Hebrew Union College-Jewish Institute of Religion. I cannot separate those who contributed to this study from the members of that body who made my years there so significant and worthwhile. There are a few individuals who merit special mention. Samuel Sandmel of blessed memory initiated me into the study of Jewish literature. He and his wife Frances also welcomed me and my wife into their home and lives. It was a rare privilege to conclude my studies at Hebrew Union as the recipient of a fellowship named in his honor. The second reader of the original dissertation, Michael Cook provided valuable advice and comments on this project, as he had throughout my years of study. His friendship was a continual source of encouragement. Ellis Rivkin gave assistance and support unsparingly and freely.

For a number of years I had the rare privilege of learning the meaning of study from Ben Zion Wacholder, my major advisor at Hebrew Union College. He and his wife Touby accepted me into their home and family. The hours spent in his study were lessons in the love, the joy, the commitment and the integrity which are the mark of a true scholar. I can only hope that this work reflects a little of his daring and insight.

This study was possible only because of generous financial support from a number of sources. Hebrew Union College provided the Dr. Samuel Sandmel Fellowship, the Julius and Hildegard Lewy Fellowship as well as the S. H. and Helen R. Scheuer Foundation Fellowship. I am indebted to the Social Sciences and Humanities Research Council of Canada for a doctoral fellowship during the 1981-82 academic year.

I am most grateful to William Adler, the editor of the series in which this volume appears, for accepting this manuscript for publication. He was most helpful throughout the process. The comments of the readers appointed by him were also appreciated. I am deeply indebted to James A. Vanderkam, who took the time to read the original dissertation and suggested its publication. The assistance of a knowledgable and courteous library staff is necessary for all research. I was fortunate to find such persons both at Hebrew Union College and United Theological Seminary.

The completion of this work was accomplished while teaching at Payne Theological Seminary. I thank former President U. A. Hughey for his appreciation of the important role of scholarship in seminary education. I am deeply grateful to former Dean Paul A. Griffin for his recognition of the time and commitment which study requires.

Of course, none of the persons listed above should be held responsible for the material which appears in the following pages.

The material presented in Chapter 4 of this work has already appeared in *HUCA* 57 (1986) 61-81. I thank its gracious editor Sheldon H. Blank for permission to use it in this publication.

It was my wife Ann who provided the encouragement which was necessary for engaging in this task. Her recognition of the commitment which was necessary to complete this study is a true example of selflessness. I will continue to try to find ways to thank her.

PREFACE

The editions of texts utilized in this study are cited in the notes where relevant. For both abbreviations and transliteration, I have generally followed the guidelines published by the Society of Biblical Literature in their "Instructions for Contributors," which appears in the *Member's Handbook* (1980), pp. 83-97. For Hebrew and Aramaic transliteration I have, with the following exceptions, followed the consonantal system: א is represented by ’, ע by ‘ and ש by *sh.* I do not think the reader should have difficulty following the manner in which the vowels are treated in the text of this work.

In addition to those abbreviations referred to in the "Instructions for Contributors," the reader will find the following list helpful:

ANRW	*Aufstieg und Niedergang der Römischen Welt: Geschichte und Kultur Roms im Spiegel der neueren Forschung*. Eds. H. Temporini and W. Haase. Berlin/New York: Walter de Gruyter, 1972-
BHWJ	*Bericht der Hochschule für die Wissenschaft des Judenthums*
BJS	Brown Judaic Studies
CRINT	*Compendium Rerum Iudaicarum ad Novum Testamentum.* Assen: Van Gorcum/Philadelphia: Fortress, 1974-
CSCT	Columbia Studies in the Classical Tradition

EJ	*Encyclopaedia Judaica*
Even-Shoshan	*A New Concordance of the Bible.* Ed. A. Even-Shoshan. 4 vols. Hebrew. Jerusalem: Kiryat Sepher, 1980
IvE	*Die Inschriften von Ephesos.* Eds. H. Wankel, H. Engelmann, D. Knibbe, R. Merkelbach et al. Vols. 1-7b. Bonn: Rudolf Habelt Verlag GMBH, 1979-81
JE	*Jewish Encyclopedia*
JPS	Jewish Publication Society
JTS	Jewish Theological Seminary
JZWL	*Jüdische Zeitschrift für Wissenschaft und Leben*
KHAT	Kurzer Hand-Commentar zum Alten Testament
OTM	Old Testament Message
REG	*Revue des etudes grecques*
Schürer-Vermes-Millar	Emil Schürer, *The History of the Jewish People in the Age of Jesus Christ.* Eds. G. Vermes, F. Millar et al. (see bibliography)
S.E.	Seleucid Era
SEG	*Supplementum Epigraphicum Graecum*
SIG	W. Dittenberger, *Sylloge Inscriptionum Graecum.* Hildesheim: Georg Olms, 1960; orig., 1915.
TCAAS	*Transactions of the Connecticut Academy of Arts and Sciences*
UCPH	University of California Publications in History
ZRIG	*Zeitschrift für die religiosen Interessen des Judenthums*

I

THE HASIDEANS IN MODERN STUDY

The history of scholarship concerning the Hasideans of the second century B.C.E. is a fitting illustration of the old adage repeated by historians that the fewer the references, the greater the number of books and articles. In the title of this study I employ the term "Hasidean," an English derivative of the Greek *Asidaioi*, which appears in Graeco-Jewish literature only in 1 Macc. 2:42 and 7:12, and in 2 Macc. 14:6. It is usually considered to be a transliteration of the Hebrew *Ḥasydym*, a noun often translated as "pious" which appears in both the singular and plural in the Hebrew Scriptures and is employed as a proper name for certain individuals and groups in Jewish history.

Prior to a detailed analysis of the references and possible allusions to the Hasideans in antiquity, we must examine the various proposals advanced in the modern era to locate this enigmatic group within the diverse streams that flowed through Judaism during the Second Temple period. I begin by looking at treatments of the term in the biblical materials.

The 'Pious' in the Psalms

One of the contentious issues in the history of the study of the Maccabean references is the biblical references to the *Ḥasydym*. The word *ḥasyd* appears thirty-two times in the Hebrew Scriptures[1] and is apparently a derivative of the much more common *ḥesed*, a word which has received a good deal of study in this century. Since the majority of the *ḥesed* references appear in the Psalms, a major question has been the relationship of the Maccabean citations to those Psalms in which these references occur, especially Ps. 79:2-3 which is cited in 1 Macc. 7:17 and Ps. 149:1 which speaks of a *qehal ḥasydym* (assembly of the pious). Some earlier modern scholars such as Duhm argued from these and other references that these Psalms were composed in Maccabean times.[2] While Schloessinger does not hazard a date for Ps. 149, he does connect the *synagōgē Asidaiōn* (company of Hasideans) with the *qehal ḥasydym.*[3] In his study of Jewish-Palestinian piety, A. Büchler accepts Gesenius's identification of the *synagōgē Asidaiōn* with some of the Psalms.[4] However, frequently an

1. *Even-Shoshan*, 2:722-23.

2. D. B. Duhm, *Die Psalmen*, KHAT 14 (Freiburg: J. C. B. Mohr, 1899), 206, 301. Note, however, that he thinks the Psalter was not closed until around 70 C.E. (see pp. XX-XXIII). A discussion of this question is to be found in H.-J. Kraus, *Psalmen*, BKAT 15:2 (Neukirchen: Neukirchener Verlag, 1960), 2:966-67.

3. *JE* 6:251.

4. A. Büchler, *Types of Jewish-Palestinian Piety from 70 B.C.E. To 70 C.E.: The Ancient Pious Men* (London: Jews' College, 1922), 7-8.

analysis of the *ḥasyd* references has been merely a byproduct of studies of the term *ḥesed.*

The groundbreaking work of Nelson Glueck is the first study of *ḥesed* which must receive mention.[5] In his work, Glueck notes that the context for understanding the meaning of *ḥesed* in the Hebrew Scriptures was that of relationship. Thus in his description of its 'secular meaning', he provides a long list of relationships in which the word is found and concludes that it refers to "conduct corresponding to a mutual relationship of rights and duties."[6] Then only the participants in "a mutual relationship of rights and duties can receive or show *ḥesed.*" Thus "*ḥesed* constitutes the essence of a covenant" and its component parts include "reciprocity, mutual assistance, sincerity, friendliness, brotherliness, duty, loyalty and love."[7] To define the religious meaning of the term, Glueck turns primarily to the prophetic literature. Here he finds that "*Ḥesed* is the reciprocal conduct of men toward one another and, at the same time, explicitly and implicitly, the proper relationship toward God."[8] It "fulfills the demands of loyalty, justice, righteousness, and honesty."[9] While it is closely related

5. N. Glueck, *Ḥesed in the Bible*, trans. A. Gottschalk (Cincinnati: Hebrew Union College, 1967); originally published as *Das Wort Ḥesed im alttestamentlichen Sprachgebrauche als menschliche und göttliche gemeinschaftgemässe Verhaltungsweise* (Giessen: Alfred Töpelmann, 1927). References in this work are to the English ed.

6. Ibid., 54.

7. Ibid., 55.

8. Ibid., 69.

9. Ibid.

to the concept of mercy, *ḥesed* is distinguished from it in that *ḥesed* is obligatory. The theological import of this view is that *ḥesed* is found in the covenantal relationship of the followers of Yahweh and their god.[10] The documentation of the covenantal context in which the term is to be understood is Glueck's magnificent contribution. However, when we look in his work for what this means for the subject of this study, we find very little discussion of *ḥasyd* and what we do find is misleading. Glueck discusses the term in his chapter on the religious meaning which, as just pointed out, is largely based on the prophetic materials. The *ḥasyd* is the one who practices *ḥesed*, which is "determined by the divinely-based ethical commandments which are the laws of human society."[11] Glueck's rooting of the *ḥesed* concept in the prophetic materials at this point gives it an ethical definition. However, as has been pointed out by Tsevat, Sakenfeld and others, *ḥasyd* is used almost exclusively in the Psalms.[12] This means more attention must be devoted to those references than Glueck saw fit, even though we must remember that a study of *ḥasyd* was not his central purpose. Clearly his major contribution was the demonstration of the integral relationship between *ḥesed* and *beryt* (covenant).

10. Ibid., 102.

11. Ibid., 69.

12. M. Tsevat, *A Study of the Language of the Biblical Psalms*, JBLMS 9 (Philadelphia: SBL, 1955), 17, 91, n. 106; L. Gulkowitsch, *Die Entwicklung des Begriffes Ḥāsîd im Alten Testament*, ACUT B XXXII.4 (Tartu: K. Mattiesen, 1934), 11; K. D. Sakenfeld, *The Meaning of Hesed in the Hebrew Bible: A New Inquiry*, HSM 17 (Missoula: Scholars Press, 1978), 241-42. Note that Sakenfeld is incorrect in finding the term in the Psalms twenty six times. This sum is most likely based on the Mandelkern concordance in which Ps. 16:10 is listed twice.

More directly related to the subject of this study is the first of two monographs on *ḥasyd* by L. Gulkowitsch.[13] He finds three stages in the development of this concept in biblical materials. He finds hints of an earlier secular usage with reference to treaties and contracts, reminiscent of Glueck's analysis, but its major use in the earlier strata of biblical texts is the more limited application to the sacral sphere, indicated by the phrase *ḥasydey WYHWH*. Once the term becomes confined to use in the sacral field, *WYHWH* is understood and no longer needs to be included in the text. What is important for our study is that Gulkowitsch understands the term in its earliest sacral usage to refer to a defined, concrete community, i.e., the cultic community in the temple which included both priestly and lay elements.[14] The usage of this term gradually changed as it became more individualized and took on an ethical religious meaning.[15] In other words, it referred to a specific community, Israel as a whole, in an earlier stage and then took on a more general orientation in later texts. This means that the term had lost any specific sociological designation by the time that the references in 1 and 2 Maccabees were encountered. For Gulkowitsch, *ḥasydym* is not a special name for a party but an archaizing and sacral designation for the army that considers itself to be fighting for the things of Yahweh; thus it appears only in contexts where it could refer to the entire people.[16] The contrast between this study and the

13. Gulkowitsch, *Entwicklung*, especially 18-38.

14. Ibid., 18-21.

15. Ibid., 22-28.

16. Ibid., 28.

many others which see a development towards a specific group of persons must be noted.

Following the work of Glueck, Bowen in his Yale dissertation spent more time on the term *ḥasyd.*[17] He found that both Glueck and Gulkowitsch depended too heavily on the contractual nature of these terms for their definition. Significant was his response to earlier scholars who had attempted to derive a definition of *ḥasyd* from its apparently antecedent passive form: the choice of restricting *ḥasyd* to either one who receives God's grace or to one who is distinguished by his own righteousness is to create a false alternative.[18] He noted that in the Psalms, where these terms appear more frequently than in any other biblical books, *ḥesed* is used almost exclusively for Yahweh and *ḥasyd* for humans; thus the latter term is preferred in the area of social relationships and is used to designate "men of ethical and religious integrity."[19] Significant was his claim that, when *ḥesed* appeared in the work of the Chronicler, a post-exilic composition, the term lost some of its religious-ethical conception and became identified with zealous activity on behalf of the cult.[20] This meant that when he discussed *ḥasyd* he found examples of the *ḥasyd* as a man of prayer and fidelity to Yahweh,[21] in addition to those cases where it referred to a person distinguished by personal, ethical and religious attain-

17. B. A. Bowen, "A Study of *Ḥesed*," Dissertation, Yale, 1938.

18. Ibid., 389.

19. Ibid., 404-405.

20. Ibid., 182-91; e.g., Neh. 13:14; 2 Chr. 32:32; 35:26.

21. Bowen, "Study," 397; e.g., Pss. 4:4; 16:10; 32:6.

ments. He did, however, in his zeal to deny Gulkowitsch's identification of this group as a cultic community, overlook some of his own arguments for ascribing to the *ḥasyd* some cultic significance, e.g., those in Psalm 79 who he says defend the temple and Jerusalem through patriotism and religious zeal.[22] For Bowen, *Ḥasydym* in the Bible were considerably different from the *Asidaioi* in 1 and 2 Maccabees. The former were all of the sons of Israel or men of either ethical integrity or religious zeal while the latter were zealots for the law.[23] In the time of the Maccabees, these warriors simply appropriated the older term and gave it a new meaning.

A similar argument is to be found a number of years later in an article by J. Coppens.[24] In his attempt to provide a chronological arrangement for those Psalms which contain the word *ḥasyd*, he concludes that this term does not refer in the biblical materials to a special category of citizens, to a particular social class or to a distinct profession.[25] In the time of the Maccabees, this biblical term caught the attention of the faithful and was adopted by them, since it had become the expression of a particular religious ideal.[26]

A closer connection among these references is hypothesized by Oesterley. In his commentary on the Psalms, he notes

22. Bowen, "Study," 398.

23. Ibid., 408.

24. J. Coppens, "Les Psaumes des Hasidim," *Mélanges bibliques rédigés en l'honneur de André Robert*, Travaux de l'Institut Catholique de Paris 4 (Paris: Bloud & Gay, 1955), 214-24.

25. Ibid., 220-23.

26. Ibid., 223-24.

that one of the distinguishing marks of the Psalter is the antagonism between the righteous and their enemies.[27] While some of the biblical references to the *ḥasydym* are used in a very general sense, i.e., they could refer to anyone in Israel, it is more common to find them employed in the more restricted sense implied in the phrase *ḥasydaw* (his pious), where the possessive pronoun indicates they are distinguished from the generality of their fellows. These passages which are not confined to the Psalms suggest a body or party which stands apart not only from their enemies but also from the remainder of Israel. Having also found a specific body of opponents of the *ḥasydym* in the Psalms, usually called the *resha'ym*, Oesterley proceeds to find evidence of the antagonism in the preexilic as well as the exilic and postexilic periods.[28] This rift becomes intensified during the Greek period. These Psalms then are accepted as evidence of religious and political feuds within Israel from preexilic times until well into the Greek period. However, he rightly challenges the hypothesis of any Maccabean Psalms,[29] thus the *Asidaioi* of 1 and 2 Maccabees are seen as late representatives of the same group of persons. They eventually become the Pharisees and the *resha'ym* the Sadducees. The identification of this antagonistic relationship as basic to any understanding of the *ḥasydym* in the Psalms becomes the springboard for a number of other studies.

Accepting Oesterley's arguments against dating any of the Psalms to the Maccabean era, B. D. Eerdmans suggests the

[27]. W. O. E. Oesterley, *The Psalms: Translated with Text-Critical and Exegetical Notes* (London: SPCK, 1939), 57-60.

[28]. Ibid., 60-66.

[29]. Ibid., 67-73. He does permit the possibility of some Maccabean additions.

Psalms which describe the *ḥasydym* are even earlier.[30] Specially chosen by Yahweh (he uses the term 'Jahu'), they are his vigorous defenders in the preexilic era. Eerdmans concludes that they, being neither prophets nor priests, were laymen deemed essential to Judaism who acted as the bodyguard of Yahweh. He cites the Mishnah and 1 and 2 Maccabees as evidence that this group continued to exist.[31] Thus for Eerdmans, the *ḥasydym* as a party survived from the preexilic period until the time of the Maccabees, and even afterwards in "their equals, the Zelotes."[32] While appearing much later, Morgenstern's article reflects an approach and reaches conclusions similar to those of Oesterley and Eerdmans, even though he makes no mention of them in his notes.[33] Taking Ps. 149:1 as a reference to all of Israel, he observes that *ḥasydym* comes to mean a portion of Israel only when it appears in conjunction with the term *resha'ym* and these texts can only be dated after 485 B.C.E.[34] They represent the poor and oppressed who consider Yahweh to be their national God and their only source of salvation. Thus the Hasidim become a defined entity within Israel only in the early postexilic period and there is no

[30]. B. D. Eerdmans, "The Chasidim," *Oudtestamentische Studien* 1 (1942) 176-257, passim (note pp. 201-205 on Maccabean dating).

[31]. Ibid., 205-207.

[32]. Ibid., 206.

[33]. J. Morgenstern, "The Hasidim-Who Were They?" *HUCA* 38 (1967) 59-73.

[34]. Ibid., 63-64.

evidence that they ever developed into a specific religious sect in the biblical era.[35]

Continuing studies based on Glueck's work contribute very little to our understanding of the term *ḥasyd* and its significance in the Hebrew Scriptures. For Stoebe, a study of *ḥasyd* adds very little to an understanding of *ḥesed*.[36] He takes issue with Glueck's emphasis on the covenantal basis of the term and suggests that it rather means good-hearted sentiment or kindness, similar to *raḥamym* (mercy).[37] *Ḥasyd* is only to be understood in the active sense of one who practices *ḥesed*, i.e., God in Jer. 3:12 and Ps. 145:17.[38] Otherwise it is used in the passive sense to refer to human beings to whom God has shown *ḥesed* and has thereby pulled them into his community. This one whom God has favored is also the active pious one. While Jacobs recognizes that in some passages the covenantal basis of *ḥesed* is not evident and that the use of *beryt* (covenant) in conjunction with the term is replaced by *ḥen* (grace) and *raḥamym* he insists, contrary to Stoebe, that Glueck's initial viewpoint should not be abandoned.[39] Arguing in a similar vein to Glueck and stressing the intimate relationship of *ḥesed* and

[35]. Ibid., 72-73.

[36]. H. J. Stoebe, "Die Bedeutung des Wortes *Häsäd* im Alten Testament," *VT* 2 (1952) 254.

[37]. Ibid., 247-48.

[38]. His reference on p. 254, n. 1 is to Jer. 52:12 (written lii:12), evidently intending to write 3:12 (i.e., iii:12).

[39]. E. Jacob, *Theology of the Old Testament*, trans. A. W. Heathcote and P. J. Alcock (New York: Harper and Row, 1958), 103-107.

beryt, Johnson argued that the best translation of *ḥesed* was 'devotion'; thus *ḥasyd* would mean "one who is devoted or devotee."[40] The term is used almost exclusively to designate the Israelite relationship with Yahweh and vice versa. For Johnson, this close connection with *beryt* is particularly evident in those passages where *ḥasyd* is contrasted with *resha'*.[41] These studies are primarily aimed at evaluating the theological significance of the term and as such add little to our evaluation of the relationship of this term to the group which appears in 1 and 2 Maccabees.[42]

In his more popular theological study, Sorg develops his notion of *ḥasyd* from a hypothesis that the *ḥasydym* and their opponents represented opposing religious and political views within the Jewish community, a perspective for which he seems to be indebted to W. O. E. Oesterley.[43] He emphasizes the differences between the *ḥasydym* whom he calls saints and the *resha'ym* whom he calls sinners.[44] The saints enjoy the

40. A. R. Johnson, "Ḥesed and Ḥasîd," *Interpretationes ad Vetus Testamentum Pertinentes Sigmundo Mowinckel* (Oslo: Forlaget Land Og Kirke, 1955), 108.

41. Ibid., 109. On *ḥasyd* and *rasha'*, Johnson lists 1 Sam. 2:9; Pss. 43:1; 97:10.

42. The recent study by C. F. Whitley, "The Semantic Range of *Ḥesed*," *Bib* 62 (1981) 519-26, does not even mention the question. Other studies on *ḥesed* include: R. Bultmann, "*Eleos*," *TDNT* 2:479-82; W. Zimmerli, "*Charis*," *TDNT* 9:381-87; H. Conzelmann, "*Charis*," *TDNT* 9:387-91.

43. D. R. Sorg, *Hesed and Hasid in the Psalms* (St. Louis: Pio Decimo Press, 1953), 29.

44. Ibid., 23-31.

knowledge of and confidence in God's *ḥesed*. The sinners deny God. The saints are the humble, the downtrodden and the poor who rely on God's *ḥesed*, while the sinners are identified with the proud, the rich and the powerful. Characterized by absolute purity and separatism, the ideology and form of government of the saints is theocratic; they are interested in the direct rule of God. Thus we do find in Sorg a theological articulation of the conflicts which Oesterley identified in the Psalms. In his discussion of the *ḥasydym*, Marvin Pope begins by discussing the biblical use of *ḥesed*.[45] Since he also accepts Ps. 149:1 and some other references as being a collective designation for Israel, he sees a stage where belonging to the chosen people merited the name *ḥasyd*; however the term gradually came to have moral and ethical implications, such as in Pss. 37:28-29 and 97:10-11 where it is paraleled by *ṣaddyqym* (righteous) and contrasted with the *resha'ym*. Pope makes no attempt to link these references with the Maccabean era. Other scholars make a more direct link between the Psalms and the group from the Maccabean era.

In his commentary on Maccabees, Abel accepts evidence from the Psalms as applicable to these Maccabean references,[46] a stance which is explained in greater detail in the introduction to the third edition written in conjunction with Jean Starcky.[47] Robert Pfeiffer, who thinks that the author of the book of Daniel was probably a leader of the *ḥasydym*, finds

45. M. H. Pope, "Hasidim," *IDB* 2:528-29.

46. F.-M. Abel, *Les Livres des Maccabées* (Paris: J. Gabalda, 1949), 43.

47. F.-M. Abel and J. Starcky, *Les Livres des Maccabées*, 3rd rev. ed. (Paris: Les Editions du Cerf, 1961), 56.

a reference to the martyrdom of the Hasideans in Ps. 79:2[48] and considers the theology of the book of Daniel to be the same as that of those Psalms which he considers to be Hasidic, dating from the same period.[49] More circumspect views of the dating question were to follow.

As already noted, some recent studies have attributed great prominence to the role of the Hasideans in the history of Jewish sectarianism during the Second Temple era; Hengel's work is the most well-known. He suggests that references such as Ps. 149:1 may be used as evidence of the pre-Maccabean existence of groups of the "pious" prior to their formation under Antiochus IV.[50] While Plöger, his predecessor, makes very little mention of the Psalms, he does suggest that the division between the righteous and the godless found in the Psalms and wisdom literature is another witness to the separation within Israel concerning the centrality of an eschatological faith.[51] This eschatological viewpoint, which is represented primarily in certain prophetic writings, later appears among the

48. R. H. Pfeiffer, *History of New Testament Times: With an Introduction to the Apocrypha* (New York: Harper & Brothers, 1949), 53.

49. R. H. Pfeiffer, *Religion in the Old Testament: The History of a Spiritual Triumph*, ed. C. C. Forman (London: Adam & Charles Black, 1961), 219.

50. Martin Hengel, *Judaism and Hellenism: Studies in their Encounter in Palestine during the Early Hellenistic Period*, trans. John Bowden, 2 vols. (Philadelphia: Fortress, 1974), 1:176 and 2:118, n. 464. W. R. Farmer similarly seems to suggest a connection between Ps. 149:1 and the Maccabean references: "Hasideans," *IDB* 2:528.

51. Otto Plöger, *Theocracy and Eschatology*, trans. S. Rudman (Richmond: John Knox, 1968), 64-66.

Hasideans as apocalypticism. Like Hengel, Blenkinsopp also finds evidence in the Psalms of pre-Maccabean Hasidic circles.[52] Earlier Louis Jacobs had already suggested that the *ḥasydym* in the Psalms "may be the group of that name in the time of the Maccabees or they may be a group out of which the latter grew."[53] However, he noted the uncertainty involved in both claims, which arose primarily from the difficulties encountered in the attempts to date accurately the various Psalms. Equal restraint is shown by S. Safrai.[54]

A connection between these Hasidic Psalms and some of those found in the Qumran Psalms Scroll is suggested by both Hengel and Blenkinsopp.[55] Neither scholar, however, suggests that the two works are to be dated to the same time period. The editor of the Psalms Scroll, James A. Sanders, had already indicated that 11QPs[a] 154 may be of "proto-Essenian or Hasidic" origin.[56] It is certainly not clear

52. J. Blenkinsopp, "Interpretation and the Tendency to Sectarianism: An Aspect of Second Temple History," *Jewish and Christian Self-Definition*, ed. E. P. Sanders et al., vol. 2 (Philadelphia: Fortress, 1981), 21 and 308, n. 107.

53. L. Jacobs, "The Concept of *Ḥasid* in the Biblical and Rabbinic Literatures," *JJS* 8 (1957) 145-46.

54. S. Safrai, "Teaching of Pietists in Mishnaic Literature," *JJS* 16 (1965) 15.

55. Ibid., and Hengel, *Judaism and Hellenism*, 1:176-77; 2:118-19, nn. 465-69.

56. James A. Sanders, *The Psalms Scroll of Qumran Cave 11*, DJD 4 (London: Oxford University, 1965), 64-70. Note also David Flusser, "Psalms, Hymns and Prayers," *Jewish Writings of the Second Temple Period: Apocrypha, Pseudepigrapha, Qumran Sectarian Writings, Philo, Josephus*, ed. Michael E. Stone, *CRINT*

that the usage of *ḥasyd* in any of the Qumran Psalms can be considered to be a reference to a party or sect. Having denied the possibility that Ps. 149:1 should be accepted as evidence concerning the Hasideans, John Collins and Philip Davies both dispute the contention that references to the Hasideans are to be found in the Qumran Psalms.[57] They argue that the author(s) of these Psalms merely adopted the term from the biblical exemplar. Prior to the publication of the Psalms Scroll, W. Zimmerli had noted the conspicuous absence of *ḥasyd* from the Qumran Scrolls.[58] This means that the use of the term in the Psalms Scroll is either not significant for identifying the group out of which it arose or its origin is not related to the rest of the Qumran literature. Due to the similarity between the Qumran Psalms and certain biblical compositions of that genre, it seems most plausible that the term, as suggested above, was adopted from its biblical exemplar and was not to be understood as the name of any particular group. While the perspectives of Davies and Collins account for the similarity of the Qumran Psalms to those found in the Hebrew Scriptures, Zimmerli's observation has implications for both the question of the relationship of these Psalms to writings accepted as literary compositions of

2:2 (Assen: Van Gorcum/Philadelphia: Fortress, 1984), 560.

[57].Collins, *The Apocalyptic Vision of the Book of Daniel*, HSM 16 (Missoula: Scholars Press, 1977), 202; id., *The Apocalyptic Imagination: An Introduction to the Jewish Matrix of Christianity* (New York: Crossroad, 1984), 62; Philip Davies, "Ḥasidim in the Maccabean Period," *JJS* 28 (1977) 131-32.

[58]. W. Zimmerli, "*Ḥesed* im Schrifttum vom Qumran," *Hommages a André Dupont-Sommer*, ed. A. Caquot and M. Philonenko (Paris: Librairie d'Amerique et d'Orient Adrien-Maissoneuve, 1971), 446.

the Qumran community and the problem of the origin of the Essenes, a matter to be addressed later in this study.

In the opinion of this writer the best summary of the biblical evidence on the use of *ḥasyd* is found in an appendix to Sakenfeld's monograph on *ḥesed*.[59] Rejecting Morgenstern's argument that the word evolved only shortly before the exile, she argues that it became fixed relatively early as a technical religious term restricted in its usage. Central for our study is her identification of three different "groups" of persons to whom this term is applied in its plural form: (a) All Israel, the entire people; (b) the faithful and/or upright, a particular group loyal to Yahweh who expressed this loyalty in its social behavior; (c) priests. She then hypothesizes "that the general application of *ḥasid* to all of God's people in covenant existed alongside of a use for special religious functionaries which only occasionally came into the foreground."[60] This term, which includes an emphasis on obedience to Yahweh and the covenant, becomes very applicable for those who, facing persecution under the Seleucids, resolve to remain loyal. Note, however, that Sakenfeld assumes the use of this term in the Maccabean era is chronologically distinct from its use in the biblical Psalms. The term in the Psalms is utilized by people in a later time period, the Maccabean era, because they think it describes their situation and their religious aspirations. The people called *ḥasydym* in the Psalms are not part of the same group that existed in Maccabean times. This seems to be the only reasonable conclusion. The use of the term in biblical materials concerns a different era from that of the Maccabees. In the biblical materials it is also not to be understood as a proper noun, a subject to be discussed in the second chapter

[59]. Sakenfeld, *Meaning of Hesed*, 241-45.

[60]. Ibid., 244-45.

of this work. Scholars have not sought, however, for the predecessors of the Hasideans only in the Psalms.

Connections with the Scribes

One of the seemingly obvious places to search for connections to the *Asidaioi* who are described in 1 Macc. 2:42 as being devoted to the law is among those people called the *soprym* (scribes). In the modern period, Frankel already thought that the two groups were identical, with "scribes" being an earlier pre-Maccabean name for this group, based on the evidence from 1 Maccabees 7.[61] Kaufmann Kohler seems to have followed his lead when producing his own view of exilic and postexilic history. For him, the Hasidim played a major role in the exilic and postexilic development of liturgy and prayer.[62] Throughout this period both the lay Hasidim and the professional *Soprym* are involved in the devotional assemblies. These two groups, under the persecution of the Seleucid rule, combine to form the Hasideans.[63] For Tcherikover, the Hasideans and the scribes are identical in the time of the Maccabees.[64] He considered it most likely that they originated in the time of, or at least go back to, Simon the Just, who himself apparently belonged to the Hasidim and who made the oral law of the

61. Z. Frankel, "Die Essäer nach Talmudischen Quellen," *MGWJ* 2 (1853) 32, 61.

62. K. Kohler, *The Origins of the Synagogue and the Church* (New York: MacMillan, 1929), 29-107.

63. Ibid., 28.

64. Victor Tcherikover, *Hellenistic Civilization and the Jews*, trans. S. Applebaum (Philadelphia: JPS, 1959), 229.

scribes "the official authoritative interpretation of the Mosaic Law."[65] Rendered purposeless by the abolition of the ancestral laws accomplished by Jason, this is the group which goes to the desert to form the first movement of national resistance.[66] After the rebellion is underway, the Hasmoneans come along and provide the leadership for the revolt.[67] While the Hasideans certainly fostered the religious zeal of the resistors,[68] Tcherikover rejects any distinction which maintains that the Hasideans were interested only in religious matters while Judah Maccabee was interested in both religious and national matters.[69] The issue for the Hasideans in 1 Maccabees 7 was rather whether Alcimus would accept them as the legitimate interpreters of the law. Tcherikover thinks they are returned to their position when Judah restores the Torah to its place in Jewish society.[70]

It is to Finkelstein that Tcherikover points when he argues for the pre-Maccabean existence of the Hasideans. Finkelstein finds the origin of this group, which he calls the *Keneset Haḥasydym* (Assembly of the Hasidim), in the activities of

[65]. Ibid., 125.

[66]. Ibid., 197-98.

[67]. Ibid., 204.

[68]. Ibid., 223.

[69]. Ibid., 229.

[70]. Ibid., 220.

Ezra.[71] This group grows out of the body of professional *soprym*, those persons who did the reading and writing. References in later postexilic literature point back to the original group from which the Hasidean movement sprang.[72] Its charter is partially reproduced in Nehemiah 9-10.[73] Its court was called *Hakkeneset Haggedolah* (the Great Assembly) and functioned as a voluntary court among its adherents, in contrast to the court of the high priest called the *Beyt Din* (House of Judgment).[74] This group was motivated by a desire to spread knowledge and study of the Torah among the people, thereby not permitting it to be limited to the Temple authorities.[75] This view is based on his theory that the internal events of Second Temple Jewish history are to be seen as a conflict between a patrician priestly class and a plebeian intellectual and merchant class. Since Simon the Righteous is called a survivor of the Great Assembly, he thinks that in addition to the Great Assembly at the time of Ezra there must have been a second Great Assembly under Simon's leadership, at which time the Hasidic scholars played a leading role and were given official

71. L. Finkelstein, *The Pharisees and the Men of the Great Synagogue* (New York: JTS, 1950), 60-65 (Hebrew).

72. L. Finkelstein, *The Pharisees: The Sociological Background of their Faith*, 3d ed. (Philadelphia: JPS, 1962), 1:261-80, 576-83.

73. *Pharisees and Men of the Great Synagogue*, 62-65; *The Pharisees*, 711; "The Origin of the Pharisees," *Cons Jud* 33 (1969) 25-36 or in *Pharisaism in the Making: Selected Essays* (New York: Ktav, 1972), 175-86.

74. *Pharisees and Men of the Great Synagogue*, 51-60.

75. Ibid., 65-77; *The Pharisees*, 500-625.

legal status within the ruling Temple hierarchy.[76] In many of his works he uses 'Hasideans' and 'Pharisees' interchangeably, since he thinks that *Perushym*, which can be translated "separatists," was a later term applied to the Hasideans by their opponents.[77] For Finkelstein, the Hasideans find their origin among the scribes at the time of Ezra.

Finding their establishment rather in the Maccabean era, other scholars still argued that the Hasideans originated in scribal circles. Finding the origin of the Hellenists and the Hasidim in the Hellenistic takeover of Palestine, E. Schürer suggested that the *Ḥasydym* held to the ideal of the scribes.[78] Bickerman refers to the Hasideans as "experts on the law," even though he makes no mention of their founding.[79] Orlinsky seems to see the Hasideans as a group within the scribal circles.[80] For Abel, the scribes are professionals with the job of

76. L. Finkelstein, "The Maxim of the *Anshe Keneset Ha-Gedolah*," *JBL* 59 (1940) 455-69, or *Pharisaism in the Making*, 159-73.

77. *Pharisees and Men of the Great Synagogue*, 33, n. 119, 77-85; "The Ethics of Anonymity among the Pharisees," *Cons Jud* 12 (1958) 1-12, or *Pharisaism in the Making*, 187-98; *The Pharisees*, 570-625.

78. E. Schürer, *Geschichte des jüdischen Volkes im Zeitalter Jesu Christi*, 4th ed., vol. 1 (Leipzig: J. C. Hinrichs'sche Buchhandlung, 1901), 190. This is followed in the later *Schürer-Vermes-Millar* edition as well, 1:145.

79. E. J. Bickerman, *God of the Maccabees*, 58.

80. H. M. Orlinsky, "Maccabees," *IDB* 3:200.

copying the law, reading it in public and interpreting it.[81] However, the Hasideans, who are older than the Maccabees, represent a broader group including scribes that resolved to practice the law and was bound together for that pious purpose.[82] Apparently following Tcherikover, F. E. Peters claims that the Hasidim seem to be connected with the scribal circles in Jerusalem.[83] Since this group had the greatest institutional investment in the law of Moses, they lost their power in the *polis* created by Jason in which the Mosaic law was no longer the basis for social and individual conduct. In this situation, the Hasideans were opposed to the Hellenized Jew and Seleucid alike. However, the argument that the origin of the Hasideans is to be found among those people called scribes in second century B.C.E. Jerusalem has certainly not always been accepted.

A number of other hypotheses concerning the relationship of the Hasidim and the scribes have been advanced. While Wellhausen argued that the Hasideans were a group of gathered, independent scribes, he considered them to be an insignificant group who joined the Maccabees only after they started to be successful.[84] Pfeiffer considered the Hasidim to

81. Abel, *Livres*, 132.

82. Ibid., 43, 132-33.

83. F. E. Peters, *The Harvest of Hellenism: A History of the Near East from Alexander the Great to the Triumph of Christianity* (New York: Simon and Schuster--Touchstone Book, 1970), 264-67.

84. J. Wellhausen, *Die Pharisäer und die Sadducäer: Eine Untersuchung zur inneren jüdischen Geschichte* (Greisswald: Bamberg, 1874), 80-81.

be laymen; hence the scribes were a different group.[85] This means that for him the references to the *Asidaioi* and the scribes in 1 Macc. 7:12-13 are to two independent groups.[86] Johann Maier works with a similar assumption,[87] as does J. Sievers in his excursus on the *Asidaioi* in his dissertation.[88] While these proposals all bear mention, one further thesis concerning the scribes demands more investigation.

The Question of Apocalyptic Literature

Prominent in recent years, although not new, has been the hypothesis that apocalyptic literature finds its origin among the *Ḥasydym.* A number of studies consider the Hasideans to be scribes who authored this particular kind of literature. In his important study, Joshua Bloch talked about the new character which this scribal movement adopted during the Hasmonean era.[89] In other words, from this perspective the essential elements of the apocalyptic viewpoint can be found among the postexilic scribes and the Hebrew prophets. In the introduction to his commentary on Daniel, Heaton followed a similar tack.

85. Pfeiffer, *History of New Testament Times*, 53-54.

86. Ibid., 16.

87. J. Maier, *Geschichte der jüdischen Religion: Von der Zeit Alexander des Grossen bis zur Aufklärung mit einem Ausblick auf das 19./20. Jahrhundert* (Berlin/New York: Walter de Gruyter, 1972), 53.

88. Joseph Sievers, "The Hasmoneans and their supporters from Mattathias to John Hyrcanus I," Dissertation, Columbia, 1981, 56.

89. J. Bloch, *On the Apocalyptic in Judaism* (Philadelphia: Dropsie College, 1952), 28-43.

He claimed that both Daniel and Ben Sira came out of the group which was called scribes, but that Daniel was closer to the Pharisaic schools.[90] The Hasidim, then, were forerunners of the Pharisees who authored the book of Daniel. Within the biblical work itself they were called the *maśkylym* (wise) who opposed the infiltration of Hellenistic culture.[91] More recently, Thoma has spoken of "two differently motivated groups of pious people: the interpreters of Scripture and founders of the liturgy, and those excitedly awaiting the early *eschaton.*"[92] The first group consists of the scribes and other forerunners of the Pharisaic movement; the second, the creators of that literature whose major interest was the endtimes. He then notes that these two groups had the same name but that we do not know of any polemics between them. He doesn't clarify whether these two groups are ever identified as one. However, in his discussion of the origin of the Pharisees, he does consider references to *Ḥasydym Hari'shonym* (the early Hasidim) in rabbinic literature to be indicative of Pharisaic views, and 1 Enoch 91-105 and 108 is also said to contain Pharisaic traditions.[93] Perhaps his view would best be expressed by

[90]. E. W. Heaton, *The Book of Daniel: Introduction and Commentary* (London: SCM Press, 1956), 23-24, 237-38.

[91]. Ibid., 237.

[92]. C. Thoma, *A Christian Theology of Judaism*, trans. Helga Croner, Studies in Judaism and Christianity (New York: Paulist, 1980), 43-44. He reached similar conclusions in his earlier study, "Der Pharisäismus," *Literatur und Religion des Frühjudentums*, 256-57.

[93]. *Christian Theology*, 65-66. Another view which emphasizes the importance of the Apocalypse of Weeks as a source for understanding the Hasideans is that of Ferdinand Dexinger, *Henochs Zehnwochenapokalypse und offene Probleme der Apokalyptikforschung* (Leiden: E. J. Brill, 1977), 45-57.

stating that both the scribes and the authors of apocalyptic literature are Hasideans. In all these cases, the Hasidim are thought to have originated among the scribes and to be the authors of that body of literature called apocalyptic.

There are other viewpoints which connect the Hasidim with apocalyptic literature but which do not relate them to the scribes. As mentioned earlier, Kohler put more distance between the Hasidim and the scribes in the pre-Maccabean era. He accepted Enoch and Baruch, along with so much of the rest of postexilic literature, as compositions of the Hasidim.[94] He considered apocalyptic literature to be the result of the influence of Persian dualism, a viewpoint to which the Hasidim, in contrast to the official priesthood--the Sadducees--were particularly open.[95] A very influential work which laid the groundwork for some of the recent perceptions of the Hasidim was that of Plöger. Tracing the Hasideans or at least their viewpoint back to the Persian period, Plöger ignores the question of the relationship of the *soprym* to the Hasideans (except for the suggestion in his historical outline that 1 Macc. 7:12 refers to the scribes and the "Pious" as if they were two different groups).[96] He credits Martin Noth with beginning to argue for the identification of a pre-Maccabean apocalyptic viewpoint with those persons called the "Pious."[97] He thinks this may be a reference to scribes who were commissioned by the Hasidim to test the legitimacy of the high priest or that

94. *Origins of the Synagogue*, 29.

95. Ibid., 43-48.

96. *Theocracy*, 8.

97. Ibid., 10; see M. Noth, *The History of Israel*, 2d ed. (New York/Evanston: Harper & Row, 1960), 395-99.

these scribes were themselves Hasidim. Relying heavily on Plöger's work and accepting his hypothesis on the early origins of hasidic thought in the Hebrew prophetic literature, Hengel speaks of the appearance of "the scribal wise men" as a group in 1 Macc. 7:12, who probably formed the elite of the Hasideans.[98] The relationship of the two terms is not spelled out. Both Plöger and Hengel seem to be following Foerster who had already proposed a connection between the Hasideans and the scribes, based on 1 Macc. 7:12.[99] He argued that details concerning the Hasidim are to be found in the apocalyptic sections of Jubilees and the Ethiopic book of Enoch, as well as in Daniel.[100] D. S. Russell also speaks of the distinction between the scribes and the Hasidim, for which he finds evidence in 1 Macc. 7:12-13.[101] While both groups are zealous for the Torah and championed Torah religion against Hellenism, he distinguishes the lay scribes, whom he considers the forerunners of the Pharisees, from the Hasidim, who are related to Daniel and apocalyptic literature.[102] A similar position is taken by Maier. Reading 1 Maccabees 7 in a way similar to

98. *Judaism and Hellenism*, 80, cf. 175-80.

99. W. Foerster, "Der Ursprung des Pharisäismus," *ZNW* 34 (1935) 35-51.

100. Ibid., 37-43; id., *From the Exile to Christ: A Historical Introduction to Judaism*, trans. G. E. Harris (Philadelphia: Fortress, 1964), 42-44.

101. D. S. Russell, *The Jews from Alexander to Herod* (London: Oxford University Press, 1967), 159-60.

102. Ibid., 45-47; id., *The Method and Message of Jewish Apocalyptic: 200 BC-AD 100* (Philadelphia: Westminster, 1964), 16, 23-28.

Russell and others,[103] he contrasts the scribes, who were prepared to accept a recreation of the old order prior to the abomination of Antiochus IV Epiphanes, with the Hasideans who initially saw in the events the anticipated end-times.[104] In all these cases, the scribes are viewed as a group that is of a different nature from the Hasideans, even though not unrelated during the time of the revolt.

Listing the scribes with some of the other groups in postexilic Judaism such as the priests, the levites, the adherents of a prophetic eschatology and those who ascribed to a deuteronomistic view of history, Schreiner maintains that the Hasideans grew out of the pious persons within these factions.[105] Specific to the Hasidean movement was a blending of priestly elements with apocalyptic to create a priestly apocalyptic. Schreiner expresses his indebtedness to Steck for the view that the Hasideans are to be viewed as a "Sammelbewegung" out of these various bodies.[106] Steck identified the element common to all four of these groups as the desire for a "Torah-true" Israel.[107] All those persons who share this conviction are then united to stand against the hellenization which, according to Steck, the priesthood and the urban population had unsealed. This rejection by the Hasideans of the reigning Sadducean

103. J. Maier, *Geschichte*, 53.

104. Ibid., 51-56, 70.

105. *Literatur und Religion*, 214-53, see 240-43.

106. Ibid., 240, n. 55.

107. O. H. Steck, *Israel und das gewaltsame Geschick*, 196-208; see also his article, "Das Problem theologischer Strömungen in nachexilischer Zeit," *EvT* 28 (1968) 445-58.

priesthood in Jerusalem is also a central thesis shared by Schreiner.[108] While not stressing the diverse backgrounds of those drawn into the Hasidic party, Plöger does also portray the intellectual history of postexilic Judaism as a struggle between (a) a theocratic view which saw the existence of the cult as a fulfillment of the divine promises which Yahweh had announced through the prophets and (b) an eschatological outlook which could only see the promises of the prophets being fulfilled in a more dramatic intervention of the Lord into the very desperate affairs of the present age.[109] Of course, the Hasideans represent the latter group. As mentioned previously, Hengel builds upon the work of Plöger. He also describes the Hasideans as the opponents of "'official' Judaism, embodied in the priestly hierarchy and the rich lay aristocracy."[110] All of the discussions just mentioned find priestly elements in the Hasidean movement, however, it is in one way or another portrayed as being in opposition to the priestly rule in Jerusalem. The scribes, on the whole, are counted as part of the cult in these studies.

The hypothesis of a conflict between the Hasideans and the Jerusalem priesthood, a viewpoint common to so many scholars, is called into question in an important critique of Hengel's work by J. C. H. Lebram.[111] He argues that Hengel's assumption that apocalyptic literature and Daniel stem from the

108. *Literatur und Religion*, 240.

109. *Theocracy*, 106-17.

110. *Judaism and Hellenism*, 176.

111. J. C. H. Lebram, "Apokalyptik und Hellenismus im Buche Daniel: Bemerkungen und Gedanken zu Martin Hengel's Buch über 'Judentum und Hellenismus'," *VT* 20 (1970) 522-24.

circles of the Hasidim is never proven. Lebram finds that the concerns of Daniel are best placed in the priestly circles, thereby challenging the framework Hengel adopted from Plöger.

The hypothesis that the Hasideans should be related to apocalyptic literature is also questioned by Collins, who remains agnostic on the question, even though he does accept as "extremely plausible" Charles's identification of the lambs in Enoch 90:6-9 with these people.[112] George Nickelsburg started to qualify his use of the term "Hasidim" after the appearance of the work by Collins. While he makes frequent reference to the Hasidim in some of his earlier works,[113] he is intentionally cautious in his later tome.[114] P. Davies claims that "it is impossible to find any concrete basis for this identification."[115] Agnostic would be the best way to characterize Stone's statements in his evaluation of Hengel's reconstruction of the

[112]. John J. Collins, *Apocalyptic Vision*, 202-05; but note *Apocalyptic Imagination*, 62-63.

[113]. George W. E. Nickelsburg, *Resurrection, Immortality and Eternal Life in Intertestamental Judaism* (Cambridge: Harvard University/London: Oxford University, 1972), 43-45, 99, etc. His use of the phrase "earlier Hasidic writings" on pp. 113 and 124 suggests that he is considering a large portion of the texts discussed in the work to be the product of the Hasidim. See also his article, "1 and 2 Maccabees--Same Story, Different Meaning," *CTM* 42 (1971) 523-25.

[114]. George W. E. Nickelsburg, *Jewish Literature between the Bible and the Mishnah: A Historical and Literary Introduction* (Philadelphia: Fortress, 1981), 95, n. 1.

[115]. *JJS* 28 (1977) 129.

third century B.C.E.[116] In his dissertation, Sievers also maintains that there is no evidence that the Hasidim were interested in apocalyptic speculation.[117] In fact, he argues that the acceptance of Alcimus as High Priest by the *Asidaioi* suggests the opposite. While many recent scholars see the *Ḥasydym* as one of the major movements of Judaism during the period of the Second Temple based on the assumption that they are the authors of at least some of the apocalyptic literature, others see only a very minor role for this group.

Within the discussion of apocalyptic literature, a more specific question is whether the author(s) or recipients of the book of Daniel were among the Hasidim. On the whole, most writers simply consider Daniel to be another apocalyptic work; thus their opinion on the book of Daniel coincides with how they resolve the question of the Hasidim and apocalyptic literature. We find a long list of people who consider Daniel, or at least parts of it, to be authored by the Hasidim and who look to this group when describing the sociological milieu for the work.[118] Most of these authors consider the *maśkylym* of Daniel

116. M. E. Stone, "The Book of Enoch and Judaism in the Third Century B.C.E.," *CBQ* 40 (1978) 480-81.

117. "The Hasmoneans and their Supporters," 55-56.

118. Foerster, *ZNW* 34 (1935) 41; id., *Exile*, 42; Pfeiffer, *History of New Testament Times*, 53; id., *Religion in Old Testament*, 218; Heaton, *Book of Daniel*, 23-24; Noth, *History of Israel*, 396-98; Russell, *Message and Method*, 16, 49; id., *Jews from Alexander to Herod*, 46-47; id., *Apocalyptic: Ancient and Modern* (Philadelphia: Fortress, 1978), 10; Bo Reicke, "Official and Pietistic Elements of Jewish Apocalypticism," *JBL* 79 (1960) 137-38; id., *The New Testament Era: The World of the Bible from 500 B.C. to A.D. 100*, trans. David E. Green (Philadelphia: Fortress, 1968), 170; W. H. C. Frend, *Martyrdom and Persecution in the Early Church: A Study of a Conflict from the Maccabees to Donatus* (Oxford: Basil Blackwell, 1965), 47-49 (this work is too unspecific to ascertain whether he

to be the Hasideans and the *'ezer me'aṭ* (a little help) of Dan. 11:34 to be the Hasmoneans. While Tcherikover also uses the book of Daniel as evidence for the important role of the Hasideans he makes no mention of any non-canonical apocalyptic literature.[119] In his hypothesis, discussed above, of the Hasidim as scribes who lead the military resistance to hellenization, Daniel has only a supporting role. The critics of that viewpoint which connect Daniel with the Hasideans are the same people who contest the apocalyptic connection already discussed above. In that group must be included Lebram,[120] Davies,[121] Collins,[122] Stone,[123] and Sievers.[124] Lack of evidence

connects the discussion of apocalyptic literature in the succeeding pages with the Hasidim); Steck, *Israel und das gewaltsame Geschick*, 207-208; Plöger, *Theocracy*, 16-20; F. F. Bruce, "The Book of Daniel and the Qumran Community," *Neotestamentica et Semitica: Studies in Honor of Matthew Black*, eds. E. E. Ellis and M. Wilcox (Edinburgh: T & T Clark, 1969), 228-30; Maier, *Geschichte*, 54-55; H. Burgmann, "Ein Schaltmonat nach 24,5 Jahren im Chasidischen Sonnenkalendar?" *RevQ* 8 (1972) 66; J. Bright, *A History of Israel*, 2d ed. (Philadelphia: Westminster, 1974), 426; Hengel, *Judaism and Hellenism*, 176; L. F. Hartman and A. A. DiLella, *The Book of Daniel*, AB 23 (Garden City: Doubleday, 1978), 44-45; Thoma, *Christian Theology*, 44, 76; id., *Literatur und Religion*, 255-57; Blenkinsopp, *Jewish and Christian Self-Definition*, 2:18.

119. *Hellenistic Civilization*, 198.

120. *VT* 20 (1970) 523.

121. *JJS* 28 (1972) 129.

122. Note that Collins differentiates between Daniel and the evidence in some other apocalyptic literature on the question of the Hasidim: *Apocalyptic Vision*, 209-14; *Apocalyptic Imagination*, 62.

123. *CBQ* 40 (1978) 481. His view would best be characterized as agnostic.

124. "The Hasmoneans and Their Supporters," 55-56.

for the connection is the most important argument in these studies rather than any identifiable negative indicators.

The circularity of the argument relating the Hasidim to apocalyptic literature in general and to Daniel is pointed out by Stephen Reid in his dissertation on Enoch and Daniel.[125] He argues that Charles's claim that the Hasidim were the authors of Daniel 7-12 and 1 Enoch 83-90 is tautological. Deciding that the Hasidim in Maccabees were persons who believed in passive resistance, Charles attributed every text in which he found that theology to the Hasidim. However there is no internal evidence in Daniel or Enoch to justify that claim. According to Reid, "Hasidim" in this case has no sociological designation. It is here merely being used as shorthand for a belief system. Perhaps the critique could be restated. If we assume that the Hasidim were the representatives of the passive resistance viewpoint, then all texts which reflect that ideology are considered Hasidic. However, since the references are too meager to permit this assumption to be anything other than an unsubstantiated hypothesis, labeling these texts as Hasidic tells us nothing more about the Hasidim. Of course, this critique applies to all those viewpoints which hold that the Hasidim were the authors of apocalyptic literature.

125. Stephen Beck Reid, "The Sociological Setting of the Historical Apocalypses of 1 Enoch and the Book of Daniel," Dissertation, Emory, 1981, 25-27.

The Pharisees and the Essenes

Until this point in the chapter, we have examined some of the arguments for the pre-Maccabean existence of the Hasideans. The question of the extent to which the *Asidaioi* in 1 and 2 Maccabees were an identifiable group or sect has already been mentioned and will be dealt with at greater length in the following chapter. The *Ḥasydym* in talmudic literature will also receive mention later in this work. However, at this point it is important to note the strictures of Davies and Collins to the effect that all study of the Hasidim must start from the three references to that group in 1 and 2 Maccabees.[126] This means that further analysis of these hypotheses about the pre-Maccabean existence of the Hasidim must follow an examination of 1 and 2 Maccabees, the topic of chapter 3. Prior to doing that, however, we shall survey the various hypotheses about the successors of these *Asidaioi*. This is necessary since this question plays a major role in discussions concerning this enigmatic group. As with so many other cases of "before" and "after" in historical writings, the divisions are not always neat. This means that in some cases, we will be jumping back into the pre-Maccabean era. However, since this division of the material brings us into the period when Josephus first makes mention of the Jewish sects, which is often accepted as evidence for the approximate time of their origin, such an organization of our material seems appropriate.[127]

I have previously mentioned the very important role in postexilic Judaism which has been ascribed to the Hasidim by

[126]. *JJS* 28 (1977) 133; *Apocalyptic Vision*, 202; *Apocalyptic Imagination*, 62.

[127]. *AJ* 13:171-73.

scholars such as Plöger and Hengel. Philip Davies has taken their viewpoint, which builds on and incorporates earlier perceptions of the Hasidim, and called it the "Hasidic hypothesis."[128] We have already looked at the one portion of this hypothesis described by him, i.e., that the Hasidim are the authors of Daniel and other apocalyptic literature. Now we need to examine the other part: the Pharisees and Essenes are both considered to be the successors of the Hasidim. This group is considered to be the "plant root" of CD 1:7, thus explaining the origin of the later Essene movement. While the description of this viewpoint by Davies, based primarily on the work of Hengel and Plöger, is one of its more recent articulations, many earlier scholars ascribed the origin of one or both of these groups to the *Ḥasydym*.

The hypothesis that the Hasidim were the forerunners of both the Pharisees and the Essenes was frequently advanced already in the nineteenth century. By the middle of the century, Zechariah Frankel had made the daring claim that there was a good deal of evidence concerning the Essenes in talmudic literature, including in that argument references to the *Ḥasydym Hari'shonym* and to certain individuals who were designated as *ḥasyd*.[129] The Pharisees, who called themselves *Ḥaḇerym*, arose out of these Essenes-*Ḥasydym* only later in opposition to the *Ṣeduqym*. Abraham Geiger took exception to the important role which Frankel had ascribed to the Essenes in Second Temple

128. *JJS* 28 (1977) 127-32.

129. Z. Frankel, "Die Essäer. Eine Skizze," *ZRIJ* 3 (1846) 441-61; id., "Die Essäer nach Talmudischen Quellen," *MGWJ* 2 (1853) 30-40, 61-73.

Judaism.[130] For him, the name *Ḥasydym* was in use for only a brief period at the height of the war with the Greek Syrians.[131] Prior and subsequent to this event, these same people were called Pharisees. However, he does, like Frankel, find the origin of the Essenes among these Hasideans. An argument similar to that of Geiger is advanced by Derenbourg. He also finds the existence of a group called the Hasideans to be short-lived.[132] They emerge out of the remnants of the Great Assembly to oppose the Hellenists. However, he finds any attempt to connect the Essenes with the Hasideans of 1 and 2 Maccabees to be ill-fated, even though the Essenes may sometimes have called themselves *Ḥasydym.*[133] While he considered the role of the Hasideans in the war with the Greeks to be a fairly minor one, Wellhausen did accept and advance the argument that the origins of both the Pharisees and the Essenes were to be found with that group called the Hasideans.[134] He claimed that the hypothesis that the *Ḥasydym* were the forerunners of the Pharisees had a high degree of probability, citing their connection with the scribes in 1 Maccabees 7 as evidence.

130. A. Geiger, "Die Essäer in der halachischen Literatur?" *JZWL* 9 (1871) 49-56.

131. A. Geiger, *Urschrift und Übersetzungen der Bibel in ihrer Abhängigkeit von der inneren Entwicklung des Judenthums* (Breslau: Julius Hainauer, 1857), 103.

132. J. Derenbourg, *Essai sur l'histoire et la géographie de la Palestine d'après les Thalmuds et les autres sources rabbiniques* (Paris: Imprimerie Impériale, 1867), 55-57.

133. Ibid., 460-62.

134. Wellhausen, *Pharisäer und Sadducäer*, 77-80.

Both Heinrich Graetz and Emil Schürer, in their monumental works, followed the course already laid out in these studies. Graetz understood the Essenes to be the form which the *Ḥasydym* took after the Maccabean revolt.[135] The Pharisees arose out of a division among these pious. A different nuance of this argument is found in Schürer. He contended that "once everyday life is organized as a continuous fulfillment of the Torah, and obedience to the Torah is regarded as the basis of religious conduct, Pharisaism already exists in principle."[136] In other words, the principles of Pharisaic Judaism were in existence some time before the Maccabean revolt. However, its appearance as a sect could only be traced back as far as the *Ḥasydym* at the time of the revolt. This same party reappeared some time later as the Pharisees. Essenism originates from this Hasidic-Pharisaic movement.[137] In other words, while Graetz considered a direct connection between the *Ḥasydym* and the Essenes, with the Pharisees an offshoot from that group, Schürer saw a continuous thread from the *Ḥasydym* to the Pharisees with the Essenes a particular later development. Both, of course, accepted the general hypothesis that the Hasidim were the forerunners of both the Pharisees and the Essenes.

We could continue to list lesser known works which also advocated this position, such as Hitzig, Ewald, Lauer and

135. H. Graetz, *Geschichte der Juden von den ältesten Zeiten bis auf die Gegenwart*, 4th ed. (Leipzig: Oskar Leiner, 1888), 3:1:83-84.

136. E. Schürer, *Geschichte des jüdischen Volkes im Zeitalter Jesu Christi*, 3d and 4th ed. (Leipzig: J. C. Hinrichs'sche Buchhandlung, 1898-1901), 2:403-404; the quotation can be found in *Schürer-Vermes-Millar*, 2:400.

137. *Geschichte*, 573-84.

Kuenen.[138] All these nineteenth century works, with the exception of Derenbourg, assumed, on the one hand, that the *Ḥasydym* had in one way or another a connection with the rabbinic tradition and, on the other, some sort of tie between the *ḥasydym* and Essenes. Most frequently this was based on the theory that *Essēnoi* or *Essaioi* was derived from *ḥasydym* via the Aramaic *Ḥasyan* or *Ḥasayya'*.[139]

The question must be asked, How in the turbulent world of nineteenth century historical study could there be so much similarity in viewpoint concerning a historical group that had such a limited attestation? Of course, an exploration of the intellectual world of the nineteenth century would be necessary to give a full answer. However, for the present study it is important to note that all these works shared a common assumption. They all assumed a polarity between the Hellenists and Hasideans. In other words, the Hasidim were portrayed as the most ardent opponents of the Greeks and those Jews who supported the adoption of Greek ways in Jerusalem. For example, Frankel argued that Jose ben Joezer's advocacy of a

[138]. These nineteenth century works have been collected by S. Wagner, *Die Essener in der Wissenschaftlichen Diskussion: Vom Ausgang des 18. bis zum 20. Jahrhunderts: Eine wissenschaftsgeschichtliche Studie*, BZAW 79 (Berlin: Alfred Töpelmann, 1960); note especially 83-117: F. Hitzig, *Geschichte des Volkes Israel von Anbeginn bis zur Eroberung Masada's im Jahre 72 nach Christus* (Leipzig: S. Hirzel, 1869), 426-28; H. Ewald, *Geschichte des Volkes Israel*, 3d ed. (Göttingen: Dieterichschen Buchhandlung, 1864), 366-67, 476-94; M. Lauer, *Die Essäer und ihr Verhältniss zur Sunagoge und Kirche* (Vienna, 1869); published separately from the *Oesterreicher Vierteljahresschrift für katholische Theologie*, 7:489-562, see 540-42; A. Kuenen, *The Religion of Israel to the Fall of the Jewish State*, trans. A. H. May (London/Edinburgh: Williams and Northgate, 1875), 3:121-36, see 130-31; id., *Volksreligion und Weltreligion* (Berlin: G. Reimer, 1883), 203.

[139]. See Chapter 4 below.

higher level of purity was an attempt to separate those Jews who remained true from the unfaithful who adopted a Greek life-style in the time of Antiochus Epiphanes. He suggested that this was the event which sparked the creation of the Essenes out of the Hasidim.[140] In other words, the Hasideans opposed the Hellenists by emphasizing purity. This point found even greater emphasis in the work of Geiger, who considered *ḥasydym* to be the name given to the Pharisees only during the height of the war against the Syrians.[141] Similarly, Derenbourg argued that the Hasideans were in existence only during this time.[142]

It is in the larger histories of Graetz and Schürer that this viewpoint received fuller expression. Graetz argued that the warfare of the time was to be seen as a battle between the Hasidim and the Hellenists, which was to continue until the extinction of one of the two parties.[143] Any moderates, which included most of the common people, were forced to take sides as this battle progressed. Similarly, Schürer found that two antagonistic parties arose within Judaism upon the encroachment of Hellenism, the Hasidim and those friendly to the Greeks.[144] Under the leadership of the Hasidim, the Jews were saved from total hellenization. Thus, we can see that the common viewpoint in these studies which found the origin of

140. *ZRIJ* 3 (1946) 453-54; *MGWJ* 2 (1853) 61-64.

141. *Urschrift*, 103.

142. *Essai*, 55-57, 461-62.

143. *Geschichte*, 2:2:240-41, 273-75.

144. *Geschichte*, 1:190.

both the Essenes and the Pharisees in this group is that the Hasidim were viewed as that party within Judaism that led the fight against hellenization.

That the Pharisees and the Essenes arose from the Hasidim has also been a dominant assumption in twentieth century thinking, continuing up to the present day. The list of persons who hold this view seems endless.[145] However, this perspective

145. K. Kohler, "Essenes," *JE* 5:225; Foerster, *Exile*, 36, n. 8, 49-52 (in his earlier article prior to the discovery of the Qumran scrolls, *ZNW* 34 [1935] 46-47, he connects the Hasidim with the Damascus Document without making mention of the Essenes); K. Schubert, *The Dead Sea Community: Its Origin and Teachings*, trans. J. W. Doberstein (London: Adam & Charles Black, 1959), 32-33; id., "A Divided Faith: Jewish Religious Parties and Sects," *The Crucible of Christianity: Judaism, Hellenism and the Historical Background to the Christian Faith*, ed. A. Toynbee (Cleveland/New York: World, 1969), 87; id., *Die jüdischen Religionsparteien in neutestamentlicher Zeit* (Stuttgart: Katholisches Bibelwerk, 1970), 18; id., "Das Zeitalter der Apokalyptik," *Bibel und zeitgemässer Glaube*, ed. K. Schubert (Klosterneuberg: Klosterneuberger, 1965), 1:276; Plöger, *Theocracy*, 20, 51; Frank Moore Cross, Jr., *The Ancient Library of Qumran and Modern Biblical Studies*, rev. ed. (Garden City: Doubleday [Anchor], 1961), 132, 141, n. 66, 154, n. 87, 198-99, 227-28; Abel-Starcky, *Livres des Maccabées*, 57; Marcel Simon, *Jewish Sects at the Time of Jesus*, trans. James H. Farley (Philadelphia: Fortress, 1967), 19; W. F. Smith, "A Study of the Zadokite High Priesthood within the Graeco-Roman Age: From Simon the Just to the High Priests appointed by Herod the Great," Dissertation, Harvard, 1961, 6-7; W. Farmer, *IDB* 2:528; J. Jeremias, *Jerusalem in the Time of Jesus: An Investigation into Economic and Social Conditions during the New Testament Period*, trans. F. H. and C. H. Cave (Philadelphia: Fortress, 1975), 247, 257; Reicke, *New Testament Era*, 67, 71, 160-61, 170; Russel, *Method and Message*, 23-28; id., *Jews from Alexander to Herod*, 160-66; R. Meyer, *Tradition und Neuschöpfung im antiken Judentum: Dargestellt an der Geschichte des Pharisäismus* (Berlin: Akadamie Verlag, 1965), 16-23; *TDNT* 7:39, n. 27; 9:14-16; H. Stegemann, *Die Entstehung der Qumrangemeinde* (Bonn: Rheinische Friederich-Wilhelms-Universität, 1965), 229-32; Steck, *Israel und das gewaltsame Geschick*, 158-59, 209-10; Hengel, *Judaism and Hellenism*, 1:176; W. F. Albright and C. S. Mann, "Qumran and the Essenes: Geography, Chronology, and Identification of the Sect," *The Scrolls and Chris-*

has not gone unchallenged. Büchler argued that the special rigor of Essene practice is absent from the rabbinic statements describing the *Ḥasydym Hari'shonym* and those individuals who are called *ḥasyd.* The use of the term in rabbinic literature is an expression of a high Jewish morality but bears no relationship to those people called the Essenes.[146] Both Noth[147] and Heaton make no mention of the Essenes when they discuss the Hasidim, "who were the forerunners of the Pharisees."[148] Reading the passage in 1 Macc. 2:29-38 in a manner similar to that proposed in chapter 3 of this work, Rabinowitz finds described there the actions of a group which was the forerunner of the Essenes, while the Pharisees arise out of the Hasideans mentioned in 1 Macc. 2:42.[149] Büchler's rejection of any connection between the Hasidim and the Essenes is accepted

tianity, ed. M. Black (London: SPCK, 1969), 18-21; 108, n. 12; E. Lohse, *The New Testament Environment*, trans. J. E. Steely (Nashville: Abingdon, 1976), 77, 85; Josef Schreiner, *Literatur und Religion des Frühjudentums: Eine Einführung*, eds. J. Maier and J. Schreiner (Würzburg: Echter Verlag/Gütersloh: Gerd Mohn, 1973), 244-48; Thoma, *Christian Theology*, 44, 65-66, 76; id., *Literatur und Religion*, 255-58; *Schürer-Vermes-Millar*, 1:212, n. 28; 2:397-401, 559, 586-87; Blenkinsopp, *Jewish and Christian Self-Definition*, 2:22-24; G. Theissen, *Sociology of Early Palestinian Christianity*, trans. J. Bowden (Philadelphia: Fortress, 1979), 87; J.-C. Violette, *Les Esséniens de Quomran* (Paris: Robert Laffont, 1983), 81-82; W. Dommershausen, *1 Makkabäer. 2 Makkabäer*, Die Neue Echter Bibel, Kommentar zum Alten Testament mit der Einheitsübersetzung, v. 12 (Würzburg: Echter Verlag, 1985), 25 et al.

146. *Types*, 33-39, 59-61, 100-102.

147. *History of Israel*, 374, n. 1; 391; 396.

148. *Book of Daniel*, 24.

149. L. Rabinowitz, "The First Essenes," *JSS* 4 (1960) 358-61.

by S. Safrai.[150] Johann Maier uses the evidence from Qumran when describing the Hasidim; however he does not think the Essenes were ever a popular party such as the one described by Josephus.[151] These Hasidim originate in priestly circles while the beginnings of the Pharisees are to be found in the circles of the lay-scribes.[152] Collins does not really enter into a discussion of this hypothesis, merely characterizing it as an oversimplification.[153] In his critique, Davies argues that the Hasidean parentage of both Essenes and Pharisees must be called into question, even though the Pharisees receive only passing mention.[154] Noting that Josephus ignores the Hasideans, Berman suggests there is no basis for identifying them with the Hasidim in the rabbinic traditions or with the Essenes.[155] In his recent dissertation, Sievers suggests that a connection with either the Essenes or the Scribes/Pharisees is uncertain.[156] The question which has guided the majority of these works is, How did the Pharisees and/or the Essenes originate? The enigmatic Hasidim have been used in various ways to answer that question.

150. S. Safrai, "Teaching of Pietists in Mishnaic Literature," *JJS* 16 (1965) 16-17.

151. *Geschichte*, 51-53, 57-63.

152. Ibid., 71-73.

153. *Apocalyptic Vision*, 202.

154. *JJS* 28 (1977) 128-31.

155. *SBLSP* (1979), 2:16.

156. "The Hasmoneans and their Supporters," 55-56.

Conclusion

The foregoing discussion began with an analysis of *ḥasyd* in the biblical materials. While noting that a number of studies rightly emphasize the use of the term in the Psalms to separate a certain group of persons within Israel from their opponents, the dating of the materials precludes the identification of them with the *Ḥasydym* mentioned in 1 and 2 Maccabees. Sakenfeld and others note that frequently *ḥasyd* in the biblical materials designates those persons who remain true to the cult of Yahweh. Evidence is cited for its employment both to point to religious functionaries and to designate the faithful and/or upright. Hence, we should not be surprised to find cultic terminology employed in the treatment of this group which found in the biblical materials a term that they could adopt as an appellation to describe themselves.

One of the obvious places for historians to look for connections with the Hasideans was the scribes, an enigmatic category in Second Temple Judaism. While some looked to the period of Ezra and immediately thereafter, others found the scribes and the Hasideans closer in time to the events of the Maccabean revolt and its aftermath. Many of these studies are characterized by the view that within the ranks of the Hasideans-scribes is to be found either the totality of or at least the ideological and in some cases the tactical core of resistance to the hellenization of Jewish Palestine, whether the source of that effort was Jew or Greek. For many students of Second Temple Judaism these hypotheses quickly led to a rather simple identification of the scribes-Hasideans with the 'resistance' viewpoint expressed in apocalyptic literature. The thrust of these analyses has been to lump all the opponents of 'hellenization' together under the category of the Hasideans thereby making them a rather broad group with influence that far supersedes the meager evidence available. Problematic also is the assumption that all of Jewish activity in the second century B.C.E. is to find explanation as a reaction to hellenism. The major recent proponent of this viewpoint is Martin Hengel whose work has already been cited. His work and perspective have been challenged by historians of Second Temple Judaism,[157] so we can only accept his hypotheses concerning the Hasideans if the evidence warrants, a task reserved for chapter 3 of this study. To explain all events in Judaea in the second century B.C.E. as a reaction to Hellenism is an unwarranted approach to resolving the many difficult problems encountered in a study of that era.

This oversimplification of the forces at play in Jewish life in the second century B.C.E. has found resistance to 'hellenization' to be an explanation for the origins of the Pharisees and the Essenes, those two groups conveniently described for us in Josephus. Their origins are frequently found in the midst of the Hasidic forces, their subsequent history written from that point of departure. Modern scholarship is increasingly aware of the limitations imposed upon it by the descriptions of Josephus; we should not limit our perceptions of the various parties involved in the events of second century B.C.E. Judaism to the four bodies listed in Josephus. It is necessary to base our understanding of the movements of this era on the evidence which can be summoned for each body. While the testimony of Josephus is important, his perceptions must be evaluated for each case independently.

The purpose of this study is to provide a starting-point for an evaluation of the Hasidim in the second century B.C.E. by examining the references to that group in 1 and 2 Mac-

157. See, e.g., L. H. Feldman, "Hengel's *Judaism and Hellenism* in Retrospect," *JBL* 96 (1977) 371-82; F. Millar, "The Background to the Maccabean Revolution: Reflections on Martin Hengel's 'Judaism and Hellenism'," *JJS* 29 (1978) 1-21; L. H. Feldman, "How Much Hellenism in Jewish Palestine," *HUCA* 57 (1986) 83-111.

cabees. A survey of the literature on the Hasidim has demonstrated the need for such an investigation. We will also need to take a brief look at the way in which *ḥasyd* and *ḥasydym* are used in talmudic literature. On the basis of such a study we can then look afresh at the viewpoints and movements of second century B.C.E. Judaism to determine the place of the Hasideans.

II

THE USE OF THE NAME - *ASIDAIOI*

In an investigation of this nature, the terminological issue is of the utmost importance and needs to be addressed at the outset. As already noted, the epithet adopted for the title of this study is "Hasidean," an English derivative of the Greek *Asidaioi*, a term which appears in Graeco-Jewish literature only in 1 Macc. 2:42 and 7:12, and in 2 Macc. 14:6. As rightly emphasized by Philip Davies in his penetrating critique of scholarship on this issue, these three references must be the starting point of any study.[1] No work of which I am aware challenges the assumption that *Asidaioi* is a Greek transliteration of the Hebrew *Ḥasydym*, a noun that appears in both the singular and plural in the Hebrew Scriptures and which is employed as a proper name for certain individuals and groups in Jewish history. What has not gone uncontested is the use of the Greek term as a proper noun in the context of 1 and 2 Maccabees.

[1]. Philip Davies, "Ḥasidim in the Maccabean Period," *JJS* 28 (1977) 128.

The Significance of the Term

Already in his *Jewish Encyclopedia* article of 1904, Max Schloessinger challenged the hypothesis that "Hasideans" could refer to a sect or party. Basing his argument on the identification of the *synagōgē Asidaiōn* of 1 Macc. 2:42 with the *Qehal Ḥasydym* of Ps. 149:1, he suggested that since the term merely means a 'congregation' in the biblical citations, it could not mean otherwise in Maccabees: "The Hasideans appear simply to have been those 'pious ones' who remained true to the customs of their fathers.... They were animated by a profound hatred for the foreign, Hellenic spirit and for those of their Jewish brethren who were filled with it."[2] Thus, these references were mere adjectives describing people with a certain level of piety. Years later, Rudolph Meyer advanced virtually the identical viewpoint, suggesting that "the *chasidim* were unrelated groups more or less strongly opposed to the dominant trend in the Jerusalem hierocracy."[3] This loose definition permitted him to find a division within the groups of the Hasideans in 1 Macc. 7:12. A similar conception of this group is maintained by other German scholars including Schreiner[4] and Schubert, the latter having labeled the group as "a catchment-area for several

[2]. "Hasideans," *JE* 6:250-51.

[3]. "Saddoukaios," *TDNT* 7:39, n. 27. This article was originally published in German in 1964.

[4]. J. Schreiner, "Die apokalyptische Bewegung," *Literatur und Religion des Frühjudentums: Eine Einführung* (Würzburg: Echter/ Gütersloh: Gerd Mohn, 1973), eds. J. Maier and J. Schreiner, 239-40.

apocalyptic groups and sects...."[5] In his discussion of the identification of the Qumran sect, Burrows seems to be indebted to Schloessinger for his use of the term.[6] Jerry O'Dell makes a similar assumption when discussing the religious background of the Psalms of Solomon.[7] What the student fails to find in all these studies is an explanation of why the Hebrew term appears in Greek letters in both 1 and 2 Maccabees.

While in agreement with their colleagues on many other questions concerning the role of the Hasideans in Jewish history, other continental scholars have vigorously challenged such a broad, unspecific definition for this group. In a major study in which the question of the origin and role of the Hasideans is central, Otto Plöger follows their development through post-exilic Judaism to 1 Maccabees. He finds that according to the testimony of this latter work, "the eschatological group of the *Ḥasidim* possessed a fairly fixed form at the time of religious conflict."[8] His entire thesis is adopted

[5]. K. Schubert, "A Divided Faith: Jewish religious sects and parties," *The Crucible of Christianity: Judaism, Hellenism and the Historical Background to the Christian Faith* (Cleveland/ New York: World, 1969), ed. A. Toynbee, 88; id., *Die jüdischen Religionsparteien in neutestamentlicher Zeit* (Stuttgart: Katholisches Bibelwerk, 1970), 19.

[6]. M. Burrows, *The Dead Sea Scrolls* (New York: Viking, 1955), 274.

[7]. Jerry O'Dell, "The Religious Background of the Psalms of Solomon (Re-evaluated in the Light of the Qumran Texts)," *RevQ* 3 (1961) 257.

[8]. Otto Plöger, *Theocracy and Eschatology*, trans. S. Rudman (Richmond: John Knox, 1968), 116; see also id., *Das Buch Daniel*

and extended in a monumental study by Martin Hengel, who also rightly argues for the *Synagōgē Asidaiōn* "as a clearly defined Jewish party."[9] While identifying four major theological strands in post-exilic Judaism, O. H. Steck concludes in his work on the tradition of the Deuteronomic worldview that these various strands were combined in the Hasidean movement, an organized group.[10] In his new commentary on 1 Maccabees, W. Dommershausen stresses the particular identity of the Hasideans already prior to the Maccabean movement.[11] Working backwards from the Pharisees and the Essenes, Marcel Simon makes a similar claim by suggesting that we are justified in recognizing the mighty warriors of 1 Macc. 2:42 as the first Jewish 'sect'.[12] The acceptance of the

(Gütersloh: Gerd Mohn, 1965), 30.

9. Martin Hengel, *Judaism and Hellenism: Studies in their Encounter during the Early Hellenistic Period*, trans. J. Bowden (Philadelphia: Fortress, 1974), 1:175; 2:116, n. 453.

10. O. H. Steck, *Israel und das gewaltsame Geschick der Propheten: Untersuchungen zur Überlierferung des deuteronomistischen Geschichtsbildes im Alten Testament, Spätjudentum, und Urchristentum*, WMANT 23 (Neukirchen-Vluyn: Neukirchen, 1967), 206.

11. W. Dommershausen, *1 Makkabäer. 2 Makkabäer*, Die Neue Echter Bibel, Kommentar zum Alten Testament mit der Einheitsübersetzung, v. 12 (Würzburg: Echter Verlag, 1985), 24-25.

12. Marcel Simon, *Jewish Sects at the Time of Jesus*, trans. James H. Farley (Philadelphia: Fortress, 1967), 19.

thesis that the Hasideans were a clearly defined body characterizes these studies.

Qualification rather than acceptance or denial is the hallmark of a number of recent works. Noteworthy are the few pages on the question by John Collins at the end of his work on Daniel.[13] While his argument is directed against those works which ascribe far too great a significance to the Hasidim in the history of Judaism during the Second Temple era, there is at the same time an acceptance of the three Maccabean references as evidence that the Hasidim were an organized party in Maccabean times.

A similar viewpoint finds expression in the work of George Nickelsburg. In earlier writings, he speaks of the very concrete role of the Hasidim as a group in the rebellion; he even makes reference to a Hasidic ideology.[14] Admittedly, he sees it as a fairly broad movement, in many ways similar to the views of Meyer and Schubert. However, this breadth is due to the longevity of the group; it comes into being as an opponent of Hellenism well before the Maccabean revolt.[15] It is an identifiable group with a specific

[13]. John J. Collins, *The Apocalyptic Vision of the Book of Daniel*, HSM 16 (Missoula: Scholars Press, 1977), 201-205. Note also *The Apocalyptic Imagination: An Introduction to the Jewish Matrix of Christianity* (New York: Crossroad, 1984), 62-63.

[14]. George W. E. Nickelsburg, "1 and 2 Maccabees--Same Story, Different Meaning," *CTM* 42 (1971) 515-26. This also seems to be his viewpoint in *Resurrection, Immortality and Eternal Life in Intertestamental Judaism* (Cambridge: Harvard University/London: Oxford University, 1972), 99-108.

[15]. *CTM* 42 (1971) 516.

outlook and ideology which he can locate in the literature of the time. More recently, Nickelsburg has begun to qualify his use of the term under study. While in a number of places he appears to accept the idea of the Hasidim as a specific group, but cautions that the evidence for that hypothesis is more limited than some scholars seem to think,[16] a view which he credits to Collins, at one point in his recent opus he uses the term 'pious' to refer to the Hasidim and suggests that it is an adjective rather than a proper noun.[17] He uses it here to refer to some pious Jews who, he claims, revolted against both Menelaus and Jason in 170/169 B.C.E., thereby bringing the wrath of Antiochus IV onto Jerusalem. However, neither the revolt nor the 'pious' are mentioned at this point in 2 Macc. 5:5-7, which rather records a military attempt by Jason to regain the high priesthood. There is no record of these events in 1 Maccabees. Nickelsburg is here following the hypothetical historical reconstructions of Bickerman and Tcherikover rather than any evidence concerning the Hasideans in 1 and 2 Maccabees.[18] Thus his reference has no bearing on the question of the use of *Asidaioi* in the

[16]. George W. E. Nickelsburg, "The Epistle of Enoch and Qumran Literature," *JJS* 33 (1982) 348.

[17]. George W. E. Nickelsburg, *Jewish Literature between the Bible and the Mishnah: A Historical and Literary Introduction* (Philadelphia: Fortress, 1981), 72, 95, n. 1.

[18]. E. Bickermann, *Der Gott der Makkabäer: Untersuchungen über Sinn und Usprung der makkabäischer Erhebung* (Berlin: Schocken, 1937), 18; in English translation, *The God of the Maccabees*, trans. H. Moehring (Leiden: E. J. Brill, 1979), 10; V. Tcherikover, *Hellenistic Civilization and the Jews*, trans. S. Applebaum (Philadelphia: JPS, 1959), 186-88.

books of the Maccabees. At other points in the book, he uses the term *Ḥasydym* without qualification.[19] Regrettably, his article on "Social Aspects of Palestinian Jewish Apocalypticism" does not clarify our understanding of his usage.[20]

Vigorous objection to the work of Plöger and Hengel has come from Philip Davies.[21] As with Schloessinger, Davies maintains that the argument for seeing the Hasideans as a sect or well-defined group rests on the use of the term *synagōgē* in 1 Macc. 2:42.[22] Also like Schloessinger, he argues that this term is a Greek translation of the biblical *qahal* or *'edah*, a valid assumption, and that this term does not mean a party or sect in the biblical materials. In other words, the term does not yet have a technical meaning. It seems to me, however, that Davies misses the point. It is true that *synagōgē* acquires a more precise meaning within Judaism in time and that the history of the term is an important question for the history of Judaism; of course, for Dav-

19. *Jewish Literature*, 101, 122.

20. George W. E. Nickelsburg, "Social Aspects of Palestinian Jewish Apocalypticism," *Apocalypticism in the Mediterranean World and the Near East*, ed. D. Hellholm (Tübingen: J. C. B. Mohr/Paul Siebeck, 1983), 641-54.

21. *JJS* 28 (1977) 127-40. His critique seems to find acceptance by Gary G. Porton, "Diversity in Postbiblical Judaism," *Early Judaism and its Modern Interpreters*, eds. Robert A. Kraft and George W. E. Nickelsburg (Atlanta: Scholars Press, 1986), 61.

22. *JJS* 28 (1977) 135.

ies also the issue is not the origin of the synagogue.[23] The argument, however, for the *Asidaioi* as a well defined group does not rest on *synagōgē* at all. As correctly noted by Solomon Zeitlin, the fact that the Greek translator uses the term *Asidaioi*, a transliteration of the Hebrew *Ḥasydym*, shows that the author had in mind a particular group who were called *Ḥasydym*.[24]

It is apparent to me that the use of the transliterated Hebrew term *Asidaioi* already assumes that it was understood as a proper noun. Had the author of 1 Maccabees understood the two references in his work as common adjectives, he would have translated them employing *hosios* or *eusebēs*, the usual Greek terms used by the LXX to render *ḥasyd*. Zeitlin has noted that the author does translate the quotation from Ps. 79:2-3 in 1 Macc. 7:17 using *hosios*.[25] Even if the Greek translator of this verse was simply following the LXX version of Psalm 79, it is clear that this passage was viewed

[23]. Summaries and bibliography of the extensive discussion on the origin of the synagogue are to be found in S. Safrai, "The Synagogue," *The Jewish People in the First Century: Historical Geography, Political History, Social, Cultural and Religious Life and Institutions*, eds. S. Safrai and M. Stern, *CRINT* 1:2 (Assen: Van Gorcum/Philadelphia: Fortress, 1976), 908-44; id., "The Synagogue and its Worship," *Society and Religion in the Second Temple Period*, eds. Michael Avi-Yonah and Zvi Baras, WHJP 8 (Jerusalem: Massada, 1977), 65- 98; *Schürer-Vermes-Millar*, 2:423-63.

[24]. S. Zeitlin, "The Essenes and Messianic Expectations: A Historical Study of the Sects and Ideas During the Second Jewish Commonwealth," *JQR* 45 (1954) 87-88; id., *The Rise and Fall of the Judaean State: A Political, Social and Religious History of the Second Commonwealth* (Philadelphia: JPS, 1968), 91.

[25]. Zeitlin, *JQR* 45 (1954) 87-88.

differently than the two which contain the term *Asidaioi*. The best explanation of the differing terminology is the argument that the translator thought 1 Macc. 2:42 and 7:12 refer to a defined group which had a name. In his dissertation on the Hasmoneans and their supporters, Sievers makes the same point: the term itself is the important piece of evidence for accepting the existence of a party of Hasideans in the second century B.C.E.[26] I find the stance of Berman somewhat puzzling when he can suggest that the name *Asidaioi* itself implies only that the persons referred to were staunch traditionalists.[27] This argument would be valid if the Greek translator used the term *hosioi* to refer to the *Ḥasydym*. But he did not.

The Antiquity of the Name

The assumption, of course, in the preceding discussion is that 1 Maccabees is a work originally composed in Hebrew and later translated into Greek. While no fragments of the Hebrew text have ever been found, the presence of Hebraisms and awkward constructions which find their best explanation as the translation of a Hebrew original all support the stance of the vast majority of scholars who assume an original Hebrew composition.[28] Both Origen[29] and Je-

[26]. Joseph Sievers, "The Hasmoneans and their supporters from Mattathias to John Hyrcanus I," Dissertation, Columbia, 1981, 57.
27.

[27]. D. Berman, "Hasidim in Rabbinic Traditions," *SBLSP* (1979), 2:21, n. 15.

[28]. C. L. W. Grimm, *Kurzgefasstes exegetisches Handbuch zu den Apokryphen des Alten Testaments* (Leipzig: S. Hirzel, 1853), 3:xv- xvii; H. W. Ettelson, "The Integrity of I Maccabees," *TCAAS*

rome[30] refer to Hebrew versions of Maccabees with which they were familiar. The relevant question for this study is how soon the Greek translation was produced. When did this translator who accepted *ḥasyd* as a proper noun render the work into Greek?

It is apparent that the Greek version was available by the time Josephus wrote *Jewish Antiquities*. Grimm discusses Josephus' use of this source and provides a list of examples where Josephus uses the Greek text of 1 Maccabees quite literally.[31] Thus we can be quite confident that the Greek translation was available and in use by the time Josephus produced *Jewish Antiquities* in 93/94 C.E.[32]

27 (1925) 290-91, 307-14; F.-M. Abel, *Les Livres des Maccabées*, Etudes bibliques (Paris: Gabalda, 1949), xxiii-xxiv; K.-D. Schunck, *Die Quellen des I. und II. Makkabäerbuches* (Halle: Veb Max Niemeyer Verlag, 1954), 8-10; J. A. Goldstein, *I Maccabees: A New Translation with Introduction and Commentary*, AB 41 (Garden City: Doubleday, 1976), 14-21; K.-D. Schunck, *1. Makkabäerbuch*, JSHRZ 1:4 (Gütersloh: Gütersloher Verlagshaus Gerd Mohn, 1980), 289-90. While raising the possibility of an Aramaic rather than Hebrew original, Grimm and Abel, along with others (see Schunck, *Quellen*, p. 10, n. 1), opt in favor of a Hebrew composition.

29. In his commentary on Psalm 1, as cited by Eusebius in *Historia ecclesiasticus* 6:25:1- 2.

30. *Praefatio Hieronymi in Libros Samuel et Malachim*, PL 28, 602-03 (Prologus galeatus).

31. *Handbuch*, 3:xxviii-xxx; see also H. W. Attridge, *The Interpretation of Biblical History in the Antiquitates Judaicae of Flavius Josephus*, HDR 7 (Missoula: Scholars Press, 1976), 31.

32. *AJ* 20:267; cf. H. St. John Thackeray, *Josephus: The Man and the Historian* (New York: Ktav, 1967 - orig. 1929), 51-52. Even if there were later editions, as suggested by R. Laqueur, *Der*

When paraphrasing 1 Maccabees, Josephus does not reproduce the term *Asidaioi.* 1 Macc. 2:42 is skipped over entirely[33] and where 1 Macc. 7:12-13 speaks of scribes and Hasideans, Josephus simply describes them as *tines...ton ek tou demou* (some...of the people).[34] There is no evidence to relate this apparent omission to any of the major historiographic tendencies that have been studied in the writings of Josephus, e.g., an anti-Zealot or pro-Pharisaic bias.[35] It seems much more probable that a group by this name simply was not considered important by Josephus and his contemporaries. In the living tradition, the purification of the temple and the miraculous happenings surrounding that event as well as the leadership of the priest Mattathias and his sons were the important recollections from the time of the Maccabean revolt. It seems much more likely that Josephus considered

jüdische Historiker Flavius Josephus: Ein biographischer Versuch auf neuer quellenkritischer Grundlange (Giessen: Münchow'sche Verlagsbuchhandlung, 1920), 1-6, and mentioned as a possibility by S. J. D. Cohen, *Josephus in Galilee and Rome: His Vita and Development as a Historian*, CSCT 8 (Leiden: E. J. Brill, 1979), 175-76, there is no reason to believe this would have affected the text where 1 Maccabees was used as a source. Note the responses to this hypothesis: D. A. Barish, "The *Autobiography* of Josephus and the Hypothesis of a Second Edition of his *Antiquities*," *HTR* 71 (1978) 61-75; T. Rajak, *Josephus: The Man and His Society* (Philadelphia: Fortress, 1984), 237-38.

33. In *AJ* 12:277-78, Josephus jumps from the decision to resist aggressors on the sabbath in 1 Macc. 2:41 to the force gathered by Mattathias to destroy pagan altars and kill the lawless in 2:44-45.

34. *AJ* 12:395.

35. Thackeray, *Josephus*, 7-22; Attridge, *Interpretation*, 6-16; Cohen, *Josephus*, 147-51; Rajak, *Josephus*, 32-45. Josephus' account will receive more extensive discussion later in this chapter.

the Hasidim unimportant in view of the towering personalities and great events of the time, rather than that he had a deliberate identifiable motive for this omission. If this is the case, the judgment of the translator of 1 Maccabees that this was a proper noun is based either on an interpretation of the text itself or on an older tradition that probably went back to the time of the Maccabean revolt.

Support for the contention that the use of the name *Asidaioi* goes back to the period of the revolt is found in 2 Macc. 14:6. Since this work was originally a Greek composition, the use of the term goes back to the time it was written. This means that the epitomist accepted the record of a group by this name. Since in 2 Macc. 2:28, the epitomist leaves the responsibility for details to the author, it is reasonable to assume that the use of this name was recorded by Jason.[36] In order to ascertain the date at which this information was available to the epitomist and probably to Jason we need to look at the question of the date of composition of their two works.

Determining the date of 2 Maccabees is a complex issue, not only because the two authors, Jason and the epitomist, need to be considered, but also because of the letters prefixed to the work, one of which contains two dates and

[36]. G. W. E. Nickelsburg, *CTM* 42 (1971) 521. Even Habicht, in his attempt to identify passages original to the epitomist, makes no mention of our passage (2. *Makkabäerbuch*, JSHRZ 1:3 [Gütersloh: Gütersloher Verlagshaus Gerd Mohn, 1976], 170-77). In fact he states that since the proper name is here utilized without an introduction or explanation, there can be no doubt that Jason had mentioned them earlier in his account, probably, as in 1 Macc. 2:42, in conjunction with the outbreak of the revolt (p. 271). Cf. Ben Zion Wacholder, *Eupolemus: A Study of Judaeo-Greek Literature* (Cincinnati: Hebrew Union College-Jewish Institute of Religion, 1974), 28, n. 5. Nickelsburg is quite content to "deal with the epitome as a unified whole, not attempting to distinguish between the sources and the editorial work of the epitomizer" (p. 521).

the other none. Opinions on the date of the history have ranged from the middle of the second century B.C.E. to the first century C.E.[37] In his classic commentary, Grimm simply suggests that the epitome was composed a good deal of time later than the events described therein, but before the destruction of the temple.[38] Keil follows him, suggesting that the epitomist probably did his work during the rule of John Hyrcanus, or shortly thereafter, and rightly notes that it had to be before Pompey's conquest of Jerusalem in 63 B.C.E.[39] He also notes that Jason of Cyrene is not to be identified with the Jason of 1 Macc. 8:17, arguing against that viewpoint which makes Jason a contemporary of the sons of Mattathias. Many others follow the lead of these continental scholars.[40]

37. R. Doran, *Temple Propaganda: The Purpose and Character of 2 Maccabees*, CBQMS 12 (Washington: Catholic Biblical Association, 1981), 111.

38. *Handbuch*, 3:19-20.

39. C. F. Keil, *Commentar über die Bücher der Makkabäer* (Leipzig: Dörffling and Franck, 1875), 275-77.

40. E. Bickermann, *The God of the Maccabees*, trans. H. Moehring (Leiden: E. J. Brill, 1979 - orig. 1937), 8, 96; Schunck, *Quellen*, 116-28; R. H. Pfeiffer, *History of New Testament Times: With an Introduction to the Apocrypha* (New York: Harper & Brothers, 1949), 516; Nickelsburg, *CTM* 42 (1971) 521; Wacholder, *Eupolemus*, 38, n. 35; J. A. Goldstein, *II Maccabees: A New Translation with Introduction and Commentary*, AB 41a (Garden City: Doubleday, 1983), 71-83. There is, of course, a long line of scholarship maintaining that Jason was a contemporary or near contemporary of Judah Maccabee: E. Schürer, *Geschichte des jüdischen Volkes im Zeitalter Jesu Christi*, 3d ed. (Leipzig: J. C. Hinrichs'sche Buchhandlung, 1898), 3:359-61; B. Niese, *Kritik der beiden Makkabäerbücher: Nebst Beiträgen zur Geschichte der Makkabäischen Erhebung* (Berlin: Weidmannsche Buchhandlung,

Eissfeldt and others argue that at least three levels of composition must be considered to explain the work we now call 2 Maccabees.[41] In his view, Jason wrote at the end of the second century B.C.E., the epitomist a generation or two later, and then about the middle of the first century B.C.E. a reviser, among other things, appended the two letters at the beginning of the book. Habicht sets out a similar scheme, even though he accepts the evidence that Jason was a contemporary of Judah.[42] He dates the work of the epitomist to 188 S.E. (124 B.C.E.), the date of the first letter. A later revision following the composition of the second letter was carried out somewhere between this date and the destruction of the temple in 70 C.E. The hypothesis that Jason was a contemporary of Judah Maccabee has been argued most vigorously by Tcherikover[43] and was also advanced by F. M. Abel.[44] In his recent commentary, this proposal is accepted by John Collins as well.[45] Since one of Tcherikover's ar-

1900), 37-38; Abel, *Livres*, XLII-XLIII; Tcherikover, *Hellenistic Civilization*, 383-90; F.-M. Abel and J. Starcky, *Les Livres des Maccabees*, La Sainte Bible, 3d ed. (Paris: Les editions du Cerf, 1961), 34; Hengel, *Judaism and Hellenism*, 1:95-99; Habicht, 2. *Makkabäerbuch*, 175.

[41]. O. Eissfeldt, *The Old Testament: An Introduction*, trans. P. R. Ackroyd (New York: Harper and Row, 1976), 581.

[42]. Habicht, 2. *Makkabäerbuch*, 169-77.

[43]. *Hellenistic Civilization*, 381-90.

[44]. *Livres*, XLII-XLIII; Abel-Starcky, *Livres*, 34.

[45]. J. J. Collins, *Daniel, First Maccabees, Second Maccabees: with an Excursus on the Apocalyptic Genre*, OTM 15 (Wilmington: Michael Glazier, 1981), 261.

guments in support of the hypothesis is that the book displays no knowledge of the historical roles of Jonathan and Simon, Jason must have composed his work before 152 B.C.E. when Jonathan became high priest. Habicht accepts this same date as the terminus ad quem for the work of Jason.[46] As for the epitomist, Tcherikover believes he composed his work between 124 and 110 B.C.E., shortly after the letter dated to 188 S.E.[47] In his monograph on 2 Maccabees, Robert Doran places the epitomist in the time when John Hyrcanus' expansionist policies may have provoked a debate within Judaism.[48]

Resolving all the issues concerning the dating of 2 Maccabees would entail adding many pages to a digression from the major arguments of this work. This writer will merely summarize his own conclusions. I find myself drawn to those arguments which connect the work of the epitomist to the first letter of 2 Maccabees dated in 188 S.E. It is not clear to me why Tcherikover, having made the connection between the two, goes on to argue that the work of the epitomist follows the composition of the letter.[49] Momigliano suggests that an official of the Jerusalem council who was asked to reiterate the invitation to the Egyptians Jews to join in the celebration of the "feast-days of the Booths of Kislev" also persuaded a writer to make a summary of Jason's work

[46]. 2. *Makkabäerbuch*, 175.

[47]. *Hellenistic Civilization*, 382-83.

[48]. *Temple Propaganda*, 111-13.

[49]. *Hellenistic Civilization*, 382-83.

to send with the letter.[50] As he himself notes, however, there is no reference in the introduction to the epitomist's volume or anywhere throughout the work to such a purpose. It is my opinion that this objection is a decisive argument against the conjecture. However, if we view the letter of 2 Macc. 1:1-10a as a cover letter to which were appended two supporting documents, first, a letter from the Jews in Jerusalem and Judaea to Aristobulus in Egypt at the time of Judah Maccabee in 163 B.C.E.,[51] and, secondly, an extant summary of the work of Jason of Cyrene, we have established the terminus ad quem for the composition of the epitome. One objection to this hypothesis would be Doran's suggestion that the letter of 188 S.E. was revised in light of the contents of the epitome.[52] Since all he demonstrates is that certain features are common to the letter and the epitome, the hypothesis that the letter was written after the epitome remains quite plausible.

Let us recall for a moment the purpose of this digression concerning the date of 2 Maccabees. What we wish to establish is how early in the historical record the knowledge of the Hasideans as an identifiable group is found. If the date advanced above is accepted, then the epitomist writing at the latest in 124 B.C.E. refers to the Hasideans employing a proper noun. However, we have also already suggested that there is a possibility that the use of this name goes back to Jason. Now those studies that date the epitomist in the first

[50]. A. Momigliano, "The Second Book of Maccabees," *CP* 70 (1975) 81-88.

[51]. B. Z. Wacholder, "The Letter from Judah Maccabee to Aristobulus: Is 2 Maccabees 1:10b-2:18 Authentic?" *HUCA* 69 (1978) 89-133.

[52]. *Temple Propaganda*, 3-5, 111.

century B.C.E. reject the arguments making Jason a contemporary of Judah.[53] If the arguments of Tcherikover and Abel are accepted, however, then Jason and the information concerning the Hasideans is placed within a few years of the Maccabean revolt. Other studies have advanced the hypothesis that a document called the "acts of Judah" or "Judasvita" may be behind the description of the life of Judah in both 1 and 2 Maccabees.[54] Other sources including Eupolemus have also been seen to lie behind Jason's account.[55] If the argument that Jason is a contemporary of Judah is accepted, then the identification of the Hasideans goes directly back to the time of Judah Maccabee.

The question of a Judasvita is more complicated. While the information supplied concerning the Hasideans in 2 Macc. 14:6 is considerably different from what we learn in 1 Macc. 7:13, thereby raising questions which will be addressed later in this study,[56] the references do appear at approximately the same point in the sequence of the development of the life of Judah in the two works, i.e., at the beginning of the reign of Demetrius after Alcimus appears on the scene.

[53]. See nn. 39 and 40 above.

[54]. Schunck, *Quellen*, 52-74, 116-28; J. G. Bunge, *Untersuchungen zum zweiten Makkabäerbuch: Quellenkritische, literarische, chronologische und historische Untersuchungen zum zweiten Makkabäerbuch als Quelle syrisch-palästinensischer Geschichte im 2. Jh. v. Chr.* (Bonn: Rheinischen Friederich-Wilhelms-Universität, 1971), 206-329; but cf. Wacholder, *Eupolemus*, 29-38; Doran, *Propaganda*, 13-17.

[55]. Goldstein, *II Maccabees*, 28-54. For an evaluation and discussion of these sources see Wacholder, *Eupolemus*, 27-40; Doran, *Temple Propaganda*, 12-22.

[56]. See Chapter 3 below.

Thus it could be argued that a Judasvita included a reference(s) to the Hasideans at that point. For the purpose of this study, the Hasidean references would then go back, or at least very near, to the time of Judah himself.

Conclusion

The significance of the use of the name *Asidaioi* in the three references in 1 and 2 Maccabees has been argued in this chapter. While much debate concerning whether the Hasideans were a distinct group has centered on *synagōgē*, a term which will be discussed in the next chapter, the appearance of the transliterated Hebrew word in the Greek text is evidence of its use as a proper noun. The question is whether its usage in the works under consideration points to the existence of the group at the time of the Maccabean revolt.

Second Maccabees supplies us with evidence that a writer in the first quarter of the first century B.C.E., using the most conservative estimates, thought that the Hasideans had been involved in the events of the Maccabean revolt. He probably wrote somewhat earlier than that and most likely he was relaying information recorded by Jason of Cyrene who may have been a contemporary of Judah or who was possibly dependent upon earlier sources. Clearly, since the information supplied by the epitomist is different from that found in 1 Maccabees, we find here an independent witness to the role of the Hasideans in the revolt against Antiochus IV. The only reasonable conclusion which can be drawn from these three references is that there was a group called the Hasidim who played an important role in Jewish affairs at the time that the Jews revolted against the tyrannical rule of Antiochus IV Epiphanes. The full significance of these texts can be appreciated only after an examination of them within their literary context, a task which is reserved for the next chapter of this study.

III

THE HASIDEANS IN FIRST AND SECOND MACCABEES

There are three references to the *Asidaioi* (Hasideans) in the books of the Maccabees, 1 Macc. 2:42 and 7:12, and 2 Macc. 14:6. In the first chapter of this study, I discussed numerous identifications and associations that have been suggested for this group. In the process of this investigation, I accepted the argument of Philip Davies that any study of the Hasideans in the second century B.C.E. must start with these three Maccabean references, since they are the most apparent direct allusions to that group in the literature of the era.[1] Then I went on to demonstrate in the second chapter that these three references should be understood to refer to a

[1]. P. Davies, "Ḥasidim in the Maccabean Period," *JJS* 28 (1977) 127-40. In this study, the Greek text of 1 Maccabees is that of W. Kappler, *Maccabaeorum liber I*, Septuaginta Vetus Testamentum Graecum, 2d ed., vol. 9:1 (Göttingen: Vandenhoeck & Ruprect, 1967) and of 2 Maccabees is that of R. Hanhart, *Maccabaeorum liber II*, Septuaginta Vetus Testamentum Graecum, vol. 9:2 (Göttingen: Vandenhoeck & Ruprecht, 1959).

definite group. Now we will examine these three texts in the context of the works in which they appear in an effort to determine more precisely what they say concerning this enigmatic group. Such a study must include some discussion of the nature and purpose of the two works in which these references are found.

The Hasideans and the Maccabees: *1 Macc. 2:29-42*

In the midst of a description of the origins of the Maccabean revolt, we find the Hasideans mentioned in 1 Macc. 2:42. The chapter begins with Mattathias, the priest who with his five sons moved from Jerusalem to Modein, presumably to escape the enforcement of the decrees of Antiochus IV forbidding upon penalty of death the practice of the Jewish religion. When confronted by the demand to sacrifice to the king, Mattathias not only refuses to comply, but kills both a Jew who tries to offer a sacrifice and one of the king's officers. With that, Mattathias and his sons flee to the hills calling for all those who are "zealous for the law and support the covenant" to follow them. In v. 29, 1 Maccabees temporarily leaves the story of Mattathias to tell us about 'many' who in search of justice and righteousness fled to the desert. Soldiers of the king pursuing them into the wilderness murdered a thousand of them when these devout Jews would not fight on the sabbath. As a result of this atrocity, Mattathias and his followers decided that they would never die in such a manner; they would resist any enemy that attacked on the sabbath day. The reference to the Hasideans follows this decision: τότε συνήχθησαν πρὸς αὐτοὺς συναγωγὴ Ασιδαίων ἰσχυροὶ δυνάμει ἀπὸ Ισραηλ πᾶς ὁ ἑκουσιαζόμενος τῷ νομῷ (Then a company of Hasideans joined them, mighty men from Israel, each one willingly devoted to the law). The account continues by describing the growing strength and activity of the Maccabean forces. The chapter concludes with the death of Mattathias.

The central issues arising from this account for our study are three: (1) Are the 'many' in v. 29 who flee to the desert the Hasideans? (2) What is the relationship in this chapter of the Hasideans to Mattathias and his followers? (3) What does the description of the Hasideans in v. 42 of this chapter tell us concerning this group? We will address each of these questions as we study the texts from which they arise.

The Desert Dwellers: 1 Macc. 2:29-38

Many studies have considered the devout persons in 1 Maccabees 2, who fled to the desert only to become martyrs, to be members of the group called Hasideans in v. 42 of that chapter.[2] 1 Macc. 2:29 describes the origin of these desert dwellers: τότε κατέβησαν πολλοὶ ζητοῦντες δικαιοσύνην καὶ κρίμα εἰς τὴν ἔρημον καθίσαι ἐκεῖ (Then many seeking righteousness and justice descended to the desert to dwell there). It is thought that the stated reason for the flight of the 'many' to the wilderness, i.e., to seek justice and righteousness, is representative of a kind of piety similar to what would be expected of a group called the 'Pious'. Corroboration for this perspective is found in the refusal of these desert dwellers to defend themselves against the king's troops because they do not want to defile the sabbath. This evidence for a connec-

[2]. See, e.g., Davies, *JJS* 28 (1977) 133, n. 33.

tion between these devout defenders of Judaism and the Hasideans becomes one of the links in the so-called Hasidic hypothesis discussed above.[3] One of the tenets of that proposal is to identify the Hasideans with the Qumran sect. While the flight to the desert recorded in 1 Maccabees 2 is not usually related directly to "the new covenant in the land of Damascus" of CD 6:19, which is often understood to signify the move by the covenanters to Qumran or some other desert location, v. 29 is used as evidence of the ascetic nature of the Hasideans, thereby making them the predecessors of the Qumran-Essenes.[4]

The refusal to fight on the Sabbath is seen by some to reflect a pacifist tendency, thereby providing a basis for the identification of the Hasideans with apocalyptic literature such as Daniel and Enoch,[5] in addition to the literature identified with Qumran. Once the connection between vv. 29 and 42 is made, the discussion about resisting aggression on the Sabbath is viewed as part of the process whereby the Hasideans became allied for a brief time with the Macca-

[3]. See Chapter 1. This connection is made, e.g., by M. Black, *The Scrolls and Christian Origins: Studies in the Jewish Background of the New Testament*, BJS 48 (Chico: Scholars Press, 1983 - orig. 1961), 16. But see Davies, *JJS* 28 (1977) 127-33.

[4]. Black, *Scrolls*, 16.

[5]. Martin Hengel, *Judaism and Hellenism: Studies in their Encounter during the Early Hellenistic Period*, trans. J. Bowden (Philadelphia: Fortress, 1974), 1:175-218.

bees.[6] The assumption, of course, is that people with otherworldly interests such as those reflected in apocalyptic literature would have no interest in allying themselves with political groups since they believed the victory would be theirs as the result of their purity and their devotion to the law.[7] This hypothesis then understands the union of these Hasideans with the Hasmoneans as temporary, terminated by the events discussed in 1 Maccabees 7, a passage which will be discussed in detail later in this chapter. From this viewpoint, the split in chapter 7 comes about because the Hasideans consider that the right of Jews to practice their religion is assured and because they have no interest in political power.[8] The alliance due to the tyranny of Antiochus IV is seen as the one exception in an otherwise pacifistic history for this group. I must note that this is a simplified version of a number of more complicated hypotheses, each with its own variations. The assumption that the Hasideans were pacifists is certainly not a part of every hypothesis that relates the Hasideans of v. 42 to the 'many' of v. 29. However, the thesis that vv. 29-41 describes events concerning the Hasidim is widely held. In order to test it, we need to look even more broadly and examine the context of those verses within the rest of the work.

6. Note the statements about not fighting on the Sabbath in Jub. 50:12 and CD 12:6.

7. Note the variety of responses to Antiochus' measures recorded in J. J. Collins, *The Apocalyptic Vision of the Book of Daniel*, HSM 16 (Missoula: Scholars Press, 1977), 192-210.

8. The viewpoint is described by Davies, *JJS* 28 (1977) 137-38. Note also W. O. E. Oesterley, "1 Maccabees," *APOT* 1:73.

While commentators have noted that a new literary unit begins with v. 29,[9] I am not certain that the implications of that fact have been brought to bear upon the issue at hand. A linguistic analysis of these verses shows that the author did not connect the activity of the *polloi* (many) in v. 29 with that of Mattathias and his sons. In v. 28, Mattathias and his sons flee to the hills while in v. 29 the 'many' go down to the desert. An examination of 1 Maccabees shows that all the activity of the Maccabees is described as taking place in the *horē* (hills), with the exception of two references in chapter 9 where Jonathan and Simon along with their troops retreat to the wilderness of Tekoa.[10] If the Maccabees were engaged in some form of guerilla warfare, the hills would have been a logical place for their sphere of activity. Goldstein has noted that most of Judah Maccabee's defensive battles take place on the roads running north and west from Jerusalem, the hill country.[11] The verb *katabainō* (to descend) in v. 29 also sets off the action, for Mattathias and his sons are described using the verb *pheugō*, they "fled to the hills." The descent of the many receives additional emphasis with the addition of the infinitive phrase *kathisai ekei* (to dwell there). This seems to reflect a different attitiude toward

[9]. See the structural chart in Nils Martola, *Capture and Liberation: A Study in the Composition of the First Book of Maccabees* (Abo: Abo Akademi, 1984), 25. One exception is Goldstein, who places the major break at v. 27: J. A. Goldstein, *I Maccabees: A New Translation with Introduction and Commentary*, AB 41 (Garden City: Doubleday, 1976), 235.

[10]. 1 Macc. 9:33, 62.

[11]. Goldstein, *I Maccabees*, 236.

possessions. While Mattathias and his sons "left behind whatever they had in the city," the many took their wives, their children and their cattle with them to the desert "to dwell there," taking up permanent residence.

One further difference requires our attention. The repeated concern of Mattathias and his sons throughout this book, and especially in chapter 2, is *Torah* (Law) and *beryt* (covenant). His cry in v. 27 seems to reflect the theme of the work, "Let everyone who is zealous for the law, supporting the covenant, come out behind me." The many who go to the wilderness are not described in this manner. They are characterized as going out to seek *dikaiosynē kai krima* (righteousness and justice). These words are notably absent from the rest of 1 Maccabees, with *krima* appearing only once more in the work, and *dikaiosynē* twice, once in a quote from Gen. 15:6. In fact, the entire *dikaios* word group only appears two more times in the work. One cannot help but be struck by the difference between the story in 1 Macc. 2:29ff. and the surrounding text. The author of 1 Maccabees did not connect the many in v. 29 with Mattathias and his sons.

Having demonstrated the differences in content between vv. 29ff. and that which immediately precedes it, we must ask how much of the material following v. 29 concerns the 'desert dwellers'. There are two possibilities. First, the death of a thousand of these residents in v. 38 may be one ending, since v. 39 begins with "Mattathias and his friends," a new subject. A second possibility is that v. 42 provides a new beginning; the adverb *tote* (then) would be evidence for this viewpoint.[12] *Tote* did mark the beginning of the story in v.

12. Both the RSV and NEB begin a new paragraph at v. 42. Note also, among others, W. Dommershausen, *1 Makkabäer. 2 Makkabäer*, Die Neue Echter Bibel, Kommentar zum Alten Testament mit der Einheitsübersetzung, v. 12 (Würzburg: Echter Verlag,

29. The use of this term could indicate that we are beginning a new subject with this verse which includes the first references to the *Asidaioi* in the books of the Maccabees. It is interesting to note that the story line of the book would follow very well if vv. 29-41 were eliminated from the work. The adverb *tote*, however, does not only have this disjunctive function in the Greek syntax of 1 Maccabees. Elsewhere in the book it plays a temporal role in the midst of a literary unit, sometimes apparently in the middle of a sentence.[13] The presence of this word is not in itself enough to signify the beginning of a new literary unit.

A much more important indicator is the sequence of events surrounding the major character of this chapter, Mattathias. We had left him and his sons in v. 28 where they fled to the hills on account of their zeal for the law to organize resistance to the measures of Antiochus. In v. 39 it is recorded that Mattathias along with his friends[14] learned about the execution of these 'desert people'. As a result, a decision is made that they will resist anyone who attacks them on the sabbath. In other words, the group who lived in

1985), 24-25.

[13]. 1 Macc. 4:41, 14:32, 16:9.

[14]. The phrase, *Mattathias kai hoi philoi autou* (Mattathias and his friends), also found in v. 45, seems to be one way in which the historian describes the response of Mattathias to the offer made by the officers of the king in v. 18. They tell Mattathias that, if he will do what the king commands, "you and your sons will be among the friends of the king." This meant that they would be under the king's direct protection and be included among his officers. The Hasmonean historian suggests that Mattathias has his own group of counselors and protectors.

the desert is not part of this decision. The author has used their case to raise the issue of resistance on the sabbath; perhaps that should be stated more strongly, to justify the stance of the Maccabees. The story about the desert dwellers ends with v. 38, and in v. 39 we get a new account concerning Mattathias and his followers. The literary unit describing the experiences of the martyred group seeking righteousness and justice includes vv. 29-38 and a new unit begins with v. 39.[15]

From the preceding literary analysis, it follows that v. 42, the center of our interest, is located in the midst of a unit which begins with v. 39 and ends with v. 48, the major characters of which are Mattathias and his friends.[16] When we look at v. 42 we read, "Then a company of Hasideans joined them." The antecedent of "them" in that verse seems to be self evident, Mattathias and his friends. What is not as clear is the antecedent in the following verses: Whom do the fugitives in v. 43 join and reinforce? Who strikes down sinners and lawless men in v. 44? Some readings of these verses assume that the antecedent of the third person plural prounoun is both the Maccabees and the Hasideans. But if we locate these verses in the context of a unit beginning with v. 39, the antecedent is simply the Hasmoneans. In

[15]. Note that v. 39 is considered a major division by most of the commentators charted by Martola, *Capture and Liberation*, 25, as well as in the list of text editions provided at the bottom of p. 28 and in the summary in p. 29, n. 31.

[16]. Martola, *Capture and Liberation*, 157-59, fails to understand this relationship when he emphasizes that vv. 39-41, 42-44 and 45-49 each constitute separate literary units. His work, for the most part, provides a needed and good literary treatment of 1 Maccabees.

other words, just as the Hasideans joined "them," i.e., Mattathias and his friends, so the fugitives in v. 43 join "them," and they, i.e., the Hasmoneans, establish an army, strike out at sinners in their anger and at lawless men in their wrath.[17] Such an understanding of the text is made explicit in v. 45 when the author again refers to the major characters of the story by name, Mattathias and his friends. This is no record of a new alliance between the Hasideans and the Hasmoneans, nor is it an account of the union of political and religious forces. What is recorded in 1 Maccabees at this point is much more simple. Within the midst of an account which describes the growth, development and early activity of the Maccabean movement, we find it mentioned that the Hasideans, among others, joined the Hasmoneans in their struggle.

The misapprehension of this section in 1 Maccabees is not only the province of modern interpreters. Apparently, Josephus did not understand this passage either. We certainly will always be puzzled by his omission of the references to the Hasideans while he utilizes 1 Maccabees as a source for his works.[18] In his brief summary in *The Jewish War* of the events in 1 Maccabees 2, we find that all the events of vv. 29-45 are simply described as Mattathias προσγενομένων δὲ ἀπὸ τοῦ δήμου πολλῶν (being joined by many of the common people.)[19] A fuller paraphrase of 1 Maccabees is

[17]. Martola, *ibid*, notes the problem of the antecedents in vv. 43 and 44, but reaches a different conclusion because of his division of the text into smaller units.

[18]. See the discussion in Chapter 2.

[19]. *BJ* 1:37.

included in *Jewish Antiquities*, where his account of 1 Macc. 2:29 reads as follows: τὸ δ' αὐτὸ καὶ ἄλλοι πολλοὶ ποιήσαντες μετὰ τέκνων καὶ γυναικῶν ἔφυγον εἰς τὴν ἔρημον (And many others having done the same thing [i.e., as Mattathias and his sons] fled with wives and children to the wilderness.)[20] In this passage Josephus explicitly links those described in 1 Macc. 2:29 with the Maccabees in v. 28, whom he also describes as going "to the wilderness" rather than "to the hills," as recorded in 1 Macc. 2:28. Similarly, at the end of this account, after the king's men have killed about a thousand of those who fled to the desert along with their wives and children, Josephus records that πολλοὶ δὲ καὶ διασωθέντες τῷ Ματταθίᾳ προσέθεντο κἀκεῖνον ἄρχοντα ἀπέδειξαν ὁ δὲ καὶ σαββάτοις αὐτοὺς ἐδίδασκε μάχεσθαι (many escaped and joined Mattathias, whom they appointed as their leader. And he instructed them to fight also on the sabbath.)[21] In other words, Josephus directly linked the story about the desert people to the account concerning Mattathias and his sons both at the beginning and at the end of the story as found in 1 Maccabees. The record of the 'many' is incorporated into the account that relates the origins of the army of Mattathias. Following the instructions to fight on the Sabbath, Josephus records that ποιήσας οὖν δύναμιν πολλὴν περὶ αὐτὸν Ματταθίας (Mattathias made a large force around himself), a reference to the *dynamis* (army) of 1 Macc. 2:44, and thereby omits any mention of

[20]. *AJ* 12:272.

[21]. *AJ* 12:275.

the Hasideans. While Josephus does not fall into the trap which has caught many modern interpreters, i.e., that 1 Maccabees 2 is the record of a grand alliance between the religious Hasideans and the political Maccabees, he does fail to note that the account of the many who go to the desert is a separate story from that of the growth of the Hasmonean movement.

The literary connection between 2 Macc. 2:29-38 and the Hasideans of v. 42 has also found substantiation in the hypothesis that the name *Essēnoi* or *Essaioi* (Essenes) is derived from the Hebrew *Ḥasydym* (Pious). While one portion of this argument is discussed in the section which follows, it will be necessary to devote an entire chapter to an analysis of this proposition.[22]

The Identity of the 'Many'

If the persons described in 1 Macc. 2:29-38 are not the Hasideans, the question arises as to whether any other identification for this group is possible. Now our knowledge of events in second-century Palestine is certainly limited. This paucity of information is even more obvious when we try to define the religious and political groups of the era. This means that many proposals concerning a historical identification must remain hypothetical, including the one which follows.

What caught the attention of this writer is that a number of the features which set off the account in 1 Macc. 2:29-38 from the rest of the chapter have been identified as particularly characteristic of those people who inhabited the caves on the shore of the Dead Sea and who are usually identified as the Essenes described in the writings of Philo and Joseph-

[22]. See Chapter 4.

us.[23] I have already noted the unique vocabulary in 2:29 which is used to describe the 'many' who descend to the desert to dwell there.[24] They are said to be seeking *dikaiosynē kai krima* (righteousness and justice), terms which are used in the LXX to translate *ṣedaqah* and *mishpat.* It was noted that these two terms are notably absent from the rest of 1 Maccabees with *krima* appearing only one other time and *dikaiosynē* twice, once in a quotation of Gen. 15:6. Now, these two Hebrew terms are ubiquitous in the Dead Sea Scrolls. Not only do they appear frequently in these works, but they have been shown to be terms central to the self-understanding of the sect.[25] Verse 29 describes the 'many' using terms that are virtually absent from 1 Maccabees but central for understanding the literature of the sect.

These dwellers in the desert apparently accepted as authoritative a prohibition of fighting on the sabbath. The only place in Jewish literature that such an absolute stance concerning warfare on the sabbath appears is in Jub. 50:12. Now Charles in his commentary on Jubilees suggests that

[23]. For a discussion of the Hasidim and the Essenes, see Chapter 4.

[24]. Note the discussion of this text in Chapter 4.

[25]. On *mishpat*, see L. H. Schiffman, *The Halakhah at Qumran*, SJLA 16 (Leiden: E. J. Brill, 1975), 42-47. On *ṣedaqah*, see Joseph Baumgarten, "The Heavenly Tribunal and the Personification of *Ṣedeq* in Jewish Apocalyptic," *ANRW* II:19:1:219-39; Ben Zion Wacholder, *The Dawn of Qumran: The Sectarian Torah and the Teacher of Righteousness* (Cincinnati: HUC Press, 1983), 135-40.

this prohibition is also found in *M. Shabb.* 6:2,4.[26] However, the issue in that text is the carrying of implements of warfare on the sabbath rather than fighting. Whether that prohibition actually made the practice of warfare on the sabbath impossible to carry out seems to me to be somewhat irrelevant to this discussion. Finkelstein notes the peculiarity of Jubilees' prohibition in contrast to other Jewish literature,[27] but believes that the book of Jubilees does provide examples of pre-Maccabean halakah. In this case, Jubilees reflects the major viewpoint of the Jewish tradition prior to certain Hasmonean innovations, of which 1 Macc. 2:41 is an example. In his major study on this question, Herr similarly assumes that the sectarian laws found in Jubilees preserved an early halakic tradition concerning this matter.[28] Neither of these studies takes seriously the notion that Jubilees, now to be considered a part of the literature of the Dead Sea sect or

26. R. H. Charles, *The Book of Jubilees* (London: A & C Black, 1902).

27. L. Finkelstein, "The Book of Jubilees and the Rabbinic Halaka," *HTR* 16 (1923) 51; see also C. Albeck, "Das Buch der Jubiläen und die Halacha," *BHWJ* 47 (1930) 11, where it is noted that rabbinic halaka and recorded incidents in Josephus agree with the decision of Mattathias and his friends.

28. M. D. Herr, "The Problem of War on the Sabbath in the Second Temple and the Talmudic Periods," *Tarbiẓ* 30 (1960-61) 247 (Hebrew). See also S. Safrai, "Religion in Everyday Life," *The Jewish People in the First Century: Historical Geography, Political History, Social, Cultural and Religious Institutions*, eds. S. Safrai and M. Stern, *CRINT* 1:2 (Assen: Van Gorcum/Philadelphia: Fortress, 1976), 805.

its affiliates,[29] may be representative merely of sectarian thinking on this question and consequently should not be used to describe the viewpoint of any other segment of Judaism.

Charles and Herr also cite evidence from Josephus to buttress the viewpoint that warfare on the Sabbath was prohibited during the Second Temple era. Scattered throughout Josephus as well as in 2 Maccabees are allusions which suggest that Jews would not fight on the sabbath.[30] However, this is qualified in *BJ* 1:146, where Josephus states that Jews fight only in self-defense on the sabbath. A similar sentiment is already expressed in 1 Macc. 2:41. An explanation of the basis for this reluctance to fight on the sabbath can be found in the correspondence recorded in *AJ* 14:225-27 wherein Dolabella, governor of Syria, exempts the Jews from military service, in part because they cannot bear arms or march on the sabbath. The problem is the halakic injunctions against carrying implements on the sabbath in *M. Shabb.* 6:2,4, already alluded to above, and the restrictions on travel. The references in Josephus certainly convey the sacred character with which the Jews held the seventh day, but these are of a different nature than the absolute prohibition recorded in Jub. 50:12.

When we turn to the early rabbinic materials, we find even less evidence of a viewpoint similar to that held by the

29. J. C. VanderKam, *Textual and Historical Studies in the Book of Jubilees*, HSM 14 (Missoula: Scholars Press, 1977); Wacholder, *Dawn*, 41-62.

30. *CA* 1:209; *BJ* 1:146; *AJ* 12:4; 13:251-52,337; 14:63-64,226; 18:323; 2 Macc. 8:25-28; 12:38; 15:1-5. 2 Macc. 6:11 is a reference to the same group as 1 Macc. 2:29-38.

desert-dwellers in 1 Maccabees or recorded in Jubilees. We have already mentioned *M. Shabb.* 6:2,4, which is concerned with the carrying of implements on the sabbath. It is a well-established principle in talmudic literature that it is permissible to suspend the sabbath laws in order to save a human life.[31] In their commentary to the Mekilta on Exod. 31:14, Horowitz-Rabin apply the principle of *pyqquaḥ nepesh* (saving an endangered life) to the situation in which Gentiles attack on the sabbath and the Jews must defend themselves.[32] This is spelled out more clearly in *T. 'Erub.* 3:5-6, where there is a discussion of the conditions under which they can carry weapons in war when the Gentiles attack on the sabbath.[33] The issue in rabbinic literature is when the normal restrictions on travel and bearing burdens are overridden on the sabbath for the sake of protecting human life. Never is there a halakic controversy over the absolute prohibition of warfare on the sabbath. The only places where we find such a viewpoint expressed are in 1 Macc. 2:29-38, 2 Macc. 6:11, an apparent allusion to the same event, and Jub. 50:12.

The most obvious connection between the account of the 'many' and the people behind the Dead Sea Scrolls is the

31. *B. Yoma* 85a; *B. Ketub.* 5a, 15b, 19a.

32. H. S. Horovitz and I. A. Rabin, *Mekylta' deRabby Yshma'e'l* (Jerusalem: Wahrmann Books, 1970), 342.

33. We find this view presented in greater detail in Maimonides' *Mishneh Torah*, where war against the Gentiles is permitted, even on the Sabbath (*Hilkot Melakym* 6:11), and where the instances in which the usual Sabbath regulations are overridden are listed (*Hilkot Melakym* 6:13).

common element of the desert. However, we do have to exercise caution in our judgment. The wilderness tradition is an important part of Hebrew literature going back to its early roots in the exodus. The concept of a wilderness group separate from the remainder of the Israelites is already to be found in the testimony of Jeremiah concerning the Rechabites.[34] Given the evidence presented above, however, we must consider the hypothesis that the 'many' of 1 Macc. 2:29-38 are to be related to those producers of scrolls on the shore of the Dead Sea who were part of a broader movement called the Essenes by Josephus. What this means is that the many studies listed in Chapter 1 which identified the account in 1 Maccabees with the Essenes may be correct, however they were incorrect in claiming that this account was also descriptive of the Hasideans.[35]

The Company of the Hasideans: 1 Macc. 2:42

The examination of 1 Maccabees 2 up to this point has demonstrated that only v. 42 of this chapter yields informa-

[34]. Jeremiah 35. See J. W. Flight, "The Nomadic Idea and Ideal in the Old Testament," *JBL* 42 (1923) 158-226; Millar Burrows, *An Outline of Biblical Theology* (Philadelphia: Westminster, 1946), 151-53; R. de Vaux, *Ancient Israel: Its Life and Institutions*, trans. J. McHugh (New York/London: McGraw-Hill, 1961), 3-15; M. H. Pope, "Rechab," *IDB* 4:14-16; S. Talmon, "'The Desert Motif' in the Bible and Qumran Literature," *Biblical Motifs: Origins and Transformations*, ed. A. Altmann (Cambridge: Harvard University Press, 1966), 31-64; F. S. Frick, "The Rechabites Reconsidered," *JBL* 90 (1971) 279-87; F. S. Frick and E. G. Martin, "Rechabites," *IDBS*, 726-28.

[35]. See Chapter 4 for a discussion of the names *Essēnoi* and *Ḥasydym*.

tion concerning the Hasideans in the second century B.C.E. The account of the desert dwellers is describing a different group of persons. Verses 39-48 chronicle the growth of the Maccabean resistance. In that account, we find mention of the Hasideans. We must now turn our attention directly to this verse to determine more precisely what it tells us concerning the *Asidaioi*: τότε συνήχθησαν πρὸς αὐτοὺς συναγωγὴ Ασιδαίων ἰσχυροὶ δυνάμει ἀπὸ Ισραηλ πᾶς ὁ ἑκουσιαζόμενος τῷ νομῷ (Then a company of Hasideans joined them, mighty men from Israel, each one willingly devoted to the law). The terms in this verse are somewhat enigmatic so each phrase must be studied seriatim.

The first phrase to demand our attention is the name used in this context, *synagōgē Asidaiōn*. This is usually (and most likely correctly) considered to be a translation of the Hebrew *qehal ḥasydym*, as recorded in Ps. 149:1.[36] While it has been suggested, because of the references to *ḥasydym*, that this Psalm and the one prior to it were composed in the Hasmonean era, more recent scholarship on the Psalms has not considered such a late date acceptable.[37] Others have

[36]. A. Kahana, *Hassep̱arym Haḥyṣonym* (Jerusalem: Makor, 1970-orig. 1936), 2:107.

[37]. For a Maccabean dating see, e.g., D. B. Duhm, *Die Psalmen*, KHAT 14 (Freiburg: J. C. B. Mohr, 1899), XX, 310 and A. Büchler, *Types of Jewish Palestinian Piety from 70 B.C.E. to 70 C.E.: The Ancient Pious Men* (London: Jews' College, 1922), 7-8. A slightly earlier dating in 332/331 B.C.E. was the particular thesis of M. Buttenwiesser, *The Psalms: Chronologically treated with a new Translation* (New York: Ktav, 1969 - orig. 1938), 690. The impossibility of dating this kind of Psalm with a good deal of reliability is stressed by H. Gunkel, *The Psalms: A Form-Critical Introduction*, trans. T. M. Horner, FBBS 19 (Philadelphia: Fortress, 1967), 32 and H.-J. Kraus, *Psalmen*, BKAT 15:2 (Neukirchen:

considered these references to be evidence of a group by this name at the time of or shortly after the first *Ḥurban* (destruction). While the reference to Ps. 149:1 seems obvious, it must be noted that the LXX uses *ekklēsia* rather than *synagōgē* in this verse. Now it is true that the LXX employs *ekklēsia* only when translating *qahal*, and uses *synagōgē* to designate both *'edah* and *qahal*.[38] Since 1 Macc. 2:42 could then originally have employed either term here, the LXX translation of Ps. 149:1 still supports the argument that the original reading of 1 Macc. 2:42 is *qehal ḥasydym.*

As has frequently been noted, the meaning of the terms *qahal* and *'edah* in the Hebrew Scriptures is for the most part virtually identical.[39] Different usages are to be attributed in most cases to the individual preferences of the various authors. Both terms function most importantly as designations for the collective Israel, in particular when it was assembled for cultic purposes. Schrage has noted, however, that *synagōgē* increasingly comes to designate "the individual congregation" as we move to the books of the apocrypha and that this may have been the context in which the translators

Neukirchener Verlag, 1960), 2:966-67. Both propose a pre-exilic dating for this psalm, as does M. Dahood, *Psalms* III: 101-150, AB 17a (Garden City: Doubleday, 1970), 356-57. See Chapter 1 above.

[38]. E. Hatch and H. A. Redpath, *A Concordance to the Septuagint and the Other Greek Versions of the Old Testament (Including the Apocryphal Books)* (Oxford: Clarendon Press, 1897), 433, 1309-10. The LXX uses *synagōgē* about 35 times for *qahal* and 130 for *'edah.*

[39]. *IDB* 1:670; *TDNT* 3:528; 7:802-03. Schrage (*TDNT* 7:802, n. 20) notes a number of passages in which both *qahal* and *'edah* appear: Exod. 16:1-10; Num. 10:1-10; 14; 16; 17:6-15,20.

of the LXX understood the term.[40] They used *synagōgē* exclusively in the first four books of the Pentateuch to designate the community of Israel, regardless of whether the Hebrew was *qahal*, *'edah* or one of the other scattered Hebrew words which they chose to translate by use of this term. Schrage apparently assumes that its use in the LXX is a midpoint in the progression from the use of the term as a translation of the biblical *qahal* or *'edah* to its later designation as the Greek equivalent of the *beyt hakkeneset* (synagogue).[41] A full analysis of the use of the term as it relates to the origin of the institution of the same name would require another study.

In the words of Ben Sira we see the use of the term with reference to designated groups of persons. In Sir. 1:30, 4:7 and 41:18 action is specified which could only occur with reference to some local group. Note, I am not saying that all these groups, e.g. 41:18, need to define their identity around a religious stance. These are cases, however, where they do not designate all of Israel but some more narrowly defined entity. This is probably how Ben Sira understood the

40. Hatch and Redpath, *Concordance*, 1309; *TDNT* 7:805.

41. A summary and bibliography of the extensive discussion on the origin of the synagogue is to be found in S. Safrai, "The Synagogue," *The Jewish People in the First Century: Historical Geography, Political History, Social, Cultural and Religious Institutions*, eds. S. Safrai and M. Stern, *CRINT* 1:2 (Assen: Van Gorcum/Philadelphia: Fortress, 1976), 793-833; id., "The Synagogue and its Worship," *Society and Religion in the Second Temple Period*, eds. Michael Avi-Yonah and Zvi Baras, WHJP 8 (Jerusalem: Massada, 1977), 65-98; *Schürer-Vermes-Millar*, 2:423-63. Note also the discussion by S. J. D. Cohen, *From Maccabees to the Mishnah*, Library of Early Christianity 7 (Philadelphia: Westminster, 1987), 111-15.

synagōgais Yakōb (assemblies of Jacob) of Deut. 33:4 when in 24:23 he, like the LXX, quotes the biblical text in the plural. Elsewhere the term is used to designate those who do not do the will of God. We do find mention of the *synagōgē Kore* (company of Korah) in 45:18, which appears in the Hebrew text of this work as *'adat Qorah*, in conformity with the biblical story in Numbers 16 which uses *'edah* as well as *qahal*. The *synagōgē hamartōlōn* (company of sinners) in 16:6 and the *synagōgē anomōn* (company of the lawless) in 21:9 are similar cases. While not specifying a collective group of persons who necessarily know one another, the latter references do point to a particular group within Israel who share a certain identity.[42] Similarly, in the Dead Sea Scrolls both *'edah* and *qahal* can be used to designate the sect or its opponents.[43] What these texts from Ben Sira and the Dead Sea Scrolls illustrate is that in Jewish texts from the second century B.C.E. *synagōgē* has come to be applied more frequently to various groups of Jews rather than to Israel as a whole.

What is most significant for our study is the use of the term in the work presently under consideration. In 3:44 it designates the group assembled by Judas for battle that engages in prayer and fasting prior to going to war against the Greeks. The mention of the use of the trumpets in this warfare suggests that *synagōgē* is used here to designate the *qahal* of Num. 10:7 that assembled for battle under the leadership of the priests. In 1 Macc. 7:12 we learn of a *synagōgē grammateōn* (company of scribes), a passage which

[42]. *TDNT* 7:804-05.

[43]. K. G. Kuhn et al., *Konkordanz zu den Qumrantexten* (Göttingen: Vandenhoeck & Ruprecht, 1960), 156-57, 190.

will be discussed later in this chapter. In both these cases, the term is used to designate a specific group of persons. In 14:28, the term signifies that assembly in which decisions are made concerning the welfare of the nation; however the fact that the adjective *megalē* (great) must be added shows that this is not its normal usage.

If *synagōgē* in our passage is a translation of *qahal*, then we also need to examine those places where *ekklēsia* appears. Here we find mention of an *ekklēsia megalē* (great assembly) in 5:16 so that, given the use of *synagōgē megalē* in 14:28, it would appear the same concept is implied in 4:59 and 14:19.[44] In other words, in the latter two references which seem to apply to the collective Israel or at least to a gathering of all of Israel's leadership, the author of 1 Maccabees assumed that they would be understood in the same way as the 'great assembly' in 5:16 and 14:28. Presumably this is how the author visualized Caleb giving witness *en tę̄ ekklēsią* (in the assembly).[45] Finally, 1 Macc. 3:13 makes mention of the *ekklēsia pistōn* (company of the faithful). This usage is similar to that of *synagōgē* in 2:42, 3:44 and 7:12 in which it sets apart a very specific group of persons. Thus *ekklēsia* and *synagōgē* are used in two ways in 1 Maccabees, either to designate a "great assembly" which makes collective decisions for all of Israel or to signify a distinct group within Israel who have some common bond or

[44]. The fact that 1 Macc. 14:28 is the greeting in an official letter may explain why *synagōgē* is used here in a context where 1 Maccabees seems to prefer the term *ekklēsia*.

Whether any of these references are related to *hakkeneset haggedolah* (the Great Assembly) mentioned in the rabbinic tradition is a question beyond the scope of this work.

[45]. 1 Macc. 2:56.

purpose. In both 1 Macc. 2:42 and 7:12 the use of the verb *synagō* is to be found in conjunction with the noun.[46] The conjunction of a verb and noun from the same root seems to be a stylistic feature of this author.[47] Since Ps. 149:1 seems to lie behind the formulation of the phrase in 1 Maccabees, the verb was chosen by the author to fit the noun, thereby emphasizing its use. We can see that *synagōgē* in 1 Macc. 2:42 gives us the sense of a group of persons with a common purpose.

These observations on the use of *synagōgē* complement our earlier discussion of the name *Asidaioi*.[48] There we had noted that the transliteration of the Hebrew into Greek means that the term was understood as a proper noun. The major linguistic argument for the distinctive character of this association of persons rests on the argument above concerning the significance of the term *Asidaioi*. Describing these persons as a *synagōgē* undergirds the conclusion that we are talking of persons with some kind of shared, common identity. Given that such is the case, the question of the place of this group in the history of Jewish sectarianism arises.

Most frequently, the Hasideans have been considered a sectarian group within Judaism. Marcel Simon felt justified in recognizing the "mighty warriors of Israel" in 1 Macc.

[46]. In 1 Macc. 7:12 it has the prefix *epi-*.

[47]. This was pointed out by one of the readers of the manuscript. An example cited was 1 Macc. 3:13.

[48]. See Chapter 2 above.

2:42 as the first Jewish 'sect'.[49] Howard Clark Kee uses the Hasidim as an example of Jewish sectarianism when he attempts to define the social and cultural setting of the Markan community.[50] When he finds "the seed of sectarian narrowness" within the eschatological circles which are characterized by a "sectarian spirit," Otto Plöger is making the Hasidim a group in conflict "not only with the official community but also with groups related by common tradition."[51] Clearly, this is also the thrust of Hengel's description.[52] In order to address this question, we must first face the problem of definition.

In common usage, sect is often used in a pejorative sense to designate "a dissenting religious body; *esp*: one that is heretical in the eyes of other members within the same communion,"[53] or "a group regarded as heretical or as deviat-

[49]. M. Simon, *Jewish Sects at the Time of Jesus*, trans. J. H. Farley (Philadelphia: Fortress, 1967), 19.

[50]. H. C. Kee, *Community of the New Age: Studies in Mark's Gospel* (Philadelphia: Westminster, 1977), 79-87.

[51]. O. Plöger, *Theocracy and Eschatology*, trans. S. Rudman (Richmond: John Knox, 1968), 50-51.

[52]. Hengel, *Judaism*, 1:176-80.

[53]. *Webster's Third New International Dictionary* (Springfield: Merrian-Webster, 1981), 2052.

ing from a generally accepted religious tradition."[54] Efforts at providing a more acceptable technical definition are found in the field of sociology of religion, beginning with Ernst Troeltsch, who developed the church-sect typology as a basis for analyzing the relationship of christian groups to their environment.[55] It is not our intention here to resolve all the issues related to the study of the definition and development of sects.[56] Rather, we merely wish to determine what sociologists of religion consider a sect to be. We do find a simple description in one of the basic articles in the field: "A church is a religious group that accepts the social environment in which it exists. A sect is a religious group that rejects the social environment in which it exists."[57] Another writer summarizes the discussion: "Almost all students of sectarianism agree that in their origin sects are to be understood as protest movements. Sects protest against 'worldliness' in the religious institutions (churches in the schema of

54. *The Random House Dictionary of the English Language: Unabridged Edition* (New York: Random House, 1981), 1289.

55. E. Troeltsch, *The Social Teachings of the Christian Churches* (London: Allen and Unwin, 1931).

56. Note, e.g., the number of articles in the last ten years in the *JSSR*.

57. B. Johnson, "On Church and Sect," *ASR* 28 (1963) 542.

Troeltsch) or the depraved host society; sometimes they protest against worldliness in both spheres."[58] Thus, in one way or another sect is understood to be a group which rejects the dominant values or mores of the society, however that entity is defined. This means that, in attempts to classify modern Judaism, traditional Orthodox Judaism is frequently considered to be a sectarian group.[59] However we must note the obvious; the church-sect typology was developed for and been applied primarily within the christian tradition.[60]

The weakness of applying this typology to Judaism is illustrated by the example just cited, i.e., traditional Orthodox Judaism. While it is sectarian in the sense mentioned above, i.e., it rejects the social environment in which it exists, this portrayal ignores any sense of historical development. While traditional Orthodox Judaism rejects the values and beliefs of Christianity and of mainstream American society, it cannot be considered to be sectarian in relationship to Judaism in the same way that the Waldensians or the Anabaptists are within Christianity. A church-sect typology implies some relationship between the value and belief systems which are evaluated on that continuum.[61] Orthodox Judaism has a

[58]. C. Redekop, "A New Look at Sect Development," *JSSR* 13 (1974) 346.

[59]. W. Herberg, *Protestant-Catholic-Jew* (Garden City: Doubleday, 1960), 95-96, n. 42; Johnson, *ASR* 28 (1963) 546.

[60]. Johnson, *ASR* 28 (1963) 546.

[61]. Johnson, *ASR* 28 (1963) 539-49; Redekop, *JSSR* 13 (1974) 345-52.

different belief system which cannot rightly be placed on the same continuum as American Christianity. There is a problem when we apply the usual sociological category of 'sect' to Judaism.

It is possible to assume that the category of 'sect' could be used within Judaism and that Jewish groups could be evaluated in relationship to one another on some kind of a continuum with 'sect' at one end. Blenkinsopp, noting the difficulties involved in defining sect, still finds it an appropriate and important designation when discussing Second Temple Judaism.[62] He suggests that the essential ingredients of a sect in contrast to a party or school are opposition to the norms accepted by the parent-body and the assertion of claims, made in a more or less exclusive way, that the group is what the parent-body alleges to be. In our case, we need to find some basis in the evidence available for calling the Hasideans a sect. Based on the discussion in the previous paragraph, there needs to be some indication that the Hasideans "reject the social environment" of the remainder of Judaism or that they protest certain aspects of it.

While admittedly all the texts in 1 and 2 Maccabees have not yet been discussed, I think that the observant student will see that there is no evidence of a protest against or of a rejection of the remainder of Judaism in the three references to the Hasideans.[63] Neither do we find any evidence of

[62]. J. Blenkinsopp, "Interpretation and the Tendency to Sectarianism: An Aspect of Second Temple History," *Jewish and Christian Self-Definition*, ed. E. P. Sanders et al. (Philadelphia: Fortress, 1981), 2:1-2. Shaye J. D. Cohen also notes the problem with the definition of 'sect', but continues to employ it with some modification in the definition: *From Maccabees to Mishnah*, 124-27.

[63]. Cohen claims to not know whether the Hasideans are a sect, but does so from the basis of the little knowledge that we

the claims for exclusive truth that Blenkinsopp's definition calls for. Now, it is possible to find evidence of a sectarian group in 1 Macc. 2:29-38; however it has already been demonstrated that these texts are not relevant for a discussion of the Hasideans. It will be shown below that a sectarian understanding of the Hasideans in 1 Macc. 7:12-17 is only misleading. Since 2 Macc. 14:6 calls Judas Maccabaeus the leader of the Hasideans it is difficult to see the group portrayed in that book as a sectarian one. One fails to find in 1 and 2 Maccabees any evidence that would place the Hasideans at that end of a continuum in relation to the rest of Judaism such that we could legitimately term them a sect.

In the discussion of the Hasideans as a sect, another piece of evidence is commonly cited. The assumption in Hengel's work is that "a large part of the priestly upper class and the lay nobility fell victim more and more to Hellenistic assimilation."[64] Similarly, Gerd Theissen speaks of "a reaction to the drift towards assimilation produced by superior alien cultures."[65] In these studies, the supposition that the Hasideans were a sect is occasioned by the assumption that

have of the group: *From Maccabees to Mishnah*, 161. See also the discussion by Devorah Dimant, "Qumran Sectarian Literature," *Jewish Writings of the Second Temple Period: Apocrypha, Pseudepigrapha, Qumran Sectarian Writings, Philo, Josephus*, ed. Michael Stone, *CRINT* 2:2 (Assen: Van Gorcum/Philadelphia: Fortress, 1984), 547, where she applies the category of 'sect' to Qumran but explicitly excludes the Hasideans.

64. Hengel, *Judaism and Hellenism*, 1:176; cf. Plöger, *Theocracy*, 44-45.

65. Gerd Theissen, *Sociology of Early Palestinian Christianity*, trans. J. Bowden (Philadelphia: Fortress, 1978), 87.

the persons they were reacting against were the products of an advanced assimilation with Hellenism. Analysis of this assumption would require a study even longer than this one and I will not attempt it. Of course, Hengel's work on this particular point has been challenged a number of times.[66] What is important to note for the purposes of this study is that it is the apocalyptic literature which is cited when the Hasideans are described as a sect reacting against the growing influence of Hellenism on the Jewish people. I have already discussed the problem of the relation of the Hasideans to these writings in Chapter 1. In this chapter, we will find no evidence in 1 and 2 Maccabees for a connection between the Hasideans and apocalyptic literature. Since the support for the hypothesis that the Hasideans were a sect is derived from outside 1 and 2 Maccabees, it cannot be used as prima facie evidence concerning the references in these works.

One of the reasons that various Jewish groups during the Second Temple era are called sects is because this is the manner in which the term *hairesis* in Josephus is frequently translated.[67] Josephus uses this word when he describes and compares the Pharisees, Sadducees and Essenes. This translation probably occasioned the choice of title for a book such

66. L. H. Feldman, "Hengel's *Judaism and Hellenism* in Retrospect," *JBL* 96 (1977) 371-82; F. Millar, "The Background to the Maccabean Revolution: Reflections on Martin Hengel's 'Judaism and Hellenism'," *JJS* 29 (1978) 1-21; L. H. Feldman, "How Much Hellenism in Jewish Palestine," *HUCA* 57 (1986) 83-111.

67. H. St. John Thackeray in *BJ* 2:162; *V* 10,12,191 (LCL).

as *Jewish Sects at the Time of Jesus.*[68] Having accepted that Josephus understood these three 'philosophies' to be sects, scholars are then willing to extend this sect designation to other groups in the Second Temple era such as the Hasideans. However, this understanding and resulting translation of *hairesis* has not been uniformly accepted. In his translation, Ralph Marcus prefers "school of thought."[69] Taking strong exception to classifying the Pharisees as a sect, Ellis Rivkin also prefers the term "school."[70] None of the three groups seems to have been considered a sect by Josephus in the sense in which the term has been defined above. Thus, we find no evidence in Josephus that sect is an appropriate term for these Jewish groups during the Second Temple period.

The foregoing discussion of the question of whether the Hasideans could be considered a sect has been resolved in the negative. At the same time, it is clear that we are dealing with a group of persons who share a common identity. It seems to this writer that the term best rendering *synagōgē* in 1 Macc. 2:42 and elsewhere in the work is "company" or "congregation." In the rest of our work, we will utilize the term "company" when referring to the Hasideans.[71]

68. Simon, *Jewish Sects.*

69. *AJ* 13:171 (LCL).

70. E. Rivkin, *A Hidden Revolution* (Nashville: Abingdon, 1978), 8, 316-18, n. 1.

71. The RSV uses "company" at 2:42, "congregation" at 3:44 and "group" at 7:12; the NEB "company" in 2:42, "assembly" in 3:44 and "deputation" in 7:12.

Mighty Men from Israel

The next phrase describing the company of Hasideans is *ischyroi dynamei apo Israēl* (usually translated-mighty warriors from Israel), which most probably is rendered in Hebrew as *gibborey ḥayil myYiśra'el.* Matthew Black has emphasized how this verse contradicts any pacifistic view of the Hasideans, suggesting instead that what we find here are actually warrior-saints, that is, the ascetic corps-elite of the Maccabean resistance.[72] He then goes on to compare them with "the Knights Templars and similar orders of the Church Militant in the Middle Ages." Considering them to be scribes, Tcherikover also saw them as the leaders of the military resistance to Antiochus IV.[73] Collins followed him in this view.[74] Any attempt to answer this question requires a more careful examination of the biblical usage of this term.

Understanding what is meant by *gibborey ḥayil* in the Hebrew Scriptures is hardly a simple matter. Neither of the words in this construct phrase finds easy definition. The term *gibbor* is often considered to be part of a 'hero' tradition.[75] It

[72]. *Scrolls*, 16-17; id., "The Tradition of Hasidaean-Essene Asceticism: Its Origins and Influence," *Aspects du Judéo-Christianisme* (Paris: Presses Universitaires de France, 1965), 24-25.

[73]. *Hellenistic Civilization*, 196-98.

[74]. *Apocalyptic Vision*, 202-03; John J. Collins, *The Apocalyptic Imagination: An Introduction to the Jewish Matrix of Christianity* (New York: Crossroad, 1984), 62.

[75]. R. Bartelmus, *Heroentum im Israel und seiner Umwelt: eine traditionsgeschichtliche Untersuchung zu Gen. 6:1-4 und ver-*

is used to describe the offspring of the union of the *beney 'elohym* (sons of God) and the *benot ha'adam* (daughters of men) in Gen. 6:4. These 'heroes' reappear continuously throughout the Enochite tradition.[76] Elsewhere we read of *haggibborym 'asher leDawid* (the heroes of David).[77] Here we read about "three" and "thirty" military heroes who compose the elite among David's troops. We probably should accept Bartelmus' assertion that in 2 Samuel the use of *gibborym* is merely a shorthand for *gibborey ḥayil*.[78] This presentation of the term would seem to find substantiation in a passage such as 2 Kgs. 24:16 where we read of the *'anshey ḥayil...gibborym 'ośey milḥamah* (men of might...heroes who make war). Now *gibbor* also appears in other contexts[79] such as in Deut. 10:17 and Neh. 9:32 as well as in Isa. 9:6 and 10:21 where it is used as an adjective descriptive of *'el* (God). It is this usage which lies behind the suggestion of Bartelmus that *gibborey ḥayil* really means the "warriors of

wandten Texten in Alten Testament und der altorientalischen Literatur, ATANT 65 (Zurich: Theologischer Verlag, 1979), 112-49; Kosmala, "*gabar*," *TDOT* 2:373.

[76]. E.g., 4Q Enoch Giants[a] 7:7; 4Q Enoch Giants[b] I:ii:13,15,20, 21; iii:3; 4Q Enoch[c] I:2.

[77]. 2 Sam. 23:8; 1 Chr. 11:11. Cf. 2 Sam. 23:9,16,17,22.

[78]. Bartelmus, *Heroentum*, 114-16.

[79]. Kosmala, *TDOT* 2:373-77.

Yahweh."[80] The term is also applied to angels in Ps. 103:20. However, it is not necessary for our purposes to probe all the nuances implied in the term, since we are interpreting the construct phrase *gibborey ḥayil* in 1 Macc. 2:42.

Before looking at this noun phrase, let us take a brief glance at the term *ḥayil*. It has frequently been noted that its basic meaning is "strength" or "might," from which issues the most common use of the term to designate a military force.[81] In 1 Chr. 12:26, 20:1 and 2 Chr. 26:13 it appears in conjunction with the term *ṣeḇa'*, which refers to an army or host. However it can also be used to designate wealth, such as in Deut. 8:18 or Ezek. 28:5. This appears also to be the case in Ben Sira 44:6 where the Hebrew reads *'anshey ḥayil wesomkey koaḥ* (men of wealth who possess power). *'Anshey ḥayil* is rendered in the LXX as *andres plousioi* (rich men), testimony that *ḥayil* was understood to mean wealth in the second century B.C.E. Thorion has noted that it also means wealth in *Mek. Yitro* 2 on Exod. 18:21: *'anshey ḥayil 'ellu 'ashyrym uḇa'aley mamon* ("men of power" are the rich and those who possess wealth).[82] However, as noted, our interest resides in both terms in this construct relationship.

The predominant context in which the *gibborey ḥayil* appear in the Hebrew Scriptures is a military one. Clearly

[80]. Bartelmus, *Heroentum*, 114-16.

[81]. H. Eising, "*ḥayil*," *TDOT* 4:348-55. Note that in the LXX *dynamis* sometimes translates *ṣeḇa'*, e.g., Gen. 21:22,32; 26:26.

[82]. Y. Thorion, "Zur Bedeutung von *gibborey ḥayil lemilḥamah* in 11Q T LVII,9," *RevQ* 10 (1981) 597-98.

the references in Joshua are to a group of warriors.[83] Josh. 8:3 indicates that the *gibborey ḥayil* are an elite troop specially chosen from the ranks of the *'am milḥamah* (people of war), the volunteer militia. This must also be the meaning of the term in Josh. 10:7, where both the *'am milḥamah* and the *gibborey ḥayil* are listed as going up with Joshua against the Amorite Kings. The *gibborey ḥayil* in Josh. 1:14 include *kol* (all) the warriors in the two and a half tribes of the Trans-Jordan.[84] It would seem that all the warriors of the king of Jericho are included in Josh. 6:2. While all the references in this book are clearly to military personnel, some seem to include the entire militia while other places suggest the presence of a selected body of troops by that name. We recall the elite troops of David called *gibborym* already mentioned above.[85] However, the term in the Hebrew Scriptures has a broader range of meaning than that found in Joshua.

A number of times in the Hebrew Scriptures, the term appears without any apparent military connection. In Ruth 2:1, Boaz is called a *gibbor ḥayil*, which the RSV translates in this instance as "man of wealth." Since Ruth is called an *'eshet ḥayil* (woman of worth?) in 3:11, it seems more likely that, if we have translated the term incorrectly in 2:1, it should mean "man of worth" or "man of virtue" rather than

[83]. Josh. 1:14; 6:2; 8:3; 10:7.

[84]. Cf. Deut. 3:18, where they are called *kol beney ḥayil* ("sons of war" or "warriors").

[85]. See the references in n. 77 above.

"man of war."[86] However, there are other apparent references to "men of wealth." In 2 Kgs. 15:20, Menahem exacts fifty shekels of silver from every one of the *gibborey ḥayil* to pay off Tiglath-pileser III, king of Assyria. The father of Saul is called a *gibbor ḥayil* in 1 Sam. 9:1, which the RSV translates "man of wealth." In 1 Kgs. 11:28, Jereboam is called a *gibbor ḥayil* which in context probably does not mean "mighty warrior" but rather designates a person of either superior ability or great industry. From these examples it is clear that a military meaning is not adequate to explain the range of usage of the term *gibbor ḥayil* in the Hebrew Scriptures.

We must remember that the military, and in particular an elite troop such as the one suggested in Josh. 8:3, was frequently related to wealth and/or position. Thus perhaps the term was used to describe a class of noblemen who had either wealth or position (or both) which derived from or resulted in military service, especially in those forces which required special armaments and/or those which were closest to the king and entrusted with his protection. In this case, the description of Ruth in Ruth 3:11 as an *'eshet ḥayil* may be related to our term, indicating the character traits or the life of virtue which would be expected of a person having the status *gibbor ḥayil.* The industry or ability implied in the reference in 1 Kgs. 11:28 may have been similarly derived. The *'anshey ḥayil* of Exod. 18:21,25 whom Moses appointed as judges could mean men of either leadership status or outstanding ability. The use of the term "nobleman" to include both of these dimensions would seem to cover more adequately the semantic range of the term in

86. I thank Millard Lind of the Associated Mennonite Biblical Seminaries for drawing the reference in Ruth 3:11 to my attention.

the books of Judges, Samuel, Kings and Ruth than would that of "warrior."[87] There are a number of individuals mentioned in these books who are called *gibbor ḥayil*, in addition to those mentioned above, including Gideon,[88] Jephthah,[89] and Naaman,[90] where "mighty warrior" seems an inadequate description. In the stories describing Gideon and Jephthah we wonder whether a quality of dynamic or charismatic leadership coupled with a personal devotion to Yahweh is not implied in their designation by this title. It is perhaps this same quality which is imparted to David in 1 Sam. 16:18 when one of the servants describes him as both *gibbor ḥayil* and *'ysh milḥamah* (a man of war),[91] i.e., the phrase *gibbor ḥayil* carries a meaning other than that of warrior. There is no way of determining whether the *gibborey ḥayil* in 2 Kgs. 24:14, who are taken into captivity in Babylon, are military personnel or not. The heroic aspect of

[87]. The translation "aristocrats" is suggested by R. G. Boling, *Judges: Introduction, Translation, and Commentary*, AB 6A (Garden City: Doubleday, 1975), 131, a proposal rejected by Soggin who says Boling goes too far. Soggin does still claim that it refers to the free man, well-off and able-bodied (J. A. Soggin, *Judges*, trans. J. S. Bowden, OTL [Philadelphia: Westminster, 1981], 115.)

[88]. Judg. 6:12.

[89]. Judg. 11:1.

[90]. 2 Kgs. 5:1.

[91]. Cf. Josh. 10:7 discussed above, where both the *gibborey ḥayil* and the *'am milḥamah* ascend with Joshua from Gilgal.

the term *gibbor ḥayil* gradually gives way, in the works of the Hebrew Scriptures from Joshua to Kings, to a meaning which designates a certain status or position in that society, one which is frequently associated with military service, often an elite group of warriors. Sometimes it also seems to refer to the character traits or personal qualities of the persons who make up the group, a meaning probably not unrelated to the original heroic aspect of the term *gibbor*.

The most frequent use of these terms is found in the later biblical books, 1 and 2 Chronicles, and they are especially prominent in 1 Chronicles 7 and 12. In 1 Chr. 12:1 we read that we will find listed "the men who came to David at Ziklag, while he could not move about freely because of Saul the son of Kish." Then it describes these men: *wehemmah baggibborym ʻozrey hammilḥamah* (and they were among the *gibborym* who aided in the war). This seems to hearken back to those select few called *gibborym* in 1 Chr. 11:10-11, which had already been mentioned in 1 Samuel 23.[92] However, when we look at the numbers listed later in chapter 12, we read about seven thousand one hundred *gibborey ḥayil* from the tribe of Simeon in v. 26 and ten thousand eight hundred from Ephraim in v. 31.[93] These certainly are not the numbers involved in a selected force personally dedicated to the protection of the king. We find here rather the numbers, whether fictive or real is not the issue, of persons from each tribe who came, as 12:24 says, "to turn the kingdom of Saul over to him." Clearly there is another definition operative here in addition to that one

[92]. See n. 77 above.

[93]. This term also appears in vv. 9, 22 and 29 of this same chapter within the same context.

which designates the elite personal troops of David. A clue to this other meaning is found in the genealogy of 1 Chronicles 7.

In 1 Chronicles 7, the *gibborey ḥayil* are also described as the *ro'shym lebeyt 'abotam*[94] or *ro'shey beyt 'abot* (heads of the house of their fathers),[95] also found in the more abbreviated form, *ro'shey ha'abot* (the heads of the fathers).[96] This wording brings to mind the census ordered by God in Numbers 1, where they are counted "according to the house of their fathers" and the names of all males twenty years old and upward are listed.[97] While in both texts the census has in part a military purpose, alluded to in 1 Chr. 7:4 and 11, it seems doubtful that calling the persons listed here *gibborey ḥayil* was intended to describe them as mighty warriors or even as military personnel. While "heads of the house of their fathers" does in a few instances in the Hebrew Scriptures refer to a representative leader from each of the tribes of Israel,[98] such is clearly not the case here. It rather refers

[94]. 1 Chr. 7:2.

[95]. 1 Chr 7:7, 9, 40. W. O. E. Oesterley, "1 Maccabees," *APOT* 1:73 cites 1 Chr. 7:2,7 when discussing the "mighty men of Israel."

[96]. 1 Chr. 7:11.

[97]. I am indebted to Ben Zion Wacholder, a most helpful advisor, for this suggestion.

[98]. Num. 1:4, 7:2, 17:18; and Josh. 22:14 where only ten tribes are represented.

to all males who are the head of the *beyt 'aḇot* (clan or extended family). It is this group, for example, that is summoned to a meeting to decide the fate of those who intermarried in Ezra 10:16. What exactly a *beyt 'aḇot* was continues to be a subject of discussion which will not be resolved in this work. The term can apply to a family, a subdivision of a clan composed of several families, a tribe or a different group.[99] For our purposes a precise definition of this group is not of great importance. The important point is that the "heads of the house of their fathers" are called *gibborey ḥayil*.

The relationship between the *gibborey ḥayil* and the *ro'shey beyt ha'aḇot* is made clearer in 1 Chr. 26:6: "and to Shemaiah his son were born sons *hammimshalym leḇeyt 'aḇyhem ky gibborey ḥayil hemmah* (who ruled over the house of their fathers for they were *gibborey ḥayil*)." Without any apparent military allusion, we find herein described certain persons who have a leadership role and the corresponding character traits and abilities to go with it. Translations of this verse have attempted to reflect this other meaning, the RSV and NEB both choosing to use the phrase "men of great ability." The difference between the two versions is that the NEB renders these terms in a similar manner in chapter 7, calling them "able men" while the RSV at this point reverts to "mighty warriors." The NEB translation is rooted in the supposition that *ḥayil* in some instances

99. H. Ringgren, "*'ab*," *TDOT* 1:8-10; J. P. Weinberg, "Das Bēit *'ĀḆŌT* im 6.-4. Jh. v. u. Z.," *VT* 23 (1973) 400-14.

such as 1 Kgs. 11:28 can be defined as meaning "ability."[100] However in the context of 1 Chronicles 7 and 26:6 such a definition does not seem adequate. Admittedly, the meaning of "nobleman" found in some earlier biblical writings[101] is too strong and perhaps applies to a more selective group of persons than that meant in 1 Chronicles. The notion, however, that we find in this term a certain leadership role and its corresponding character traits and abilities does explain these references in 1 Chronicles 7 and 26.

An interesting substantiation of a leading role for the *gibborey ḥayil* is to be found in 2 Chr. 26:12-13 where we read that "the number of the heads of the fathers of the *gibborey ḥayil* was 2,600 and under them was an army of 307,800 who made war." While the context is clearly military, the word does not simply designate soldiers but rather those who are in command. In 2 Chr. 25:6, the *gibborey ḥayil* from the Northern Kingdom are hired by Amaziah, while everyone twenty years old and up from Judaea is drafted. While in these references in Chronicles, the position of "nobleman" is no longer accurate and perhaps an overstatement, there is in all of them a certain sense of authority and self-determination. These are free men who are in a position to make decisions about their own and sometimes about other's lives, probably "landed proprieters,"[102] persons

[100]. *TDOT* 2:374.

[101]. See above.

[102]. This term is used by E. L. Curtis and A. A. Madsen, *The Books of Chronicles* (New York: Charles Scribner's Sons, 1910), 450.

who own land, or craftsmen and artisans who are self-employed and perhaps have some slaves or hired workmen. Such a meaning would be appropriate for references such as 1 Chr. 5:24, 7:5, 8:40 and 26:31.[103] It is also worthwhile to check the usage of these terms in an extra-biblical source, the Temple Scroll.

In a reference to the phrase *gibborey ḥayil lemilḥamah* in 11Q Torah 57:9, Thorion has noted that the writer has to add *lemilḥamah* (for war) to *gibborey ḥayil* when he wants it to designate warriors, i.e., the latter phrase itself, in a manner similar to the later biblical books, does not imply this.[104] In 11Q Torah 58:16-17 we find the phrase *'anshey hammilḥamah wekol gibborey ḥayil*, where *gibborey ḥayil* is clearly intended to give us information that supplements the first phrase, "men of war." It seems that the information provided is quite similar to the meaning of the phrase in Chronicles. The other references in 1 and 2 Chronicles,[105] while they appear in military contexts, seem to describe persons of a certain status and perhaps sometimes character. The use of this term to describe "their kinsmen, heads of the house of their fathers, *gibborey ḥayil* for the work of service in the house of the Lord," in the midst of a list of priests in 1 Chr. 9:13 is then very natural and appropriate given the kind of

[103]. This is in direct contrast to the view of H. G. M. Williamson, *1 and 2 Chronicles*, NCB (London: Marshall, Morgan & Scott/ Grand Rapids: Eerdmans, 1982), 67.

[104]. Thorion, *RevQ* 10 (1981) 597-98. He cites 1 Chr. 12:9 and 26 as examples. These terms also appear in CD 2:17 and 3:9.

[105]. 2 Chr. 13:3; 17:14,16,17; 32:21.

meaning implied above. This term is also used to describe some of the priests in the list found in Neh. 11:14. This book is, of course, closely related to Chronicles.[106] A similar case is found in 1 Chr. 26:6 where the term is used to describe those divisions of the Levites who were gatekeepers. In 1 Chr. 28:1 the *gibborey ḥayil* are included among the officials who serve the king in a variety of capacities, both military and civilian. Thus in the later biblical books, a category of persons who have the designation "free men" with a certain status and responsibility would best seem to fit the overall use of the term *gibborey ḥayil.*[107] That this definition grows out of the earlier usages of the term discussed above certainly seems possible.

It is now time to return to our text in 1 Macc. 2:42 where the Hasideans are called *ischyroi dynamei*, which we have already indicated is most probably a rendering of the Hebrew *gibborey ḥayil.* The same phrase appears in 2:66, where Judah Maccabee is called *ischyros dynamei ek neotētos autou* (a mighty man [warrior?] from his youth) which qualifies him as commander of the army that will fight against the Gentiles. "Mighty warrior" may be an appropriate translation at this point, given that it is the term chosen to validate his role as commander of the army. Certainly this is the point of the description found a few verses later in 1 Macc. 3:3-9. Elsewhere in this book we find in 10:19 the phrase *dynatos ischyi* and in 8:1, 2 and 11:44 the same

106. Kosmala, *TDOT* 2:374, thinks *gabbay sallay* in Neh. 11:8 should probably be read *gibborey ḥayil.*

107. The meaning of the *gibbarey hayil* in Dan. 3:20 appears to be confined to the more narrow military definition, even though that would not contradict the conclusions of the above paragraph.

phrase in the plural. While *ischyi* is in the dative case in these instances rather than *dynamei*, Kahana is correct in also translating this phrase *gibborey ḥayil*, the same as in 1 Macc. 2:42 and 66.[108] While all these references appear in a context which suggests a certain level of military prowess, with the possible exception of 11:44 they also seem to allude to the leadership qualities of the persons described.

It is not clear to this writer that the use of the term in 1 Macc. 2:42 should be limited to the military definition. Granting the above discussion of the use of this phrase in the biblical materials, especially in the books of Kings, Chronicles and Nehemiah, and allowing that Kings and Chronicles provided the model for the composer of 1 Maccabees, the question of other possible meanings of this phrase in this context must still be addressed. It may be that "leading citizens" is as appropriate a translation as "mighty warriors." As noted by Kosmala, the use of this phrase is diverse enough that its meaning must be determined from the immediate context.[109] In this case, we must then move on to an examination of the other half of this description of the Hasideans.

Devoted to the Law

In 1 Macc. 2:42 the Hasideans are also described as *pas ho hekousiazomenos tǭ nomǭ* (each one willingly devoted to

[108]. Kahana, *Hasseparym*, 2:134, 144, 154.

[109]. *TDOT* 2:374.

the law). In Hebrew, this is rendered *hitnaddeḇ lattorah.*[110] In order to understand what this phrase might mean, we must investigate the biblical usage of the term *hitnaddeḇ*. Particularly in its verbal form, this word is not that common in the Hebrew Scriptures. The oldest reference is found in the Song of Deborah, Judg. 5:2 and 9. Clearly the context is the military victory of Deborah, and Boling is most certainly correct when he suggests that *'am* (people) in these two verses is a reference to the *'am milḥamah* (people of war).[111] He cites Joshua 8 where *'am milḥamah* appears in vv. 1, 3 and 11 while the same general group of fighting personnel is simply called *'am* in vv. 5, 9, 10 and 13. Rabin suggests the term in Judg. 5:2 should be understood as meaning "to go to war in answer to a call."[112] This call is one of duty so the usual voluntary element assumed in the translation of this word is incorrect. In this case the use of *hitnaddeḇ* implies the willingness to leave one's house, family, vineyard and flock and go to fight on behalf of the cause of Yahweh, implied as well in the story of Gideon's choice of troops, Judg. 7:1-8, which seems to be rooted in the stipulations of Deut. 20:1-8.[113]

110. F. Hauck, "*Hekousios*," *TDNT* 2:470.

111. Boling, *Judges*, 71, 107.

112. C. Rabin, "Judges V, 2 and the 'Ideology' of Deborah's War," *JJS* 6 (1953) 128-30. See also R. M. Good, *The Sheep of his Pasture: A Study of the Hebrew Noun 'Am(m) and its Semitic Cognates*, HSM 29 (Chico: Scholars Press, 1983), 60, 146.

113. M. Lind, *Yahweh is a Warrior: The Theology of Warfare in Ancient Israel* (Scottdale: Herald Press, 1980), 155.

The majority of the references to this term have a cultic connection. The qal form of the verb only appears three times, all in the book of Exodus,[114] and refers to voluntary contributions of the Israelites for building the tabernacle. Elsewhere the verb is only found in the hitpael form. The most concentrated set of references is found in 1 Chronicles 29 wherein is described the giving of gifts by both David and the people for building the temple in Jerusalem.[115] Similarly in Ezra, the gifts given by the Jewish people as well as the Persian king for the rebuilding of the temple are described using this verb.[116] In the Aramaic section of the book the verb is used in the same manner utilizing the hitpaal form.[117] In Exodus and Ezra the noun form *nedabah* is used to designate these voluntary contributions.[118] Elsewhere the noun can designate a sacrifice given as a freewill offering.[119]

114. Exod. 25:2; 35:21,29.

115. 1 Chr. 29:5,6,9,9,14,17,17.

116. Ezra 1:6; 2:68; 3:5.

117. Ezra 7:15,16,16.

118. Exod. 35:29; 36:3; Ezra 1:4; 3:5; 8:28.

119. E.g., Lev. 7:16; 22:18,21,23; 23:38; Num. 15:3; 29:39; Deut. 6,17; 16:10; 23:24.

The cultic use of this word group to designate either freewill offerings given for sacrifices or contributions for the building of a sanctuary, the common use in the verbal form, raises questions about how the term in 1 Macc. 2:42 has usually been understood.

In the previous paragraph, the discussion of the verbal form of *nadab̲*, with the exception of Judg. 5:2 and 9, has been related to the giving of objects, either money, building materials or sacrificial animals. Even when the subject of the verb *hitnaddeb̲* is a person, such as in 1 Chr. 29:5, the request made is that individuals would "voluntarily devote themselves" to donating materials for building the temple. However, in the text of 1 Maccabees under discussion in this work, no objects are mentioned: *kol hammitnaddeb̲ lattorah* (all who voluntarily devote themselves to the law). This forces us to look at the other passages in the Hebrew Scriptures where this term appears in contexts concerning persons.

Its meaning in 2 Chr. 17:16 is obscure, due to the fact that no additional information about Amasiah, the person described as *hammitnaddeb̲* is provided.[120] However, we also find the term in more suggestive contexts. In Ezra 7:13, Artaxerxes gives permission for any of the Israelites or priests or levites who *mitnaddeb̲* (freely offer) to go to Jerusalem to leave. When we turn to Neh. 11:2, we read of all the men who "freely offered" to dwell in Jerusalem. Since Neh. 11:1 says that the leaders of the people dwelt in Jerusalem and that the rest of the people cast lots, apparently for the privilege of living in Jerusalem, described in the text as the "holy city," we get the impression that these residents of the newly rebuilt city had special responsibilities in addi-

[120]. Williamson notes that this phrase is not typical of the chronicler and that it finds no explanation in its present form (*1 and 2 Chronicles*, 248).

tion to the honor which came from living in that place. From the book of Nehemiah, it would appear that those responsibilities derived from the fact that the city provided the site for the temple, the center of the cult. In other words, the *hammitnaddeḇym* of Neh. 11:2 had a special responsibility for and role in the maintenance of the cult. To summarize, these references to persons as well as the use of this term discussed in the previous paragraph all point to a primarily cultic but non-professional (i.e, not priests or levites) context for understanding the meaning of *hitnaddeḇ* in the Hebrew Scriptures.[121] Of course, the sense of voluntarism, of giving of self or possessions beyond that which is required or demanded, is a meaning which pervades this cultic usage.

When we return to 1 Macc. 2:42 we immediately recognize that we have not encountered the phrase *hitnaddeḇ lattorah* in the Hebrew Scriptures. When we look for further clues as to the meaning of this phrase, we find one in a closer examination of the LXX text. The Hebrew *hitnaddeḇ* is not always translated by *hekousiazomenos* in the LXX. In Chronicles we find rather that some form of *prothumeomai* (to be willing or eager) is employed.[122] This term is also used in 1 Macc. 1:13: προεθυμήθησάν τινες ἀπὸ τοῦ λαοῦ καὶ ἐπορεύθησαν πρὸς τὸν βασιλέα καὶ ἔδωκεν αὐτοῖς ἐξουσίαν ποιῆσαι τὰ δικαιώματα τῶν ἐθνῶν (and some of the people were eager and went to the king. He gave

[121]. This conclusion agrees with that of A. Fitzgerald, "*MTNDBYM* in 1QS," *CBQ* 36 (1974) 495-502. He suggests that this term was used by Qumran because of the group's self-perception as a temple.

[122]. 1 Chr. 29:5,6,9,14,17; 2 Chr. 17:16.

them authority to observe the decrees of the Gentiles.)[123] These people then built a gymnasium in Jerusalem. Here also the original text would have read *hitnaddeb̲*, but the willing zeal finds a very different focus.

A comparison of the use of *hitnaddeb̲* in 1 Macc. 2:42 with that in 1:13 is instructive. In 1:11 we read of the *paranomoi* (lawless or those against the law) Israelites who advocated the making of a *diathēkē* (covenant) with the gentiles. In v. 15 these same Israelites removed the marks of circumcision *kai apestēsan apo diathēkēs hagias* (and fell away from the holy covenant). In other words, v. 13 is saying that these rebellious Israelites are *hitnaddeb̲ leḥuqqey haggoyim*,[124] which includes denying the law and forsaking the holy covenant for one with the gentiles. The author chooses to spell out what this means in greater detail in the decree of Antiochus IV found in vv. 41-49. He summarizes the decree in the last verse: ὥστε ἐπιλαθέσθαι τοῦ νόμου καὶ ἀλλάξαι πάντα τὰ δικαιώματα (so that they would forsake the Law [*Torah*] and alter all the commandments [*ḥuqqym*]). The details enumerated in this section include following foreign customs, the prohibition of sacrifices in the sanctuary, the profanation of the sabbaths

[123]. Why they have to appeal to the king "to observe the decrees of the Gentiles" is difficult to explain. Goldstein (*I Maccabees*, 200) may be correct in suggesting that this is a reference to the abolition of the decree of Antiochus III that Judaea be governed according to the ancestral laws (*AJ* 12:142; cf. 2 Macc. 4:11). On the other hand, Josephus understood this line as a petition to build the gymnasium, a project which receives mention in the next verse of 1 Maccabees.

[124]. *Ḥuqqey haggoyim* is most likely the Hebrew phrase which the author in 1:13 translates as *ta dikaiōmata tōn ethnōn*, since LXX usage normally translates *ḥoq* as *dikaiōma*.

and feasts, the defilement of the sanctuary and the priests, building altars and shrines for idols, the sacrifice of swine and unclean animals, and the neglect of circumcision.[125] In other words, forsaking the law in this context included activities associated with the temple cult, in addition to other stipulations based on the Torah such as circumcision. What is clear is that, for the author of 1 Maccabees, the Torah encompasses not only that way of life which came to be known as Judaism, but also the entire cultic system which was centered in the temple of Jerusalem. When the Hasideans in 1 Macc. 2:42 are said to be willingly devoted to the Torah, they are being contrasted with those people in chapter 1 who are devoted to the commandments of the gentiles, who deny the law and defile the temple.

We recall that the discussion of the *gibborey ḥayil* had been left open, pending the examination of the phrase which follows it in the text. Having completed that study, we must combine the conclusions of these two sections. While ample evidence had been found in the biblical materials to justify the translation of the term *ischyroi dynamei* in 1 Macc. 2:42 as "leading citizens" instead of "mighty warriors," we did observe that most of the other places where this phrase appears in the work do suggest the military definition. In these cases, however, the *context* is clearly a military one. With regard to v. 42, we already demonstrated that it is constructed in such a manner as to contrast the Hasideans who are "devoted to the law" with the lawless and the sinners who go against the law in chapter 1. In this case, the significance of this verse could well be that there were "leading citizens devoted to the law" who supported the

125. The literary connection between 1 Maccabees 1 and 2 is also noted by Martola, *Capture and Liberation*, 221-25, even though he bases his case on the earlier verses of chapter 2.

Maccabean efforts.[126] This support was based in their commitment to the law and the temple. While we should not totally exclude the military component from this definition, we also need not make it the exclusive meaning of the term. The identification of the Hasideans with the scribes proposed in the next section of this study would undergird the claim that the primary focus of this verse is on the prominence of the members of this identifiable group who are distinguished by their devotion to the temple and the law.

The Hasideans in Jewish Historiography: 1 Macc. 7:12-18

The literary problems associated with the second and only other reference to the Hasideans in 1 Maccabees are no less formidable than those encountered in 2:42. In 1 Maccabees 7, we find that Demetrius I murders the child ruler Antiochus V and his guardian Lysias and then takes over as ruler of the Seleucid Empire. Demetrius is approached by some *andres anomoi kai asebeis* (lawless and impious men) from Israel that are led by Alcimus who wishes to be high priest. They warn the king that he must take decisive action against Judah and his brothers. Demetrius responds by sending Bacchides, a trusted adviser, to Judaea and by appointing Alcimus to the position he desired. These two come with a large force and send messengers to Judah and his brothers bearing *logois eirēnikois meta dolou* (words of peace with deceit). Being aware of the large army behind the

[126]. Note that neither *prothumeō* nor *hekousiazō* is used to describe the zeal for the law on the part of Mattathias. The writer rather prefers the verb *zeleō* to describe their efforts (1 Macc. 2:27,50). Note the discussion of the importance of *zeleō* in 1 Maccabees 2 by Martola, *Capture and Liberation*, 208-21.

peaceable words, Judah and his brothers ignore the message. It is at this point that our Hasideans again enter the picture. Contrary to Judah Maccabaeus, this group seeks peace with Bacchides and Alcimus, who in turn betray these trusting souls and kill sixty of them. There are a number of problems in this apparently straightforward account that impinge upon our understanding of the story as a whole.

In most studies, support is found in this account for the view that the Hasideans were a group inclined towards a pacifism which was based on an apocalyptic world view. They departed from their pacifist stance for only a brief period under the most adverse circumstances and eagerly embraced it again upon the restoration of a high priest they considered legitimate and upon the recognition of the right to again freely observe their religious practices.[130] This view will be tested and found incorrect when we examine issues such as those which follow: (a) the relationship of the scribes in v. 12 to the Hasideans in v. 13 including the meaning and significance of the term *prōtoi* (first) in v. 13; (b) the meaning of the Hasideans' recognition of Alcimus in v. 14; (c) the meaning of the use of Psalm 79 in v. 17. These problems will be addressed in turn as we attempt to understand this account of the people known as the Hasideans.

The Hasideans and the Scribes: 1 Macc. 7:12-13

One problem concerning the Hasideans which arises from the text of 1 Maccabees is whether they are related to

[130]. This summary is similar to that of Collins, *Apocalyptic Vision*, 202.

the group called *grammateis* (scribes).[131] Since the scribes are mentioned in v. 12 and the Hasideans in v. 13, the resolution of this issue may rest on the literary relationship between these two verses: καὶ ἐπισυνήχθησαν πρὸς Ἄλκιμον καὶ Βακχίδην συναγωγὴ γραμματέων ἐκζητῆσαι δίκαια καὶ πρῶτοι οἱ Ασιδαῖοι ἦσαν ἐν υἱοῖς Ισραηλ καὶ ἐπεζήτουν παρ' αὐτῶν εἰρήνην (a company of scribes was assembled before Alcimus and Bacchides seeking just terms. 13. The Hasideans were the first among the Israelites and they sought peace from them.) In his noteworthy commentary, C. L. W. Grimm remarked on the literary similarity between v. 12 and 2:42, but failed to find any significance in the connection.[132] Both Plöger and Hengel understand the scribes and the Hasideans as two different groups, even though probably related.[133] In this case, the Jewish resistance movement is portrayed as representing a coalition of two distinct parties or bodies, the Maccabees and the Hasideans. The latter only joined the revolt for a brief period of time until they thought their religious rights were again assured. The Maccabees are

131. I have mentioned already in Chapter 1 the many studies which see a connection between the Hasideans and the scribes.

132. C. L. W. Grimm, *Kurzgefasstes exegetisches Handbuch zu den Apokryphen des Alten Testaments* (Leipzig: S. Hirzel, 1853), 3:110.

133. Plöger, *Theocracy*, 8; Hengel, *Judaism and Hellenism*, 1:80; 2:119, n. 474. For a recent expression of this general view see I. Gafni, "The Historical Background," *CRINT* 2:2 (Assen: Van Gorcum/Philadelphia: Fortress, 1984), 12-13 and H. W. Attridge, "Historiography," 173 in the same volume. This seems to also be the case with Dommershausen, *1 Makkabäer. 2 Makkabäer*, 54.

seen to be interested in political power as well as religious rights.

It is Tcherikover who has vigorously challenged this picture of the Hasideans and he has done it on the basis that the Hasideans and the scribes were the same group.[134] He bases the connection between the scribes and the Hasideans on the similarity of the phrase in 7:12, *ekzētēsai dikaia* (to seek the just [or right]), to *zētountes dikaiosynēn* (those seeking justice), found in 1 Macc. 2:29. Of course, Tcherikover believes the account of the 'many' in 1 Macc. 2:29-38 is referring to the Hasideans in 2:42. This permits him to view the Hasidim-scribes as the initiators and leaders of the forces of national resistance who rose up against the decrees of Antiochus IV. Earlier in this chapter, the hypothesis that the Hasideans were to be seen in the account of the 'many' in 1 Macc. 2:29-38 has been found unacceptable. Does this mean that there is no literary basis for a connection between the scribes and the Hasideans?

A reexamination of these two verses shows that they can serve as the basis for understanding the link between the Hasideans and the scribes. To properly understand the two, they need to be viewed in a complementary relationship where v. 13 serves not only to restate but also to elaborate on v. 12. When we look more closely at the latter, we see that, contrary to Tcherikover, it bears more similarities to 1 Macc. 2:42 than to 2:29. The verb used in 7:12, *episynagō* (to gather or join), is the same as that in 2:42.[135] In this passage, as mentioned earlier, the discussion is of a *synagōgē* (company) of Hasideans, while in 7:12 we find a *synagōgē grammateōn* (company of scribes). Since *synagōgē* only

[134]. *Hellenistic Civilization*, 196-98.

[135]. It does have a prefix in 7:12 which is absent from 2:42.

appears twice more in the book, we must conclude that the author's use of this term in both these verses is more than coincidental. What we find is that both the noun and the verb used to describe the Hasideans and their activity in 1 Macc. 2:42 are used for the scribes in 7:12. The *grammateis* are to be found only once more in this work at 5:42. However, in this instance the term is probably not a translation of the Hebrew *soprym* (scribes), but rather of *shoṭrym* (officers), as found in Deut. 20:5-9.[136] In Josh. 1:10 we read of the *shoṭrey ha'am* (officers of the people), rendered in the LXX as *grammateusi tou laou*, the same phrase as in 1 Macc. 5:42. Thus we find references to the scribes only in 2:42 and 7:12. The connection of 7:12 to both 2:42 and 7:13 suggests that these scribes are to be linked with the Hasideans in the following verse.

When we turn to v. 13, we encounter new difficulties. First of all, this passage says that the Hasideans are *prōtoi* (first), a very suggestive description whose meaning is not immediately apparent. Equally obscure is the second part of the passage, *kai epezētoun par autōn eirēnēn* (and they were seeking peace from them). In his extensive commentary on 1 and 2 Maccabees, Abel summarizes the variety of opinion on the meaning of this verse under five options:[137] (a) The scribes were the first Hasideans. (b) The Hasideans were the first among that company (of scribes). (c) The Hasideans, as the leaders among the sons of Israel, negotiated for peace. (d) Outside of the scribes, the Hasideans were the first

[136]. F.-M. Abel and J. Starcky, *Les Livres des Maccabées*, La Sainte Bible, 3d ed. (Paris: Les editions du Cerf, 1961), 140; Goldstein, *I Maccabees*, 303.

[137]. F.-M. Abel, *Les Livres des Maccabées*, Etudes Bibliques (Paris: Gabalda, 1949), 132-33. A similar list of alternatives is provided by Davies, *JJS* 28 (1977) 136-37.

among the faithful to ask for peace. This was argued by Grimm, along with many others, who maintained that the company of Hasideans was a lay movement.[138] (e) This viewpoint was disputed by Keil who argued that the scribes were nothing other than the literate and teaching Hasideans.[139] He considered any option which set one off from the other unacceptable. Given the argument above which shows the literary connection between the account of the scribes in v. 12 and that of the Hasideans in 2:42 and 7:13, we have no alternative but to accept Keil's point that any proposal which disengages the Hasideans from the scribes does not stand up to scrutiny.

To understand more clearly what was meant in these two verses, we need to probe the use of the term *prōtoi* (first). The so-called Hasidic hypothesis lies behind many translations of this verse--e.g., the RSV: "The Hasideans were the first among the sons of Israel to seek peace from them." The assumption behind the translation seems to be that the Hasideans were ideological pacifists who took the first available opportunity to break with the Hasmoneans and return to a stance more in keeping with their own beliefs. The implication is that 'first' is used either with chronological significance (i.e., the Hasideans were the first in time to seek peace) or in the sense of status (they were the leaders or chieftains who sought peace). In either case the phrase *epezētoun par autōn eirēnēn* (and they were seeking peace from them) is understood to be a subordinate clause modifying *prōtoi*. When the RSV translation accepts this as a subordinate clause, it ignores the fact that *epezētoun* (were

[138]. Grimm, *Handbuch*, 3:110.

[139]. C. F. Keil, *Commentar über die Bücher der Makkabäer* (Leipzig: Dörffling and Franck, 1875), 128.

seeking) is a finite verb, not a participle, and that it is connected to the preceding clause by the word *kai* (and).

Abel is of course correct when he argues that behind the Greek *kai* stands a Hebrew *waw*.[140] What is not as certain, in the opinion of this writer, is that the *waw* introduces a relative clause or that, even if the clause is interpreted in this manner, it would modify *ri'shonym*, the Hebrew word for *prōtoi*. There is no doubt that relative clauses are frequently introduced by the conjunctive *waw* in biblical Hebrew.[141] However, the relevant phrase contains a finite verb so there is no necessary reason to interpret it as a relative clause. There is an additional problem with Abel's argument. He assumes that the *waw* follows the adjective *ri'shonym*. However, *prōtoi* stands at the beginning of v. 13, so Kahana rightly puts *ri'shonym* at the beginning of the sentence when he translates it into Hebrew.[142] In this case, *wayyeḇaqqeshu* (and they sought) follows *beney Isra'el* (Israelites). This means there is no necessary reason to relate "first" to the fact that they "sought peace." In that case, a more appropriate translation of the verse would be as follows: "The Hasideans, who sought peace from them, were first among the Israelites." However the most likely version is one which has two co-ordinate clauses: "The Hasideans were first among the Israelites and they were seeking peace from them." What we find here are two statements both descriptive of the Hasideans. In this case, *prōtoi* is to be understood in the context of the phrase, "The Hasideans were first among the

[140]. Abel, *Livres*, 133.

[141]. *GKC*, 484-89; J. Blau, *A Grammar of Biblical Hebrew* (Wiesbaden: Otto Harassowitz, 1976), 106-07.

[142]. Kahana, *Hasseparym*, 2:131.

Israelites." This conclusion coincides with that reached earlier in this chapter when we examined the references to the Hasideans in 2:42 where they are called the *gibborey ḥayil* (mighty men). This would also seem to describe the scribes in 7:12. The Hasideans according to 1 Maccabees were scribes who were leading citizens.

We have suggested earlier that there is limited evidence to show that the Hasideans were adherents of a pacifist ideology. The second half of 1 Macc. 7:13 is an important piece of evidence for evaluating that hypothesis. Having already established the meaning of the claim that the Hasideans were "first among the Israelites," we are still left with the question of what it meant for them to be "seeking peace." Perhaps we should look at the immediate context for an answer to this question. Recall that we have earlier demonstrated the link between vv. 12 and 13, based in part on the similarity between the description of the scribes in v. 12 to that of the Hasideans in 2:42. This led us to conclude that the scribes in v. 12 are the same persons as the Hasideans described in v. 13. When we examine these verses in light of the question presently under consideration we note another similarity. The verb *zētēo* (seek) is used in both instances; in v. 12 the scribes are seeking *dikaia* (righteousness? just terms?) while in v. 13 it is peace. The RSV translation using "just terms" is clearly preferable, in light of the context of the story, to the NEB which uses the abstract "justice." As already mentioned, this story appears after Alcimus and Bacchides have come to Judaea with a large force. They send a messenger to Judah and his brothers with an offer of peace, however the author of 1 Maccabees labels it "words of peace with deceit." This message is ignored by Judah because "they saw that they had come with a large force." It is in this context that the scribes ask for "just terms." It seems that the Hasideans are aware of the large force of

Alcimus and Bacchides and rather than seeing this as a reason for rejecting their offer, as was the case with Judah, they understand the threat posed by this force and wish to discern the terms whereby disaster might be averted. They are afraid that the Greek military forces will destroy Israel and they wish to head off the attack. This is what is meant both by "seeking just terms" in v. 12 and "seeking peace" in v. 13. Both verses reflect a pragmatic response to the fact that Bacchides and Alcimus were marching into Judah with a large force and that Judah Maccabee refused to talk peace terms with them. From vv. 12 and 13 we learn that the Hasideans were scribes, leading citizens who were willing to respond to the threat of Greek force by means other than military resistance.[143] While their action is pacifistic, the evidence suggests it is taken for pragmatic reasons.

A Priest of the Seed of Aaron: 1 Macc. 7:14

In the hypothesis which understands the resistance movement of 167 B.C.E. to be a union of the Maccabees and the Hasideans, a political and religious party respectively, 1 Macc. 7:14 is understood to represent the breakdown of the coalition: εἶπαν γάρ "Ἄνθρωπος ἱερεὺς ἐκ τοῦ σπέρματος Ααρων ἦλθεν ἐν ταῖς δυνάμεσι καὶ οὐκ ἀδικήσει ἡμᾶς (For they said, "A priest from the seed of Aaron has come with the troops and he will not treat us unjustly.")[144] Let us examine this verse in light of the claims espousing such a hypothesis.

[143]. See, e.g., Hengel, *Judaism and Hellenism*, 2:119, n. 471.

[144]. Perhaps similar to the Pharisaic response to the cessation of sacrifices to Rome in *BJ* 2:411-16.

It has sometimes been argued, e.g., by Starcky and Zeitlin, that this conciliatory attitude on the part of the Hasideans was due to the rights granted to them in 1 Macc. 6:59 by Lysias and Antiochus V: καὶ στήσωμεν αὐτοῖς τοῦ πορεύεσθαι τοῖς νομίμοις αὐτῶν ὡς τὸ πρότερον (and agree to let them live by their laws as they did before).[145] However, both of these commentators seem to ignore the reference only three verses later stating that the king ἠθέτησε τὸν ὁρκισμόν ὃν ὤμοσε (broke the oath he had sworn). Verse 62 only mentions directly the orders which the king gave to tear down the wall around the temple. The passage does appear to imply, however, that in so doing he revoked entirely his earlier promise. It is possible, of course, to interpret v. 62 as a temporary lapse in the process of returning the rights of religious practice to the Jews. In this case, Alcimus is then viewed as the person who makes possible the reinstatement of the rights suggested in 6:59 and granted in v. 61. On the basis of that hypothesis which makes the Hasideans the religious wing of a coalition party, this reinstatement is sufficient cause for the group to abandon the coalition and the rebellion. However, 1 Macc. 7:15 says nothing about the rights of religious practice, so we have no evidence to support the view that Alcimus had anything to do with getting these rights reinstated, or that such things even occurred during his tenure. We must turn our attention more directly to the text of 1 Macc. 7:15.

145. Abel and Starcky, *Livres*, 140; S. Tedesche and S. Zeitlin, *The First Book of Maccabees*, Jewish Apocryphal Literature, Dropsie College Edition (New York: Harper & Bros., 1950), 138. J. C. Dancy suggests that the scribes' request in v. 12 for 'justice', as he translates the term *dikaia*, may have been a request for the recognition of this earlier settlement (*A Commentary on 1 Maccabees*, Blackwell's Theological Texts [Oxford: Basil Blackwell, 1954], 122).

The most common interpretation of this line is rooted in the by now familiar hypothesis, i.e., that the Hasideans made up the religious faction of a coalition whose other member was the politically-motivated Maccabees. Most frequently, commentators have argued that the statement calling Alcimus "a priest of the line of Aaron" is related to the issue of the legitimate, hereditary priestly succession.[146] In order for us to evaluate such a hypothesis, however, we need to discuss further two claims: first, that Menelaus, the high priest prior to Alcimus, was not of priestly lineage; and secondly, that Alcimus was. While the second is probably true, even though the record is not clear, the first may well be false. Of course, it may be argued that the Hasideans put their support behind Alcimus as the legitimate high priest for reasons other than those connected with Menelaus, e.g., as just mentioned Alcimus may have secured their rights of religious practice. We must remember that Menelaus is never mentioned in 1 Maccabees.

Let us first examine the claim that Menelaus was not of Aaronide lineage. Substantiation for this viewpoint is found in 2 Macc. 4:23 where Menelaus, persuading the king to make him instead of Jason high priest, is described as being the brother of the *prosēmainomenou* (previously mentioned) Simon, the temple treasurer. In 3:4 this Simon is said to be *ek tēs Beniamin phylēs* (from the tribe? of Benjamin) in the Greek manuscripts, thereby excluding the possibility that he is a legitimate Aaronide of the tribe of Levi. However, it has been observed that, given the infamy of Menelaus in Jewish

[146]. Abel, *Livres*, 133; R. H. Pfeiffer, *History of New Testament Times: With an Introduction to the Apocrypha* (New York: Harper & Brothers, 1949), 16; Abel and Starcky, *Livres*, 140; W. Foerster, *From the Exile to Christ: A Historical Introduction to Palestinian Judaism*, trans. G. E. Harris (Philadelphia: Fortress, 1964), 39; Collins, *Apocalyptic Vision*, 203-04.

tradition, had he not been of priestly lineage, this fact would have received considerable mention in Jewish and early Christian writings.[147] Instead, we find in the rabbinic tradition that the *mishmeret kehunah* (priestly course) of Bilgah was held in disrepute and replaced because of activities which may be dated around the time of the reign of Antiochus IV.[148] This evidence has led Hanhart to take seriously the witness of the Latin and Armenian versions which have "Bilgah" instead of "Benjamin," so that his preferred text of 2 Macc. 3:4 reads *ek tēs Balgea phylēs* (from the tribe? of Bilgah).[149] If Hanhart is correct in his proposed reading, we are then left with the question of what a *phylēs Balgea* might be. Usually, *phylē* does refer to one of the twelve tribes of Israel. In this case "tribe of Benjamin" would certainly be the correct reading. However, *phylē* is also used in some instances to refer to the twenty-four priestly divisions.[150] In view of these brothers' apparent interest and involvement in the affairs of the temple it is most reasonable to assume that Menelaus was from a legitimate priestly lineage, unless evidence can be found to the contrary. We

[147]. M. Stern, "Aspects of Jewish Society: The Priesthood and other Classes," *CRINT* 1:2:592-93; J. A. Goldstein, *II Maccabees: A New Translation with Introduction and Commentary*, AB 41a (Garden City: Doubleday, 1983), 201.

[148]. *M. Sukk.* 5:8; *T. Sukk.* 4:28; *B. Sukk.* 56b.

[149]. R. Hanhart, *Maccabaeorum liber II*, Septuaginta Vetus Testamentum Graecum (Göttingen: Vandenhoeck & Ruprecht, 1959), 9:2:55.

[150]. Stern, *CRINT* 1:2:593; *BJ* 4:155; *V* 2; *CA* 2:108 uses *tribus*, the Latin translation of *phulē*.

have found no convincing case for such an opposing viewpoint.

When we turn our attention to Alcimus, we also find some indications, contrary to the conclusions usually drawn from 1 Macc. 7:14, that he was not of Aaronide lineage. In *AJ* 12:387 Josephus tells us that Alcimus *ouk ek tēs tōn archiereōn onti geneas* (was not from the lineage of the high priests). What Josephus meant by this statement has been the subject of considerable discussion.[151] However, it seems that Josephus resolves this problem when in *AJ* 20:235 we read, *genous men tou Aarōnos ouk onta de tēs oikias tautēs* (of Aaronide lineage but not being of this house [or family]). Evidently Josephus understood Alcimus to be an Aaronide, but not of the family of Onias, of which Menelaus had been a member.[152] This is what one would conclude on the basis of the evidence in 2 Maccabees as well; Alcimus was of priestly stock.

Having established that Menelaus was probably, and Alcimus most certainly, of the Aaronide clan, we must return to the text of 1 Macc. 7:14 to see whether we really find here evidence either that the Hasideans sided with Alcimus against the other claimants for the high priesthood or that their apparent embracing of Alcimus was related to a rupture with the Maccabees. An examination of this verse in context suggests that both these possibilities are doubtful.

In 1 Maccabees 7 we read that Alcimus and Bacchides, who are appointed by Demetrius to deal with the problem in Judaea, are on their way to that province with a large force. They send messengers with an offer of peace to Judah Mac-

151. Grimm, *Handbuch*, 3:110; Keil, *Commentar*, 129.

152. Goldstein, *I Maccabees*, 332; Abel and Starcky, *Livres*, 140.

cabee and his brothers, who ignore these emissaries. Then we find that the Hasideans, also called scribes, enter the scene. It has already been established that the two phrases describing the activity of the Hasideans, "seeking just terms" and "seeking peace," are complementary. They have been found to be not the expression of a desire for the abstract notions of peace and justice, but the very concrete request for terms whereby the slaughter and destruction of a large approaching army might be averted. The concerns of the Hasideans in vv. 12 and 13 are pragmatic. They must stop the destruction of their people and their country. This is the context for the statement, "A priest from the seed of Aaron has come with the troops and he will not treat us unjustly." Such a setting makes it very doubtful that the author intended that we should understand this line to reflect a dispute over the legitimacy of anyone's claim to the high priesthood. There is no evidence in the story to suggest any kind of dynastic struggle. The question is rather whether he is trustworthy in his negotiations. The events of the last few years prior to this time, as described in 1 Maccabees, would have created ample reason to distrust the Greek governors and whatever they might say. 1 Macc. 6:62, for example, records that the king, Antiochus V, broke the oath he had sworn and gave orders to tear down the walls of Mount Zion. That oath had been made only one verse earlier. It is in response to this concern of mistrust that the Hasideans recognize the importance of Alcimus's presence in the company of the Greek army and Bacchides. Since Alcimus is a priest of the Jewish people his word can be trusted in negotiations.[153] Because Alcimus is accompanying Bacchides and the Greek troops, the Hasideans feel they can discuss peace terms. The recognition of Alcimus as a priest of the line of

[153]. Davies, *JJS* 28 (1977) 137.

Aaron is significant only to explain why the Hasideans could trust him. Of course, as the story unfolds, we find this trust was misplaced. The Maccabean author stresses that Alcimus as well as the Greek rulers could not be trusted.

It seems that the interpretation of 1 Macc. 7:14 just suggested is not original with this study. The text of *AJ* 12:395 suggests that Josephus read this line in the same manner when he speaks of Alcimus *ontos homophylou* (who was a countryman). In this case Josephus does not even make the claim that he is a priest; they are willing to trust him merely because he is of the Jewish people.[154] Josephus certainly corroborates the view that at this point there is no struggle for the hierocratic succession involved, the issue is simply one of a trustworthy negotiator. The Hasideans feel they can confidently deal with the Greek forces because there is "a priest from the seed of Aaron" with them.

Misguided Martyrs: 1 Macc. 7:15-17

The constant repetition of major themes in 1 Maccabees helps the reader to ascertain those points which its author was wishing to emphasize. This repetition provides a unity for the work which permits us to evaluate the reaction of this Hasmonean historian to the various events and personalities of the time. We have already noted the importance of the repetition of 1 Macc. 2:42 and 7:13 in 7:12. Before directing our attention to the proof-text in 1 Macc. 7:17, we must examine vv. 15 and 16 to determine what the author is trying to say in this instance. Such an examination includes paying attention to other instances in the work where similar material appears. 1 Macc. 7:15-16 reads as follows: καὶ ἐλάλησε μετ' αὐτῶν λόγους εἰρηνικοὺς καὶ

[154]. Contrary to Abel (*Livres*, 133), who claims that Josephus missed the point.

ὤμοσεν αὐτοῖς λέγων Οὐκ ἐκζητήσομεν ὑμῖν κακὸν καὶ τοῖς φίλοις ὑμῶν καὶ ἐνεπίστευσαν αὐτῷ καὶ συνέλαβεν ἐξ αὐτῶν ἑξήκοντα ἄνδρας καὶ ἀπέκτεινεν αὐτοὺς ἐν ἡμέρᾳ μιᾷ. . . . (And he spoke words of peace with them and he swore to them, "We will not seek to harm you and your friends." They trusted him and he seized sixty of their men and killed them in one day....).

The phrase *logous eirēnikous* (words of peace) is in the first instance clearly to be contrasted with v. 10 of this same chapter, where Bacchides and Alcimus send (the verb is in the singular but the context suggests both of them) a message to Judah and his brothers *logois eirēnikois meta dolou* (of words of peace with deceit). The Hasmonean historian here contrasts the approach of the Maccabees (who see the words of peace as a means of deception) with the Hasideans (who apparently accept them at face value). Later in chapter 7 Nicanor is sent to Judaea by Demetrius to destroy the people. In v. 27 he also speaks "words of peace with deceit" to Judah and his brothers. Again this verse informs us that Nicanor is accompanied by *dynamei pollę̄* (a large force). Judah learns of the deceit in the words of peace and does not meet with Nicanor a second time. The actions of the Hasideans who naively accept the peaceable words and neglect to see the deceit, i.e., a large force approaching, are contrasted with those of Judah who is cognizant of the accompanying army and pays no attention to the words of peace. A similar contrast is also found in 1 Macc. 1:30, where the Greeks speak "words of peace with deceit" as well.

All three passages in 1 Maccabees 7 just discussed need to be read in the light of chapter 1. We have already noted how central themes of the work such as Torah and covenant are prominent in 1 Maccabees 1.[155] Also recorded in this section is the story of a revenue officer sent to Judaea by Antiochus IV. After it is recorded in v. 30 that this officer, accompanied by a large force, spoke "words of peace with deceit" to them, the verse goes on to say *kai enepisteusan autǭ* (and they trusted him), the same phrase as we find describing the reaction of the Hasideans in 7:16. The parallels do not end here, however. While in 7:17 we find Alcimus killing sixty of the Hasideans, in 1:30-35 we see that the deputy of Antiochus IV, having spoken words of peace, suddenly falls upon the city, destroys many Israelites, plunders and burns the city, takes the women and children captive and turns the city of David into a citadel for the Greek army. What we find is that the Hasideans in chapter 7 react to the words of peace in the same way as the leaders in Jerusalem had earlier. The actions of these leaders had resulted in the plundering and burning of Jerusalem, in the slaughter of many Israelites, in the captivity of women and children, and in the establishment of an *akra* (citadel) for the foreign troops in Israel's holy city. From the viewpoint of the Hasmonean historian, the results of the response to the words of peace in 1 Maccabees 1 had been disastrous and the actions of the Hasideans were a repeat of this earlier mistake. As observed repeatedly by the author of this dynastic chronicle (see also 1 Macc. 2:40-41), the Maccabees did not make the same mistake as some of these other groups of not resisting this defilement and repression.

There is a further similarity between the accounts in 1 Maccabees 1 and 7. Following the respective sequences of events described in the previous paragraph, each chapter inserts a poetic piece which makes some allusion to Psalm 79. The first reference is in 1 Macc. 1:37: καὶ ἐξέχεαν

[155]. 1 Macc. 1:11,15,49,52,56,57,63.

αἷμα ἀθῷον κύκλῳ τοῦ ἁγιάσματος καὶ ἐμόλυναν τὸ ἁγίασμα (They poured out innocent blood round about the sanctuary and defiled the sanctuary.) In his study of the poetic sections of 1 Maccabees, Günther Neuhaus notes that the phrase, "and they defiled the sanctuary," is similar to Ps. 79:1, which reads, *ṭimme'u 'et heykal qodsheka* (they have defiled your holy temple).[156] The first half of the verse in 1 Maccabees, "they poured out innocent blood round about the sanctuary," is found to be a direct citation of Ps. 79:3: *Shap̱eku damam kammayim sebybot Yerushalayim* (They poured out their blood like water round about Jerusalem). Neuhaus also finds an allusion to Psalm 79 in 1 Macc. 3:45e, *kataluma tois ethnesi* (a lodging place for the Gentiles), which he translates into Hebrew as *mishkan laggoyim* (tabernacle for the Gentiles).[157] This is understood to be based upon Ps. 79:1a: *'elohym ba'u goyim benaḥalateka* (Oh God, the heathen have come into your inheritance). He does seem to be stretching the evidence in this last example when he sees fit to translate *kataluma* (lodging place) as *mishkan* (tabernacle), even though the LXX does use that Greek term for tabernacle at 1 Chr. 17:5, where it seems to fit the context. It is worth noting, however, that the theme of the Gentile pollution and destruction of the sanctuary is common to both passages in 1 Maccabees as well as the Psalm.

A clear citation of Psalm 79 is found in 1 Macc. 7:17, where it concludes the account of the Hasideans: κρέας ὁσίων σου καὶ αἷμα αὐτῶν ἐξέχεαν κύκλῳ

[156]. G. O. Neuhaus, *Studien zu den poetischen Stücken im 1. Makkabäerbuch*, Forschung zur Bibel 12 (Würzburg: Echter Verlag, 1974), 182-83.

[157]. Ibid.

Ιερουσαλημ καὶ οὐκ ἦν αὐτοῖς ὁ θάπτων (The flesh of your pious and their blood they poured out round about Jerusalem, and there was none to bury them.) The similarity of this passage to Ps. 79:2b-3 becomes clear when we look at the LXX text which, in this case, is a quite literal translation of the Hebrew: τὰς σάρκας τῶν ὁσίων σου τοῖς θηρίοις τῆς γῆς ἐξέχεαν τὸ αἷμα αὐτῶν ὡς ὕδωρ κύκλῳ Ιερουσαλημ καὶ οὐκ ἦν ὁ θάπτων (the flesh of your pious to the beasts of the earth. They have poured out their blood like water round about Jerusalem and there was none to bury.)[158] Here we find that part of the second stich of v. 2, which contains the term *ḥasydeyka* (your pious), is added to the lament in v. 3.[159] In fact, the presence of the term *ḥasyd* (pious) seems to be the reason for the inclusion of the biblical verse. This factor points to a number of differences between this verse and the others in 1 Maccabees that are said to have similarities to Psalm 79.

A number of studies have noted the uniqueness of the phrase that we have omitted from our discussion up to this point which appears at the end of 1 Macc. 7:16: *kata ton logon hon egrapsen auton* (according to the word which he had written). Grimm already observed that this emphasis on the written word means that the Psalm was considered to be

158. The Greek text is from Rahlfs's edition. In the LXX text, this is Psalm 78.

159. A detailed discussion of the differences is found in W. Kappler, *Maccabaeorum liber I*, Septuaginta Vetus Testamentum Graecum, 2d ed. (Göttingen: Vandenhoeck & Ruprect, 1967), 9:1:38-39.

Holy Scripture.[160] It seems we have here an early example of the midrashic style of biblical exposition.

The citation of Ps. 79:2-3 as scripture distinguishes 1 Macc. 7:17 from 1:37 and 3:45, the passages discussed above. Clearly, v. 17 is much closer to the text of Psalm 79 than either of the other citations. In both of the earlier examples, the allusion to this particular biblical text appears in the context of a poetic piece which alludes to other biblical passages as well or imitates biblical style (e.g., 1 Macc. 1:39-40 betrays similarities to Amos 8:10).[161] 1 Macc. 1:37 and 3:45 are also different in content. Both of them are concerned with the defilement of the sanctuary and the gentile conquest of God's dwelling place. These verses tend to be poetic restatements of the events just described that highlight the impact of those occurrences and serve to impress upon the reader the major points of this history. While there are some similarities between 1:37 and 7:17, the reason the latter is brought into the text is because it refers to the *ḥasydym* (pious-Hasideans). Rather than an original piece of poetry, 7:17 is a proof-text which stands in an exegetical

160. Grimm, *Handbuch*, 111. See also Keil, *Commentar*, 130; Neuhaus, *Stücken*, 172.

It does not seem to me that the ambiguity in the Greek phrase introducing the biblical citation is sufficient to warrant Goldstein's theory that Alcimus wrote Psalm 79 (*II Maccabees*, 332-36). The citation of Psalm 79 without attribution in 1 Macc. 1:37 and perhaps in 1 Macc. 3:45e discussed above argues against any recognition by the author of the Hasmonean history of Alcimus as its author. The recent dating of biblical Psalms also argues against Goldstein's proposal.

161. This view is in contrast to that of Neuhaus (*Stücken*, 182-83), who sees them all as similar biblical allusions, even though he does grant that in 7:17 the psalm is cited as scripture (p. 172) and that 7:17 is different from the other poetic pieces in 1 Maccabees (p. 234).

relationship to the description of the events. The verse explains the event and the event explains the verse.

In this case, Collins may be incorrect when he says that this quotation "throws us back again to the paradigm of the destruction of Jerusalem which was invoked so often at the beginning of the book."[162] If he means that 1 Macc. 7:17 cites Psalm 79 because the author in one way or another sees the destruction of Jerusalem and the profanation of the temple in the death of the sixty Hasidim, Collins is mistaken. If he is rather saying that the author quoted from Psalm 79 in part because he saw some similarities between the events in Jerusalem described in chapters 1 and 3 of 1 Maccabees and the lot of the Hasideans, he may have a point. But we dare not forget that the presence of the term *ḥasydeyka* (your pious) in Psalm 79 was the ostensible reason for the choice of these verses. The material is structured in such a way that it applies directly and only to the Hasideans. The lines from Psalm 79 which mention Jerusalem and the sanctuary are not quoted in 1 Maccabees 7. What does this mean for our understanding of the role of the Hasideans in this story?

This investigation of 1 Macc. 7:17 undergirds what is already concluded above in the comparison of the events in chapters 1 and 7. The Hasideans are held in high regard by this Hasmonean author but ultimately they are deemed wrong. Just as in chapter 1 where the destruction of Jerusalem and the profanation of the temple are the result of some wrong decisions on the part of the city leaders, so the martyrdom of the Hasideans is the result of incorrect decisions on their part. The Hasmonean historian does not question

162. J. J. Collins, *Daniel, First Maccabees, Second Maccabees: with an Excursus on the Apocalyptic Genre*, OTM 15 (Wilmington: Michael Glazier, 1981), 198-99.

their loyalty to the covenant and the Torah; he truly reckons them as martyrs of the faith. But he also considers their martyrdom to have been their own fault and unnecessary. Is this an intentional effort to discount their role and significance in the life of the Jewish state?

In 1 Maccabees we find the Hasideans are described as leading citizens of Israel, scribes who are devoted to the law. Their early support of Mattathias and his sons is set in the context of an account which chronicles the origin and growth of the Maccabean movement. However, in contrast to Judah Maccabee, they naively expect to be able to negotiate with the Greeks because these foreigners have a leading Jewish figure with them. They are mistaken. In the eyes of the Hasmonean historian the Hasideans turn out to be of little help in the further development of the nation. The question which lingers unanswered is whether he considered them to be a threat.

Judah Maccabee and the Hasideans:
2 Macc. 14:6

The third reference to the Hasideans, the only mention of the group in 2 Maccabees, is found in the opening line of a speech by Alcimus, an aspirant to the office of high priest, addressed to Demetrius I (162-150 B.C.E.): οἱ λεγόμενοι τῶν Ἰουδαίων Ἀσιδαῖοι ὧν ἀφηγεῖται Ἰούδας ὁ Μακκαβαῖος πολεμοτροφοῦσι καὶ στασιάζουσιν οὐκ ἐῶντες τὴν βασιλείαν εὐσταθείας τυχεῖν (Those of the Jews who are called Hasideans, that are led by Judah Maccabee, are fighting and causing insurrection, not permitting the kingdom to find stability). In 2 Maccabees 14 Demetrius has just done away with Antiochus V and his guardian Lysias in a successful bid for the rule of the Seleucid empire, a set of events already familiar to us from 1 Maccabees 7. Alcimus approaches this new ruler and is invited to apprise him of the Jewish situation. Alcimus begins his speech with the charges we have just read in v. 6.

The questions raised by this passage are numerous. The first and most obvious question: Why is Judah Maccabee here called the leader of the Hasideans, a claim which finds little or no support in other sources? Second, what is the connection between this account and the report narrated in 1 Maccabees 7, which contains some corresponding information? Third, what is the significance of the fact that the epitomist attributed this claim to Alcimus? Finally, what does this passage mean in the light of the rest of 2 Maccabees? It is these questions that we shall seek to answer in the following pages.

Before we can answer the question of why Judah Maccabee is here called the leader of the Hasideans, we must address the prior issue, the relationship of this account to 1 Maccabees 7. It has frequently been noted that there is some correspondence between a general outline of 1 Maccabees 3-7 and 2 Maccabees 8-15.[163] This has led scholars such as Schunck, followed by Wacholder and Bunge, to posit the existence of a common source behind the two accounts.[164]

[163]. E. Schürer, *Geschichte des jüdischen Volkes im Zeitalter Jesu Christi*, 3d ed. (Leipzig: J. C. Hinrichs'sche Buchhandlung, 1898), 3:360 attributes this similarity to common oral sources, while E. Meyer speaks of written sources that had not yet been put into a literary format (*Ursprung und Anfänge des Christentums* [Stuttgart/Berlin: J. G. Cotta'sche Buchandlung, 1921], 2:457-58). Note his earlier discussion of the sources and date of 2 Maccabees, pp. 39-43.

[164]. K.-D. Schunck, *Die Quellen des I. und II. Makkabäerbuches* (Halle: Veb Max Niemeyer Verlag, 1954), 52-74, 116-28; Ben Zion Wacholder, *Eupolemus: A Study of Judaeo-Greek Litera-*

They have referred to this source as the "Judasvita" or "Acts of Judah."[165] Goldstein simply refers to it as the "Jewish Common Source."[166] In contrast to these studies, Doran has questioned the hypothesis of a common source because it is based on the similarity in the ordering of events rather than on linguistic likenesses.[167] He comments "that source criticism is being applied here in an unusual way." He then goes on to argue that even the order of events is often not the same, and where it is it is not necessary to posit a common source. While I admit the difficulties involved in knowing and identifying precisely the nature and content of this common source, it seems to this writer that what Doran has called the "ordering of coincidences" is hard to explain without such a hypothesis. The only other explanation would be that either 1 Maccabees is dependent on 2 Maccabees or vice versa,[168] or that both works are dependent upon inde-

ture (Cincinnati: Hebrew Union College-Jewish Institute of Religion, 1974), 29-38; J. G. Bunge, *Untersuchungen zum zweiten Makkabäerbuch: Quellenkritische, literarische, chronologische und historische Untersuchungen zum zweiten Makkabäerbuch als Quelle syrisch-palästinensischer Geschichte im 2. Jh. v. Chr.* (Bonn: Rheinischen Friederich-Wilhelms-Universität, 1971), 206-329; Goldstein, *II Maccabees*, 37-54.

165. A chart of this source in 1 Maccabees can be found in Schunck, *Quellen*, 64-65, and in both books in Wacholder, *Eupolemus*, 30.

166. Goldstein, *II Maccabees*, 37-54. His chart of all the sources utilized in 1 and 2 Maccabees can be found on pp. 50-53.

167. R. Doran, *Temple Propaganda: The Purpose and Character of 2 Maccabees*, CBQMS 12 (Washington: Catholic Biblical Association, 1981), 13-17.

168. Wacholder, *Eupolemus*, 29.

pendent sources, both of whom were eyewitnesses to and/or participants in the events surrounding the life of Judah Maccabee. Since there is no evidence to support either of these suggestions, I think it is more plausible to postulate a common source for the two accounts. The possibility of reconstructing that source or of identifying its content is much more remote and may be beyond the scope of present-day methodology. What is important for this study is the much simpler task of comparing the accounts in 1 Maccabees 7 and 2 Maccabees 14, watching for evidence of a common source but not expecting to reconstruct it.

Let us begin the comparison of these two passages concerning the Hasideans by looking not only at the accounts themselves but also at the surrounding materials. It is first of all apparent that while the information concerning the Hasideans in the two accounts is considerably different, in both cases it immediately follows some common material. Both 1 Macc. 6:55-61 and 2 Macc. 13:23-24 relate that Antiochus V, at the suggestion of Lysias, settled terms of peace with the Jews because he had to return to Antioch to protect his throne from Philip. While the results of that offer are described much differently in 1 Macc. 6:62-63 and 2 Macc. 13:25-26, we return to common material at the beginning of both of the following chapters. 1 Macc. 7:1-4 and 2 Macc. 14:1-2 describe Demetrius' seizure of the throne and the murder of Antiochus and Lysias. This is followed by an account of Alcimus and the Hasideans in both works; however there is no similarity in the content of the two on this matter. Finally, we return to common material in 1 Macc. 7:26 and 2 Macc. 14:12, where we find Demetrius appointing Nicanor to go to Israel at the head of an armed force. While there is a considerable divergence in the two accounts of the conflict between Nicanor and Judah, both culminate with the public display of the head of Nicanor and the proclamation of a festival to celebrate the day of his death.[169] What we find in this outline are two divergent narratives concerning the Hasideans framed by similar accounts of a parallel sequence of events. Let us look more closely at these two different records concerning the subjects of this study.

The account of the Hasideans in 2 Maccabees appears within a speech in which Alcimus is complaining to Demetrius about Judah Maccabee. In this speech he refers to Judah as the leader of the Hasideans who is a troublemaker and the cause of insurrection in Israel. A question concerning this diatribe of Alcimus arises when we look at the corresponding record in 1 Maccabees. There we find that Alcimus appeals two times to Demetrius: first, in 1 Macc. 7:5-7 *andres anomoi kai asebeis* (lawless and impious men) led by Alcimus tell Demetrius about the harm Judah and his brothers are doing; secondly, in v. 25 of that same chapter Alcimus returns to Demetrius to bring *ponēra* (wicked charges) against Judah and those with him. Now, 2 Maccabees does record a second appearance of Alcimus before Demetrius; however since the subject of the complaint is Nicanor rather than Judah, there is no reason to consider it when looking at the two passages in 1 Maccabees.[170] We must address the question: Which of the instances recorded in 1 Maccabees is described here in 2 Maccabees 14?

There is no unanimous answer to this question. While Grimm argued that 7:5 provides the occasion for the speech recorded in 2 Macc. 14:6-10,[171] most scholars have accepted

169. 1 Macc. 7:47-49; 2 Macc. 15:35-36.

170. 2 Macc. 14:26.

171. Grimm, *Handbuch*, 3:193.

7:25 as the better possibility.[172] Grimm rests his case on three arguments:[173] (1) Alcimus brings gifts to demonstrate his allegiance to the king; (2) the manner in which Alcimus expresses his relationship to the Jewish institutions, i.e., there is no mention of an unsuccessful mission for the king; (3) in v. 13, Nicanor is first ordered to install Alcimus as high priest. Grimm considers this verse to be parallel to 1 Macc. 7:9. None of these arguments, however, is convincing.[174]

The assertion that Alcimus brought gifts to the king is not a very convincing point in favor of the hypothesis that this was his first visit to the king. Following the failures of Alcimus recorded in 1 Macc. 7:23-25, it may have been necessary for him to take extra measures to ingratiate himself with the king. Similarly, it is not surprising that this speech makes no mention of a previously unsuccessful mission on behalf of the king. Of course, given the nature of Hellenistic historiography, it is more likely that the speech in 2 Macc. 14:6-10 was composed by Jason than that it was found in a source common to Jason and the author of 1 Maccabees. In that case, the content of the speech in particular needs to be understood in light of the purpose and nature of 2 Maccabees. Since there is no reference to a mission of Alcimus in this work prior to his speech, there would be no reason for Jason to include such material in a

172. Keil, *Commentar*, 414; Zeitlin, *First Book*, 228; Christian Habicht, 2. *Makkabäerbuch*, JSHRZ 1:3 (Gütersloh: Gütersloher Verlagshaus Gerd Mohn, 1976), 272; Goldstein, *II Maccabees*, 486; Dommershausen, *1 Makkabäer. 2 Makkabäer*, 170. While Abel-Starcky (*Livres*, 308, n. b) argues that the author put together the two accounts, he lists 7:25 as the parallel reference in the margin.

173. *Handbuch*, 3:193.

174. See Keil's response, *Commentar*, 414.

speech which he composed. As to the third point, the appointment of Alcimus as high priest in 2 Macc. 14:13, it should first be noted that Grimm himself argued that the author of 2 Maccabees considered Alcimus to have formerly been a high priest.[175] Most scholars consider this to be an appointment to succeed Menelaus, as mentioned by Josephus but not by either of the works discussed here.[176] 1 Macc. 7:9 also mentions the appointment of Alcimus, a passage Grimm considers parallel to 2 Macc. 14:13. However, regardless of when Alcimus was appointed high priest, he seems to have had difficulty retaining the post or, at least, of realizing the power of the office. 1 Macc. 7:21 claims that Alcimus *ēgōnisato* (struggled) for the high priesthood. According to the same author, as already mentioned, he had previously been appointed in v. 9. We are not given any more details. In any case, it is clear that the argument cannot rest on 2 Macc. 14:13 which could mean that Nicanor was charged either with appointing or reappointing Alcimus as high priest or with helping him actually realize the power of his office. Under close examination, Grimm's arguments do not provide a very convincing case for identifying Alcimus' speech in 2 Maccabees with 1 Macc. 7:6-7.

Additional arguments could be advanced in favor of his hypothesis. (1) The charges in 1 Macc. 7:5-6 concerning the destruction of friends of the king and the ruin of the land seem to be quite similar to those found in 2 Macc. 14:6-7. (2) In the sequence of events laid out in both works, the charges of Alcimus against Judah follow immediately after the accession to the throne by Demetrius. (3) There is some reference in both 1 Macc. 7:5 and 2 Macc. 14:3 to Alcimus'

175. *Handbuch*, 3:193.

176. Habicht, 2. *Makkabäerbuch*, 270-71.

desire to be high priest. Can any of these claims be considered decisive evidence in favor of identifying 2 Macc. 14:6-10 with 1 Macc. 7:6-7?

When we turn to the first argument we see that in addition to the destruction mentioned in 1 Macc. 7:6-7, Judah takes vengeance on the followers of Alcimus in v. 24 of that chapter and seizes control of the countryside. The latter episode, however, is just as adequate a basis for the charges of Alcimus concerning Judah's threat to the peace of the realm as the former, perhaps better. Concerning the sequence of events in the two works, no parallel development of 1 Macc. 7:5-25 is to be found in 2 Maccabees 14. While Alcimus' speech follows the accession of Demetrius in 2 Maccabees, this diatribe leads immediately to the appointment of Nicanor, an event recorded in 1 Macc. 7:26 as well. In fact, the appointment of Nicanor in 2 Macc. 14:12 is the result of the charges of Alcimus, just as it is in 1 Macc. 7:26. Perhaps the strongest argument in favor of this identification is the third, that in both cases Alcimus is aspiring to gain the high priesthood. As just noted, however, determining when Alcimus was appointed high priest and when he was struggling to actualize that power is not a simple matter. There is no clear case for identifying the speech in 2 Maccabees with 1 Macc. 7:5 over 7:25. What should be obvious to the reader by now is that in this discussion we have not found indisputable evidence for the other case either, that the speech in 2 Macc. 14:6-10 is to be identified with Alcimus' appeal in 1 Macc. 7:25. Since, however, the appointment of Demetrius immediately follows both 1 Macc. 7:25 and 2 Macc. 14:10 and in both cases results from the charges of Alcimus, I favor the more commonly-held view.[177] Regardless of how that issue is resolved, the primary objec-

[177]. See n. 168 above.

tive in this study must be to make sense of the speech within the context of 2 Maccabees itself.

Within that composition Bacchides, the governor who according to 1 Maccabees 7 is appointed along with Alcimus to take care of matters in Coele-Syria, receives no mention. The work's only interest at this point is in Alcimus and Nicanor. As presented, the speech of Alcimus provides the motive for Demetrius' commission of Nicanor; this serves to make Alcimus responsible for the atrocities of Nicanor. This motive is clearly expressed in 2 Macc. 14:26, where Alcimus brings charges of disloyalty against Nicanor in an effort to destroy the agreement he had made with Judah. While we cannot resolve the original question, Does this speech reflect 1 Macc. 7:5 or 7:25? it is important to note the points which result from this investigation. At the point in the development of the historical record of 1 Maccabees where an account of the Hasideans is found we also discover Alcimus' accusations against Judah Maccabee and the Hasideans. It is safe to conclude that the original source included some record of the Hasideans at this point, even if the exact content of that report cannot be recovered. In light of the subject of this study the question is rather, Why, in the midst of the charges Alcimus makes against Judah Maccabee, is he called the leader of the Hasideans?

Any attempt to reconcile the information that Judah was the leader of the Hasideans with the material in 1 Maccabees is bound to run into difficulty. Tcherikover, arguing that 2 Maccabees was dependent on an earlier source close to the life of Judah, accepted this information at face value and argued that the Hasideans, after initiating the revolt, did place themselves under his leadership.[178] Tcherikover finds corroboration for the stance that the Hasidim were the in-

[178]. *Hellenistic Civilization*, 198, 206-07, 218.

stigators of the revolt in Dan. 11:33.[179] Other studies, while not accepting Tcherikover's hypothesis, find the Hasidim with Judah as their leader in 1 Enoch 90:6-12.[180] The hypothetical nature of these identifications does not permit us to use them as evidence in the interpretation of our passage.[181] For this very reason, Tcherikover has not found wide acceptance. The claim in 2 Macc. 14:6 must rather be examined in the context of the nature and purpose of the work within which it is found.

It is not a simple matter to evaluate this passage in the light of the rest of the work. The importance of the speech for understanding the opinion of the author of 2 Maccabees has been previously noted.[182] Since these charges are placed in the mouth of Alcimus, the villain in this particular account, we can see that the work's author is making a positive statement about Judah and the Hasideans in a negative way. By placing these words in the mouth of Alcimus the writer is saying that this is exactly what Judah and the Hasideans are not about, they are not the ones who are responsible for the warfare and rebellion, they are not the ones that do not let the kingdom attain tranquility. In fact, as Doran has noted, in 2 Maccabees Gorgias and the Idumeans are blamed for a continual state of warfare and the local military com-

[179]. Ibid., 198.

[180]. See Chapter 1 above. Note Charles, *APOT*, 1:257; Goldstein, *I Maccabees*, 41, 237; G. W. E. Nickelsburg, *Jewish Literature Between the Bible and the Mishnah: A Historical and Literary Introduction* (Philadelphia: Fortress, 1981), 92-93; Goldstein, *II Maccabees*, 322, 479, but note p. 86, n. 16.

[181]. But see Collins, *Daniel, Maccabees*, 202-03.

[182]. Doran, *Propaganda*, 68-70; Goldstein, *II Maccabees*, 485.

manders prevent the Jews from living in peace and quiet.[183] Furthermore, later in chapter 14 we find that Judah does settle down and lead a normal life, a situation interrupted by the machinations of Alcimus.[184] Doran also notes that Alcimus' charge against Judah parallels the accusation made by Onias III against the impious Simon who had told Apollonius about the temple treasury.[185] In 2 Maccabees, Judah is and does the exact opposite of what Alcimus claims concerning him. In order to see why in this defense of Judah he is linked with the Hasideans we need to look further into his treatment in 2 Maccabees.

Judah Maccabee is one of the heroes in this work. However this does not mean he is recognized only or even primarily as a military personage. As has been noted, the rebellion in 2 Maccabees does not begin with the leadership of Mattathias but with the martyrdom of Eleazar as well as the mother and her seven sons.[186] In this work, the reason these persons choose to become martyrs is to keep themselves free from pollution and to obey the commandments.[187]

183. *Propaganda*, 68-70; 2 Macc. 10:14,15; 12:2.

184. 2 Macc. 14:25.

185. 2 Macc. 4:6; cf. 2 Macc. 3:11.

186. George W. E. Nickelsburg, "1 and 2 Maccabees--Same Story, Different Meaning," *CTM* 42 (1971) 522; Goldstein, *I Maccabees*, 33; Collins, *Daniel, Maccabees*, 265. Elsewhere the obvious and related point is noted that Mattathias is omitted from this work, e.g., Goldstein, *II Maccabees*, 322. The prominence of Judah in this history is emphasized by Joseph Geiger, "The History of Judas Maccabaeus: One Aspect of Hellenistic Historiography," *Zion* 49 (1984) 1-8 (Hebrew).

187. 2 Macc. 6:19,21-22; 7:1 pass.

These themes of purity and of adherence to the law pervade the entire work. In addition to noting Judah's military leadership and accomplishments, we find that his piety and purity are emphasized. Judah Maccabee appears in this story for the first time when he and his companions flee to the mountains *pros to mē metaschein tou molysmou* (so as to not share in the defilement.)[188] In 2 Maccabees we also find that under Judah's leadership the Jewish forces do not fight on the sabbath.[189] There is an apparent effort on the part of the author to emphasize the piety of Judah in contrast to certain impious and defiled persons such as Alcimus and Simon, the temple treasurer. This portrayal of the central personage of 2 Maccabees may provide the clue whereby we can understand that verse which is the center of this portion of our study.

In most studies of the Second Book of Maccabees we find the significance of this verse is considered to be that Judah is made the leader of the Hasideans, i.e., the statement is evaluated as to what it says about the Hasideans.[190] In light of the statements just made concerning the role of Judah in 2 Maccabees, it is not clear that this is the case. It seems much more likely that this information is included in Alcimus' speech to make a point about Judah Maccabee rather than about the Hasideans. In this speech, which we can assume is the composition of the epitomist or of Jason,

[188]. 2 Macc. 5:27. Note the contrast with Alcimus who "had wilfully defiled himself" (2 Macc. 14:3).

[189]. 2 Macc. 8:26; cf. 12:38, 15:1-5.

[190]. Solomon Zeitlin and Sidney Tedesche, *The Second Book of Maccabees*, Jewish Apocryphal Literature, Dropsie College Edition (New York: Harper & Bros., 1954), 229; Hengel, *Judaism and Hellenism*, 1:97; Collins, *Daniel, Maccabees*, 347; Goldstein, *II Maccabees*, 18, 486.

it is said that the Hasideans are led by Judah Maccabee in order to add to his general portrayal as a pious person, in contrast to the impious Alcimus. In other words, Judah is said to be leader of the 'Pious' to add to his image of piety and purity. This means that we learn relatively little about the Hasideans from this passage; the author rather wished to teach us something concerning Judah.

The major objection which could be raised against this hypothesis would be by those who consider this book to be written by an author who was from the Hasideans, or that the work is at least reflective of that viewpoint.[191] They could argue that this information was inserted into the speech by Alcimus in order to claim Judah as a representative of the viewpoint advanced by the author. It does appear that the portrayal of Judah is reflective of the sympathies of the author. However, that does not mean that we should claim this work for the Hasideans. Earlier in this study, it has been argued that the evidence supports the premise that there was a group by the name *Ḥasydym* in existence in the second century B.C.E.[192] If this were the case, then an author who was a member or supporter of this group would certainly have found places to insert references to it throughout the work. As it now stands, there is no other mention of the

[191]. B. M. Metzger, *An Introduction to the Apocrypha* (New York: Oxford, 1957), 139; Nickelsburg, *CTM* 42 (1971) 523-25, but note the discussion of his work in Chapter 2 above; Hengel, *Judaism and Hellenism*, 1:97; Goldstein, *I Maccabees*, 33, 48-54, 65, 79-80, 88; Blenkinsopp, *Jewish and Christian Self-Definition*, 2:18; Goldstein, *II Maccabees*, 18, 486.

[192]. See Chapter 2 above.

Hasideans in the book.[193] Thus there is no evidence to support the claim that 2 Maccabees was the product of a member of the Hasidim. In this case, we are left with the premise that the Hasideans were included in this speech to augment the image of Judah as a figure of piety and purity. What does this tell us concerning the Hasideans?

Conclusion

In Chapter 2 we had established that the evidence indicates there was a group called the Hasideans in the second century B.C.E. The task of this chapter was to determine what 1 and 2 Maccabees tell us concerning the persons who bore this name. Contrary to many commentators, a literary study of 1 Maccabees suggests that vv. 29-38 are not be used as evidence concerning the Hasideans. While there is some evidence to suggest that the "many seeking righteousness and justice (who) descended to the desert to dwell there" in v. 29 may be a reference to the Essene movement, the literary structure of the chapter precludes any connection of that account with the Hasideans in v. 42. The Hasideans are rather described as part of a growing body of persons who attach themselves to the Maccabean movement in an effort to resist the unjust demands of Antiochus IV.

From 1 Maccabees we learn that the 'company' of the Hasideans was composed of leading citizens devoted to the law. While they can certainly not be regarded as paci-

193. This fact also provides the justification for the ordering of the materials in this study. It could be argued that the evidence of 2 Maccabees takes priority because the date advanced for its composition (see Chapter 2 above) is earlier than that discussed in connection with 1 Maccabees (see Chapter 6 below). Since, however, the evidence concerning the Hasidim in 2 Maccabees is so scanty, this study is warranted in beginning with the major body of evidence, 1 Maccabees.

fists, *ischuroi dynamei* in 1 Macc. 2:42 probably points to their stature in the society rather than to their military prowess. The evidence suggests that they were regarded as leaders. This stature is confirmed in 1 Macc. 7:12-13 where we can see in the verbal connections with 2:42 that the author of the Hasmonean history is referring to them as scribes. When we turn to the more lengthy story in 1 Maccabees 7 concerning the Hasideans we find that its purpose ultimately is to discount the significance of the Hasideans. While he portrays them as leading citizens (*prōtoi*-first) willing to seek some accomodation with the Greek conquerors based on the fact that there is a Jewish priest with whom to negotiate, the author of this dynastic history claims that the Hasideans are unaware of the guile and deceit of which the leaders of these forces are capable. In a dramatic turn of events interpeted in the light of Psalm 79 sixty of the Hasideans are seized and killed. The Hasmonean historian is rendering the leadership abilities of this significant group as ineffectual and dangerous for the survival of the nation.

Understanding that the Hasideans were used in 2 Macc. 14:6 to heighten the image of Judah as a man of piety and purity has certain implications for the subject of this study. Given the discussion of the relationship of 1 and 2 Maccabees, as well as the fact that the transliterated Greek *Asidaioi* is here employed, we can be quite certain that the listing of the group is very intentional. The writer of this letter thought that by citing the Hasideans, the regard for and prestige of Judah Maccabee would be enhanced. Thus we see that the author of 2 Maccabees regarded the Hasideans to be well-known people, renowned for their purity in the time of hellenization and for their piety. In order to be utilized by either Jason or the epitomist in the manner in which they were, the Hasideans must not have been some people who separated themselves from the affairs of the nation but rather an influential group, leading citizens of Israel, who bore some weight in matters concerning the Jews of Judaea. In 2 Maccabees the Hasideans must be considered to be among the leading religious personalities of the era.

IV

THE ESSENES AND THE HASIDIM?

The origin of the name *Essēnoi* or *Essaioi* (Essenes) continues to be a problem which vexes those scholars who attempt to classify and describe the various religious and sociological groupings within Second Temple Judaism. A prominent issue in the discussion of this question has been the relationship of the Essenes attested in the works of Philo and Josephus to those persons described in the writings said to be found in the caves around the site of Qumran. While the majority of scholars have resolved this question in favor of some connection between the two groups,[1] most frequently basing it on a hypothesis concerning the Hasidim, such a proposal does not clearly resolve the issue of the use of the name 'Essene' in Philo and Josephus, since it is not found in

[1]. A. Dupont-Sommer, *The Essene Writings from Qumran*, trans. G. Vermes (Cleveland: World, 1962), 39-67; F. M. Cross, Jr., *The Ancient Library From Qumran*, rev. ed. (Garden City: Doubleday, 1961), 49-106; G. Vermes, *The Dead Sea Scrolls: Qumran in Perspective* (Cleveland: Collins & World, 1978), 125-30. Y. Yadin claims that the Temple Scroll resolves any outstanding issues in favor of an identification: *The Temple Scroll* (Jerusalem: Israel Exploration Society, 1983), 1:398-99; id., *The Temple Scroll: The Hidden Law of the Dead Sea Sect* (New York: Random House, 1985), 232-39.

the Qumran scrolls or fragments. This is not to say that scholars have not tried to find evidence of the name in these documents. The discussion of the etymology of the epithets *Essēnoi* and *Essaioi* was a matter of debate, of course, even before the discoveries near Wadi Qumran in 1947.[2] In this chapter I shall examine briefly some of the etymologies of the word that have been proposed, evaluate the historical evidence for those which have been most broadly accepted, and then go on to discuss an avenue which has largely been overlooked for the resolution of this problem. Interest in the question of the meaning and origin of *Essēnoi* and *Essaioi* goes back to Philo of Alexandria.

Ancient and Modern Proposals

Philo mentions the Essenes in three of his works, always utilizing the term Essaioi.[3] In *Quod omnis probus liber sit*, we find Philo's explanation of the name: λέγονταί τινες παρ' αὐτοῖς ὄνομα 'Εσσαῖοι πλῆθος ὑπερτετρακισχίλιοι κατ' ἐμὴν δόξαν--οὐκ ἀκριβεῖ τύπῳ διαλέκτου 'Ελληνικῆς--παρώνυμοι ὁσιότητος (Some of them are called by the name Essene...which in my opinion corresponds to *hosiotētos* [holiness], though not in the best

[2]. Note the proposals advanced in the nineteenth century that are listed by J. B. Lightfoot, *Dissertations on the Apostolic Age* (London: MacMillan & Co., 1892), 325-31 and by S. Wagner, *Die Essener in der wissenschaftliche Diskussion: Vom Ausgang des 18. bis zum Beginn des 20. Jahrhunderts: Eine wissenschaftsgeschichtliche Studie*, BZAW 79 (Berlin: Alfred Töpelmann, 1960).

[3]. *Prob.* 75,91; *Vita* 1:1; *Hyp.* 11:1, 3, 14.

form of the Greek language.)[4] For Philo, these people are called Essenes because of their holiness or piety. While he does not say that *Essaioi* is a Hebrew term, Philo does not recognize it as Greek. The most obvious implication of this statement in its context is that Philo thought this term was of Hebrew or Aramaic origin.

It is in Josephus that we find both *Essēnoi* and *Essaioi* employed. In the introduction to his most extensive discussion of the Jewish sects, we find that he alludes to the reputation of the Essenes for piety, but he does so using the term *semnotēta* (in addition to "holiness," this term can mean "reverence" or "dignity").[5] Nowhere does Josephus claim to know the origin of the name Essene. Neither Josephus nor Philo identify a Semitic term that explains the origin of the word presently under consideration. Modern scholarship has not been so restrained.

Within the last two centuries, we see that numerous proposals have been advanced to explain the origin of this name, some already present in earlier centuries, some original with the modern period.[6] Common to the majority of these hypotheses is the assumption that the Greek term must represent a Hebrew or Aramaic original which was then transposed into the Greek language. For example, the only possibility from the Greek that Lightfoot presented in his list

[4]. *Prob.* 75. See also *Prob.* 91 and *Hyp.* 11:1. Since this article deals with the name Essene, there is no need to discuss the complicated relationship between the Essenes and the *Therapeutai* described in *De vita contemplativa.* See Geza Vermes, *Post-Biblical Jewish Studies*, SJLA 8 (Leiden: Brill, 1975), 8-36.

[5]. *BJ* 2:119.

[6]. See the references in n. 2 above. Note also G. Vermes, *Post-Biblical*, 8-36; *Schürer-Vermes-Millar*, 2:555-61.

of etymologies advanced by nineteenth century scholars was the one already mentioned by Philo, i.e., *hosios* from *hosiotētos*, and Lightfoot considered it very doubtful.[7] In his survey Geza Vermes did not include any proposals based on a Greek etymology.[8] Scholarship has looked to Hebrew and Aramaic for an explanation of this term.

Dupont-Sommer advanced the argument that the name was derived from the term *'eṣah* (council), which appears frequently in the scrolls.[9] Brownlee notes the difficulty of getting a gentilic form from that term which would yield *essēnoi* and then goes on to propose that both *'eṣah* and *essēnoi* could be derived from *'eṣym* or *'eṣyn* (trees), for which Lebanon was noted from the time of Solomon.[10] He admits that this hypothesis has difficulty accounting for the form *Essaioi* and then goes on to point out the attractive features of the widely accepted proposal which finds the etymology of the two terms for Essene in the Hebrew *Ḥasydym*, a hypothesis to be discussed shortly.

While originally accepting the *ḥasyd* hypothesis discussed below, Geza Vermes has proposed rather that the appellation has its origin in the term *'asya'* (healer).[11] He points to the *Therapeutai* described in Philo's *De vita contemplativa* as "healers of the spiritually sick" and identifies

7. Lightfoot, *Dissertations*, 325-31.

8. *Post-Biblical*, 8-29.

9. Dupont-Sommer, *Essene Writings*, 21, n. 3; 43.

10. W. H. Brownlee, *The Midrash Pesher of Habakkuk*, SBLMS 24 (Missoula: Scholars Press, 1979), 199-201.

11. Vermes, *Post-Biblical*, 11-36.

them with the Essenes, based on the use of the term *therapeutai* in the description of that group in *Quod omnis probus liber sit.* Rejecting this proposal, Cross has noted that the first three letters of the Greek name *ess-* suggest that it is derived from the Semitic *ḥas-* rather than from *'as-*.[12] While Vermes is correct when he protests that he has been misunderstood as suggesting that the Essenes were physicians,[13] when he argues that the *Therapeutai* are 'healer worshippers', with an emphasis on the latter term 'worshippers', he severs the connection with *'asya'*, thereby casting doubt on the etymology he has proposed. Certainly we do not find here a clear case for using *'asya'* to explain *essēnoi* or *essaioi.*

A recent proposal by Stephen Goranson in *Revue de Qumran*,[14] previously mentioned by Brownlee,[15] merits mention. The suggestion is that the terms under discussion are derived from the Hebrew verb *'aśah* (do), a well-attested term in the scrolls from Qumran. While he is certainly correct in pointing out the importance of the verb in some Qumran writings, for example in 1QpHab 8:1 which speaks of *kol 'ośey hattorah* (all who do the law), we do not find evidence of its use as a name, i.e., as a proper noun, as we do for example with regard to the Pharisees and the Sadducees in Tannaitic texts. While we find in the documents the use of the verb primarily in its participial form *'ośey* to

12. Cross, *Ancient Library*, 38-39, n. 1. He cites the example of Josephus using *essen* as the transcription of *ḥoshen.* See below.

13. Vermes, *Post-Biblical*, 30-31; Cross, *Ancient Library*, 38-39, n. 1.

14. S. Goranson, "'Essenes': Etymology from *'śah*," *RevQ* 11 (1984) 483-98.

15. Brownlee, *Midrash Pesher*, 119.

describe the members of the sect, it is not clear that this term is as central a self-designation as some other phrases are such as *'anshey hayyaḥad* (men of the Commune).[16] Furthermore, an etymological explanation utilizing the term *'óśey* is more likely for the forms *Ossaioi* and *Ossēnoi* attested in Epiphanius than it is for those forms found in Josephus and Philo.[17] The evidence linking *'aśah* with essene also fails to be convincing.

The most broadly accepted hypothesis concerning the etymology of *Essēnoi* and *Essaioi* considers these terms to have been derived from the Hebrew *ḥasydym* (Pious) via its Aramaic form.[18] The theory is that the Greek *Essaioi* is a transliteration of the Aramaic *ḥasayya'*, the determined plural form, and *Essenoi* of *ḥasyn*, the absolute plural. This hypothesis finds support in Philo's repeated suggestion that *Essaioi* is related to *hosios*, the Greek term which is usually employed to translate *ḥasyd* in the LXX. However, as Vermes and others have pointed out, the Aramaic term is attested primarily in Syriac and there is no evidence of it in Palestinian usage. While Milik has noted that the word is

16. 1QS 5:1,3,16; 6:21; 7:20,24; 8:11,16; 9:6,7,8,10,19; 1Q 31:1:1; 4QPBless 5; CD 20:32. Note the list of names collected by G. Sharvit, "Names of the Judean Desert Sect and its Designations," *Beyt Miqra'* 28 (1982-3) 134-39.

17. Goranson, *RevQ* 11 (1984) 496.

18. E. Schürer, *Geschichte des jüdischen Volkes im Zeitalter Jesu Christi*, 3d and 4th ed. (Leipzig: J. C. Hinrichs, 1898-1901), 2:559-60; J. T. Milik, *Ten Years of Discovery in the Wilderness of Judaea*, trans. J. Strugnell (Naperville: Alec R. Allenson, 1959), 80, n. 1; Wagner, *Essener*, 83-88; Cross, *Ancient Library*, 51-52, n. 1; R. Meyer, "*Saddoukaios*," *TDNT* 7:39, n. 27; M. Hengel, *Judaism and Hellenism: Studies in their Encounter in Palestine during the Early Hellenistic Period*, trans. J. Bowden (Philadelphia: Fortress, 1974), 1:175; 2:116, nn. 455-56.

attested once in a Palmyrene inscription published by Cantineau,[19] we must note that Cantineau considers it a participle and not a noun.[20] This certainly does not constitute evidence that it was actually used as a name for a specific group of persons.[21]

In this particular hypothesis, we find that the historical evidence discussed above has been advanced in favor of the suggested etymology. I have already discussed the widely accepted hypothesis that the *Asidaioi* of 1 Macc. 2:42, 7:13 and 2 Macc. 14:6 are the forerunners of both the Essenes and Pharisees.[22] I listed some of the many studies that considered the devout persons in 1 Maccabees 2:29-38, who fled to the desert only to become martyrs, to be members of the group called Hasideans.[23] It has been thought that persons described as seeking *dikaiosynē kai krima* (righteousness and justice) in the desert would have been interested in the kind of pious life represented by those called the *Ḥasydym.* Corroboration for this perspective is found in the refusal of these desert dwellers to defend themselves against the king's troops because they did not want to defile the sabbath. Allusions to these events are then found in the Qumran scrolls. For example, Matthew Black connects the 390 plus 20 years re-

19. Milik, *Ten Years*, 80, n. 1.

20. J. Cantineau, "Tadmorea," *Syria* 14 (1933) 177.

21. The proposal by Takamitsu Muraoka, "'Essene' in the Septuagint," *RevQ* 8 (1973) 267-68 does not significantly strengthen the case for this identification.

22. See Chapter 1 above.

23. See Chapter 3 above.

corded in the first folio of the Damascus Document with the emergence of the Hasidim.[24] Certainly he is not alone in positing such a relationship.[25] If this is true, the Hasidim are considered to be a first stage in the development of the Essene movement as described by Philo and Josephus, and witnessed to in the scrolls found near the Dead Sea. Of course, retreating to the desert in search of righteousness and justice and then being willing to die in order not to violate the Sabbath is certainly compatible with such a portrait. That does not mean, however, that they were considered to be *Ḥasydym.*

Earlier in this study I have shown that 1 Maccabees 2:29-38 is one literary unit and that v. 42 which contains the reference to the Hasideans is encompassed within the next section which includes vv. 39-48.[26] The literary structure of 1 Maccabees 2 is such that the discussion of the desert dwellers concerns a different group of persons than the Hasideans mentioned in v. 42. What we have seen up to this point is that there is no necessary connection between the Hasidim and the Essenes that can be supported from either an etymological or a historical basis. I have also pointed out that the major proposals to explain the etymology of 'essene' have been advanced on the basis of a Semitic original. While each of the words discussed above is to be taken seriously if we assume that a Semitic original is involved, I do not think that adequate reasons have been advanced for limiting our

[24]. M. Black, *The Scrolls and Christian Origins: Studies in the Jewish Background of the New Testament*, BJS 48 (Chico: Scholars Press, 1983-reprint of 1961 ed.), 16-20.

[25]. Milik, *Ten Years*, 59; Hengel, *Judaism*, 1:175-76, 179, 225; Vermes, *Dead Sea Scrolls: Qumran in Perspective*, 142-50.

[26]. See Chapter 3 above.

study to this assumption. Since *essēnoi* and *essaioi* are attested only in Greek sources, other uses of the term in Greek literature should at least be considered in our investigations. We do not have far to look.

When we turn to Josephus, we see that he has used the term *essēn* in another context as well as the one which we have been discussing. He uses the word *essēn* to render the Hebrew *ḥoshen* (breastplate).[27] Now Vermes,[28] citing a reference to this possibility in an article by Grintz,[29] has noted this word in his list of possible Semitic originals. However, Vermes merely deals with the issue of whether the name *essēnoi* could have been derived from *ḥoshen*. Now Josephus himself does not connect his Greek translation of *ḥoshen* with the name of the sectaries.[30] He thinks *essēn* in this context means *logion* (oracle, prophecy).[31] This leads both Zeitlin and del Medico to think that it was this power of prophecy or divination that accounts for the name of the sec-

[27]. *AJ*. 3:163,166,170,171,185,216,217,218.

[28]. Vermes, *Post-Biblical*, 11-12.

[29]. Y. M. Grintz, " 'אנשי היחד'-איסיים-בית אסין." *Sinai* 32 (1952) 43, n. 77.

[30]. This important detail is missed by Allen H. Jones, *Essenes: The Elect of Israel and The Priests of Artemis* (Lanham/London: University Press of America, 1985), 50-62.

[31]. *AJ* 3:217.

tarian group.[32] Vermes similarly in his discussion concentrates on the power of divination and prophecy, however he rejects the proposal because there is no evidence that the Essenes wore anything like a *ḥoshen* or a bag for holding implements of divination.[33] His objection to the proposal is based on his assumption that we are searching for a Semitic original. The most important observation at this point is to note that Josephus finds no connection between this use of *essēn* and the description of the sectarians in his work. Why does Josephus use this term for *ḥoshen*?

It seems that Josephus considered *essēn* to be a transcription of *ḥoshen*. This is what the anonymous Hebrew author of the column in Origen's Hexapla which contained the Hebrew text in Greek transcription did. This is what Josephus seems to be saying when he states: ἐσσὴν μὲν καλεῖται σημαίνει δὲ τοῦτο κατὰ τὴν Ἑλλήνων γλῶτταν λόγιον (it is called *essēn*, this signifies according to the language of the Greeks oracle).[34] In other words, the term *essēn* is not Greek. It must then be Hebrew or Aramaic. *Essēn* at this point is Josephus' transcription of *ḥoshen*. Where then did he get his Greek translation of the term? From the LXX which translates *ḥoshen* as *logion*, derived from the fact that it contained the 'urim and thummim', instruments of divination. However, since he doesn't make the connection with the sectaries we cannot accept this explanation as valid for explaining the name of

[32]. S. Zeitlin, "The Essenes and Messianic Expectations: A Historical Study of the Sects and Ideas During the Second Jewish Commonwealth," *JQR* 45 (1954-55) 89-90; H. E. del Medico, "Une étymologie du nom des Esséniens," *ZRGG* 11 (1959) 269-72.

[33]. Vermes, *Post-Biblical*, 11-12.

[34]. *AJ* 3:163.

the sectaries. Let us rather turn to other possible uses of the term in Greek.

IN THE SERVICE OF ARTEMIS AT EPHESUS

It is when we turn to the Greek inscriptions related to the cult of Artemis at Ephesus that we again encounter the term under discussion.[35] It is well-known that Artemis was the major god of that city for a number of centuries and that the temple to her dominated the city skyline.[36] In the excavations of that city numerous inscriptions have been found which are a tremendous aid in understanding its history.[37] Within those inscriptions, the noun *essēn* and its

[35]. Certainly this is not the first time that it has been suggested that we look to the cult of Artemis for an explanation of the name of the Jewish sect. Nineteenth century scholars were quick to notice this connection: J. B. Lightfoot, *St. Paul's Epistles to the Colossians and Philemon*, rev. ed. (London: Macmillan & Co., 1904), 94, n. 1; E. L. Hicks, *The Collection of Ancient Greek Inscriptions in the British Museum*, Part. 3, Section 2, *Ephesos* (Oxford: Clarendon Press, 1890), 85. We now have also the recent work by Jones, *Essenes*. While he has collected a lot of material, many of the arguments are less than convincing. I will discuss some of those in further notes. He does not rely on the important evidence of the inscriptions for his portrait of the *essēn* in Ephesus.

[36]. There is a good deal of material on growth of the Artemis cult at Ephesus. I list here only a few selected works: W. K. C. Guthrie, *The Greeks and their Gods* (Boston: Beacon, 1955), 99-106; L. R. Farnell, *The Cults of the Greek States* (New Rochelle: Caratzas Brothers, 1977), 2:425-86. See also the note by L. R. Taylor in F. J. Foakes-Jackson and K. Lake, *The Beginnings of Christianity* (London: Macmillan & Co., 1933), 5:251-56.

[37]. For a recent collection of these inscriptions see *IvE*. Note that the bibliography for each inscription is included in that volume, thus I have not repeated all the references with each inscription. I have only documented points which I considered important

derivatives are not uncommon terms.[38] We now turn our attention to those references.

The earliest inscription pertinent to this study that can be dated with some certainty is to be ascribed to 307/306 B.C.E.[39] In a decree which gives Anaxakrates, the archon of Athens, the right of citizenship in Ephesus, we read: δεδόχθαι τῆι βουλῆι καὶ [τῶι δήμωι] εἶναι ᾿Αναξικράτει αὐτῶι καὶ ἐγγόνοις πολιτείαν καὶ ἔγκτησιν ἐφ' ἴσηι κ[αὶ ὁμοίηι] καθάπερ καὶ τοῖς ἄλλοις εὐεργέταις καὶ ἐπικληρῶσαι αὐτὸν εἰς φυλὴν καὶ χιλιαστὺν τοὺς ἐσσῆνας τὸ δὲ ψήφισμα ἀναγράψαι τοὺς νεωποί[ας] εἰς τὸ ἱερὸν τῆς ᾿Αρτέμιδος (It is resolved by the council and [the assembly] that Anaxakrates and his descendants are to have citizenship and the right to property on terms equal a[nd similar] to those of the other benefactors; the *essēnas* shall allot him a place in a tribe and a thousand;[40] the temple

to the subject under discussion.

38. The most extensive collection of references to *essēn* is that of G. P. Oikonomos, "*Naopoioi kai Essēnes*," *Archaiologikon Deltion* 7 (1921-22) 329-46. That collection is now somewhat dated.

39. *IvE* 1443. *IvE* 1451 may be dated as early as 319 B.C.E., however it is not certain that the Arridaios in the inscription is the one referred to by Diodorus (see note to that inscription). While 2011 might be dated to ca. 318 B.C.E. (see note to that inscription), *essēnas* appears there only in reconstruction.

40. The *chiliastys* was a subdivision of the tribe. See Hicks, *Collection*, 68-70.

[wardens][41] shall inscribe the decree in the temple of Artemis).[42] What is evident here is that these "essenes" play a prominent role in the city-cult of Ephesus which is dedicated to Artemis. It is they who assign the new citizen a place in the organization of the citizenry, the tribe and the 'thousand'. This description of the role of these essenes is not a solitary one. A number of other inscriptions dated to the end of the fourth and to the third centuries B.C.E. allude to the same function for these officials within the political structure of the city of Ephesus.[43] A leading role is also ascribed to them in an inscription from ca. 297 B.C.E where they along with the *synedroi* (councillors) are charged with receiving the money for the right of citizenship from the people of Priene

[41]. For an explanation of this translation, see Hicks, *Collection*, 80-81. J. T. Wood, *Discoveries at Ephesus: Including the Site and Remains of the Great Temple of Diana* (London: Longmans, Green & Co., 1877), also uses this term in his translations: e.g., app. 2, "Inscriptions from the Temple of Diana," no. 1=*IvE* 1455:9, no. 7=*IvE* 1453:15, no. 8=*IvE* 1448:20, no. 9=*IvE* 1451:4, no. 26=*IvE* 1471:3; app. 4, "Inscriptions from the Augusteum," no. 2=*IvE* 1578b:4; app. 8, "Inscriptions from the City and the Suburbs," no. 16=*IvE* 1447:18.

[42]. *IvE* 1443:4-8.

[43]. The term is included in whole or in part in the following inscriptions: *IvE* 1408, 1409, 1440, 1447(=Hicks, *Collection*, #447), 1451, 1453, 1455 (=Hicks, *Collection*, #455 and *SIG* 354), 1457 (=Hicks, *Collection*, #457), 1467, 1471, 2005 (which has *esēnas* rather than *essēnas*). The editors have included it in their reconstructions of the following inscriptions from the same era: *IvE* 1413, 1441, 2009, 2010, 2011, 2013.

A puzzling reference is the partially reconstructed text of *IvE* 2007 which states ἀναγράψ[αι δὲ τὰς δεδομένας αὐτῶι τιμ]ὰ[ς] τοὺς ἐσσῆνας (the *essēnes* shall inscri[be the hono]r[s which have been determined for him]). In all the other inscriptions this is a task which is ascribed to the *neopoioi* (temple wardens).

in Charax.[44] The assignment of their place to the new citizenry is probably also alluded to a few centuries later, in a decree dated to either 98/97 or 94/93 B.C.E., where *tous essēnas* has been reconstructed in the text, probably correctly, since the inscription charges them with granting to those from Sardis who are granted citizenship in Ephesus a tribe and a thousand.[45] This is not the only function, however, which these persons perform.

In an inscription dated to either 306 or 302 B.C.E. we read: [θύειν δὲ καὶ εὐ]αγγέλια τῆι Ἀρτέμιδι τοὺς ἐσσῆνας (the *essēnas* [sacrifice an offering of good] tidings to Artemis).[46] In addition to the task of induction referred to in the many instances listed above, we find that these persons perform priest-like functions in the cult of Artemis, being responsible for the administration of the sacrifices.[47] It does not seem to be an overstatement when Hicks, in his description of the *essēnes* based on his study of the inscriptions from Ephesus, suggests that they were really to be viewed as representatives of the goddess. In the activities referred to in the previous para-

[44]. *IvE* 2001:10=*SIG* 363:10. Concerning the date see note to 2001:12 and introduction to *SIG* 363.

[45]. *IvE* 7:Sardis 6:2. While it is tempting to reconstruct *essēnas* in cases like *IvE* 1438:3, 1452:3 and 1456:5, it must be noted that the person being granted citizenship can be allotted a place in a tribe and a 'thousand' without the agent being specified, such as in *IvE* 1454. Perhaps Hicks (p. 85) is correct in suggesting that *essēnes* should be understood in such cases.

[46]. *IvE* 1448:5-6=*SIG* 352:5-6.

[47]. M. P. Nilsson, *Geschichte der griechischen Religion*, vol. 2, 2d ed. (Munich: C. H. Beck'sche Verlagsbuchhandlung, 1961), 342, states that the Essenes were responsible for the cultic meals.

graph, "it was as if the goddess herself, by their hands, welcomed him (i.e., the new citizen) into her city and assigned him his place within it."[48] This relationship between the city and the cult has also been noted by Fergus Millar. In discussing the inscription erected by the citizens of Ephesus to Hadrian, Millar notes that "it is representative also in regarding the rights and privileges of the main temple of the city (i.e., of Artemis) as an extension or expression of those of the city itself."[49] These *essēnes* are officials of the cult of Artemis and as such have certain responsibilities in the life of the city of Ephesus. This has led to considerable debate about the origin of the term.

In the Hymn to Zeus from the pen of Callimachus (third century B.C.E.), we read: οὔ σε θεῶν ἐσσῆνα πάλοι θέσαν ἔργα δὲ χειρῶν (nor were you made ruler of the gods by casting of lots but by the works of your hand).[50] Here *essēn* is translated 'ruler'. This seems to be related to the popular etymology of *essēn* which was related to the term *hesmos* (bee) and connected with the bee found on the back of Ephesian coinage.[51] The precise history of

[48]. Hicks, *Collection*, p. 85.

[49]. Fergus Millar, *The Emperor in the Roman World: 31 BC - AD 337* (Ithaca: Cornell University, 1977), 447.

[50]. *Hymn to Zeus* 65. Note the comments concerning this passage of Jones, *Essenes*, 72.

[51]. *Etymologicum Magnum* 383, 13; B. V. Head, *On the Chronological Sequence of the Coins of Ephesus* (London: Rollin and Feurdent, 1880), 41; R. D. Barnett, "Early Greek and Oriental Ivories," *JHS* 68 (1948) 20-21. Jones, *Essenes*, tries to establish a connection between Philo's reference to the Essenes being among other things bee-keepers and the 'bee' in Ephesus (p. 6). Note also his discussion of the Artemis cult, 85-100.

this etymology continues to be a matter of dispute,[52] however that discussion does not impinge on its use in the inscriptions.[53] Regardless of the original etymology of the term, it is clearly attested that *essēn* was the term used to designate certain cultic officials from the cult of Artemis in Ephesus beginning at least as early as the latter portion of the fourth century B.C.E.

When we turn to the first few centuries C.E., we begin to find evidence of the use of this word in verb form. The earliest record of this usage may appear in a decree that is probably to be dated to the time of Caesar Augustus (27 B.C.E.-14 C.E.), in which the editors of these inscriptions have reconstructed the participle *essēneuontōn*.[54] As a verb, it is clearly present in a decree probably to be placed in the late second century C.E.: . . . Σκάπτιος φροντεῖνος νεοποιὸς [β]ουλευτὴς σὺν καὶ τῇ γυναικί μου Ἑρεννίᾳ Αὐτρωνίᾳ ἐσσηνεύσας ἁγνῶς καὶ εὐσεβῶς [σ]πονδοποιοῦντος θεοπόμπου. . . . (...I Scaptius Frontinos, temple warden, senator, with also my wife Herennia Autronia, *essēneusas* in an undefiled and pious manner, Theopompos performing the [dr]ink offer-

[52]. Hicks, *Collection*, 77, 85; R. Muth, "*Essēn*," *Anzeiger für Altertumswissenschaft* 5 (1952) 61-64, 123-28.

[53]. This fact is ignored by the historical conflation found in Jones, *Essene*, 85-100, who thinks that the meaning 'bee' was still current at the time of Josephus and Philo (pp. 61-62).

[54]. *IvE* 3513:3 where *essēneuontōn* is reconstructed. Since elsewhere the verb is only used in the aorist tense, the form of the reconstruction is suspect. The date of this inscription rests on the paleographic evidence (see notes to the inscription in *IvE*).

ing....)[55] Two features in this inscription attract our attention. The first is to note that this person says that he carried out the function of the *essēn* while Theopompos did the drink offering. The clear implication is that his function as an *essēn* was some role in the sacrificial cult, probably the offering of the major sacrifice. Secondly, we observe that he refers to himself as a *neopoios* (temple warden), which had been a distinct function in the earlier inscriptions cited above.[56] It seems that these later references reflect a lessening of the distinctiveness between these two offices. A similar phenomenon is to be observed in other instances from roughly the same time period.[57] While this may be evidence of some shift in the roles of these cultic officials around the beginning of the Common Era, we must not lose sight of the

[55]. *IvE* 1578b:3-10. For the date see Hicks, *Collection*, #578c (p. 208).

[56]. A possible exception to the two distinct roles may be *IvE* 2007 discussed above (n. 45), where the *essēnes* perform a task that has been reserved for the *neopoioi* in the other inscriptions of that time period.

[57]. *IvE* 2926, 3263, 4330; perhaps also *IvE* 969 and 1582.

On the dating of *IvE* 2926, see Franz Miltner, *Ephesos: Stadt der Artemis und des Johannes* (Vienna: Verlag Franz Deuticke, 1958), 39 and Joseph Keil, "Vorläufiger Bericht über die Ausgraben in Ephesos," *Jahreshefte des Österreichischen Archäologischen Institutes in Wien (Beiblatt)* 27 (1932) 54.

Concerning *IvE* 3263, there are no datable references in the text. However, from this collection of inscriptions from Almura, *IvE* 3250 is from the time of Caligula (37-41 C.E.) and 3252 is to be dated ca. 140 C.E. This inscription is also found in *SEG* 31 (1981) #957, where it is dated in the late second to third century C.E. on onomastic grounds.

It is suggested that *IvE* 4330 is perhaps from Annius Anullinus Geminus Persennianus (231-239 C.E.). See the notes to that inscription.

major point: these inscriptions attest to a continuous cultic role for officials known as *essēnes* over a period of at least six centuries.

Some of the examples of the verbal use of the term *essēn* also contain a derivative form referring to the position which this official held. On a statue, probably from the end of the first century B.C.E., erected by a *neopoios* of "our lord Artemis," we read: *essēneusanta tas duo essēneias.*[58] The same phrase, partially reconstructed, is to be found in a third century C.E. reference: *essēneusas ta[s duo essēnias*].[59] Another inscription, probably from the same era, reads: *[essēneusas tas duo essē]nias.*[60] Understanding the meaning of this phrase is problematic. In the first reference, Aurelius Salluvius Timotheos could not have carried out the functions of the office of two *essēnes*, thus it would be nonsensical to translate it, "he served in the capacity of two *essēnes*." Since the following phrases in the inscription read: *kai klērōsanta panta ta synedria kai po[lei]tas kalesanta* (and he appointed by lot all the council and named [man]y citizens), the verb *essēneusanta* could refer to the appointment of persons to the *essēnia*, the office filled by the *essēn*. However other inscrip-

58. *IvE* 3263:8-9=*SEG* 31 (1981) #957. See also J. and L. Robert, "Bulletin épigraphique," *REG* 95 (1982) 374. For the date of this inscription see previous note. *Essēneia* in this reference should be understood the same as *essēnia* elsewhere. See Hicks, *Collection*, p. 214.

59. *IvE* 4330:4-5. See note to l. 9 for the suggested date. This is based on J. Keil, *Forschungen in Ephesos*, 4:3 (Vienna: Österreichischen Archäologischen Institut, 1951), 283-84. See also L. Robert, "Bulletin épigraphique," *REG* 66 (1953) 168.

60. *IvE* 1582:3-4. In the light of these three references, we should perhaps reconstruct *IvE* 969:2: *ess[ēneusas tas duo essēnias*...].

tions containing the term *essēnia* make that interpretation doubtful.

When we look at other places where this word appears, we see that it can be used in conjunction with verbs other than *essēneuō*. These other words provide a clue as to the meaning of this puzzling phrase. In references from the second and third centuries C.E. we read, *ektelesas* (carry out) *tas duo essēnias*[61] and *plērōsas* (fulfil) *tas duo es[s]ēn[i]as.*[62] Elsewhere, the editors of these inscriptions have reconstructed the verb *[epitelesas* (complete) *tas duo es]sēnias.*[63] In another reference, probably from the second century C.E., we even find the phrase, *[n]eopoiēsas eusebōs tas [duo ess]ēneias.*[64] These phrases seem to be referring to carrying out or fulfilling a term of office. In other words, these references in the last two paragraphs suggest that the person named in the inscription completed two terms of office as an *essēn*. The reason for the consistent reference to the number 'two' remains a puzzle, however we do have some help in interpreting what 'term of office' meant.

[61]. *IvE* 957:12-13. See also G. P. Oikonomos, *Archaiologikon Deltion* 7 (1921/2) 258; J. Keil, *Forschungen*, 284; Friedrich Frhr. Hiller von Gaertringen, *Philologische Wochenschrift* 45 (1925) 184-85; *SEG* 4 (1954) #535.

[62]. *IvE* 958:4-5. See also Joseph Keil, "Zur ephesischen *essēnia,*" *Jahreshefte des Österreichischen Archäologischen Institutes in Wien (Beiblatt)* 36 (1946) 13-14; Keil, *Forschungen*, 284. The same word is reconstructed in *IvE* 956:1-2, which may be dated as early as the end of the first century C.E. (see note in *IvE*).

[63]. *IvE* 963:6-7.

[64]. *IvE* 1588:6-7. See Hicks, *Collection*, 213, on the date. On the form *essēneia*, see n. 57 above.

It is the second century C.E. recorder of various
customs and peoples, Pausanias, that gives us a clue to the
meaning of 'term of office'. He records: τοιαῦτα οἶδα
ἕτερα ἐνιαυτὸν καὶ οὐ πρόσω Ἐφεσίων
ἐπιτηδεύοντας τοὺς τῇ Ἀρτέμιδι
ἱστιάτορας τῇ Ἐφεσίᾳ γινομένους
καλουμένους δὲ ὑπὸ τῶν πολιτῶν Ἐσσῆνας
(I know Ephesians who are members of a religious association dedicated to Artemis the Ephesian that practice a similar
way of life for a year and no more who are called *essēnes*
by the citizens).[65] What Pausanias is telling us is that the
term of office for an *essēn* was limited. He thought that the
period of time was a year. Regrettably, we have no other
confirmation of that piece of evidence.[66] The major point is
that it was not a life-long profession, as we assume from
Jewish sources about the priesthood. Did certain leading
citizens who were *neopoioi* (temple officials) hold this position for a year? Or would it be rather for two years, *tas duo
essēnias*? We do not know the answer to that question. All
the evidence does suggest that it was an office held for a
limited period of time by certain officials of the temple cult.
Clearly the inscriptions attest that it was a position of honor,
but probably not honorary in the modern sense of that term,
since the expectations of the persons holding this office seem
to have been rather severe.

[65]. Pausanias, *Ellados Periēgēseōs* 8:13:1. Note that Hicks,
Collection, 85, considers the aorist form, *essēneusas*, also to be
indicative of a term of office.

[66]. Hicks, *Collection*, 208, suggests that the use of the aorist
tense, *essēneusas*, in the inscriptions proves that the office was not
permanent. Note also H. J. Rose, *Religion in Greece and Rome*
(New York/Evanston: Harper & Row, 1959), 44-45, on the nature
of the priesthood in Greece.

We note that Pausanias speaks of 'a similar way of life'. What is he talking about? That similar way of life is found in his prior description of the Mantineans: τούτοις οὐ μόνον τὰ ἐς τὰς μίξεις ἀλλὰ καὶ ἐς τὰ ἄλλο ἁγιστεύειν καθέστηκε τὸν χρόνον τοῦ βίου πάντα καὶ οὔτε λουτρὰ οὔτε δίαιτα λοιπὴ κατὰ τὰ αὐτά σφισι καθὰ καὶ τοῖς πολλοῖς ἐστιν οὐδὲ ἐς οἰκίαν παρίασιν ἀνδρὸς ἰδιώτου (For these not only in sexual matters but also in all other things live their lives in purity and neither baths nor other aspects of their way of life are done in the same manner as the common people. They do not enter the house of a private person). Pausanias says that these *essēnes* permit concerns of purity to dominate their lives for one year, including remaining celibate and not having anything to do with private property. Perhaps this is what is meant when a late second century inscription reads *essēneusas hagnōs kai eusebōs* (served in the office of *essēn* in an undefiled and pious manner).[67] Perhaps this is a reference to the purity which was assumed to be part of the life of the person while he held this office. We must recall that Pausanias wrote during the same era as that in which these inscriptions containing the verbal use of *essēn* originated.

[67]. *IvE* 1578b:7-8. See n. 55 above.

When we summarize the evidence from Ephesus,[68] we see a continual cultic role for persons who were known as *essēnes* who served the office of *essēnia* over a period of at least six centuries. The evidence from after the beginning of the Common Era suggests that the holders of that office served for a limited time, however that did not detract from the rigorous demands of purity that were placed on them, even allowing for a certain amount of exaggeration of that aspect on the part of Pausanias. How does this evidence relate to the problem which sparked this investigation, the origin of the name of the Jewish sect?

The Essenes and Temple Cult

Despite great differences, we immediately observe certain similarities between the accounts of the Essenes and the *essēnai* from Ephesus, including the manner in which

[68]. This discussion is limited to Ephesus because evidence for the cult of Artemis in other locations does not include the name *essēn*, e.g., Carl H. Kraeling, *Gerasa: City of the Decapolis* (New Haven: ASOR, 1938), Ins. nos. 27, 28, 32, 43, 50, 62.

In the prior publication of this material (*HUCA* 57 [1986] 61-81), I had not adequately accounted for the reference in Callimachus, who spent most of his life in Alexandria. At the 1987 SBL meeting Stephen Goranson responded to the initial article. At that time he argued that rather than Nicolaus Josephus probably used his other major source in *AJ* 13, Strabo (Attridge, *CRINT* 2:2:213-14). Posidonius, who wrote a history beginning in the 140's B.C.E. (*GLAJJ* 1:141-44), is usually considered to be a source of Strabo's account for the Hasmonean period (cf. *GLAJJ*, 1:264-67). Now most likely Philo also had some familiarity with Posidonius's writings (*CRINT* 2:2:245). This evidence suggests a broader non-Jewish usage for the term *essēn* than Ephesus, but I have not been able to establish more precisely the significance of this information.

they are described in Pausanias.[69] The Essenes are said to disdain marriage[70] and to despise riches in order to have a common community of goods.[71] We find continual reference to the ways in which purity and piety dominate their lives,[72] just as we have already observed with regard to the *essēnes*

[69]. We use the term Essene to refer both to the persons who we assume lived the kind of life described in the documents found at Qumran and to those persons by that name described in Josephus and Philo. While there are occasional divergences and contradictions in the information supplied by the two sources, they are surely witnesses to a movement of which Qumran was an important representative. There are, of course, divergences and contradictions within the material from Qumran itself, e.g., 1QS and the Damascus Document.

[70]. *BJ* 2:120; *AJ* 18:18-21. The evidence of the scrolls is not as clear. There are clear references to legislation regarding divorce and remarriage in the Damascus Document and the Qumranic Torah.

[71]. *BJ* 2:122,124; *AJ* 18:20. This seems also to be the thrust of passages such as 1QS 1:11-12; 3:2; 5:2-3; 6:2,17,22,25; 8:23; 9:7-9. See Ben Zion Wacholder, *The Dawn of Qumran: The Sectarian Torah and the Teacher of Righteousness* (Cincinnati: HUC Press, 1983), 84-85. However, C. Rabin, *Qumran Studies* (London: Oxford University Press, 1957), 21-36, and L. H. Schiffman, *Sectarian Law in the Dead Sea Scrolls: Courts, Testimony and the Penal Code*, BJS 28 (Chico: Scholars Press, 1983), 174-76, nn. 16-18, argue that the property was required to be listed with the overseer and that the actual property was not turned over to the sect. The evidence for this viewpoint rests primarily on the legislation regarding *hon* found in CD 10:18, 11:15, 12:7 and 13:11 where, they argue, these ordinances would only be applicable if the members of the sect were permitted to retain their property. These references probably refer to different stages and/or geographical locations in the life of the Essene movement, which was more widespread and diverse than often assumed.

[72]. *BJ* 2:123,128-33,138. This theme is the center of much of the Qumran literature. See, for example, Wacholder, *Dawn*, 9-13.

in Pausanias. It would be a mistake, however, to find a direct relationship between the persons described in Pausanias and the Essenes.[73] Concerns about purity and piety were too widespread in antiquity to argue for some kind of direct dependence between the two groups.[74] The more pervasive and important evidence is found in the inscriptions as well: that these were religious functionaries, priests, in the cult of Artemis at Ephesus who were called *essēnes*. It seems, then, that we should rather understand the name *Essēnoi* to be an attribution given by a Greek observer who knew something of the famous cult of Artemis at Ephesus to a group that was viewed as being priests of a similar nature.

The possibility of some connection between these two uses of the term has been denied by a scholar such as Feldman because he maintains that there is no connection between the Essenes and the priesthood.[75] The priestly aspects of the sectarian lifestyle were not always immediately apparent in the Community Rule, the Hymns and the War Scroll, which formed the basis of most of our perceptions of the Qumran community, even though the centrality of the cultic theme was recognized by some scholars such as Joseph Baumgarten,[76] Matthew Black,[77] Frank Moore Cross[78]

[73]. This is the major problem with the overall argument of Jones, *Essenes*, who assumes a direct connection because of the similarities, e.g., pp. 61-62.

[74]. Note, for example, the lifestyle of certain ascetics described in Strabo, *Geography*, 7:3:3-5.

[75]. L. H. Feldman, *Josephus and Modern Scholarship (1937-1980)*, (Berlin/New York: Walter de Gruyter, 1984), 588-90.

[76]. Joseph Baumgarten, "Sacrifice and Worship among the Jewish Sectarians of the Dead Sea (Qumran) Scrolls," *Studies in Qumran Law*, SJLA 24 (Leiden: E. J. Brill, 1977), 39-56; originally

and others.[79] The fact that some of the eschatological expectations of the group centered on a priestly messianic figure was also seen to require explanation.[80] However, these priestly aspects were frequently viewed primarily in the context of a struggle for the control of the temple and the high priesthood in Jerusalem and not as a vehicle for understanding the life and theology of the sect.[81] A very common perspective is that of Bertil Gärtner who says that in the texts from Qumran the spirit of God is no longer confined to the temple in Jerusalem but rather is tied to the true and pure Israel repre-

appeared in *HTR* 46 (1953) 141-59.

77. *Scrolls and Christian Origins*, 16, 29-30, 104-11.

78. Cross, *Ancient Library*, 100-02, 127-60, 240-41.

79. W. F. Albright and C. S. Mann, "Qumran and the Essenes: Geography, Chronology, and Identification of the Sect," in *The Scrolls and Christianity*, ed. M. Black (London: SPCK, 1969), 16-22; J. Murphy-O'Connor, "La genèse littéraire de la Régle de la Communauté," *RB* 76 (1969) 533-37; id., "The Essenes and their History," *RB* 81 (1974) 228-33, 236-39.

80. Cross, *Ancient Library*, 89-90, 116, 219-30; R. E. Brown, "The Teacher of Righteousness and the Messiah(s)," *The Scrolls and Christianity*, 37-44; G. Vermes, *Dead Sea Scrolls: Qumran in Perspective*, 185.

81. This is not as true for Baumgarten and Black as for the others listed above. Black in particular emphasizes the priestly elements to explain his view, even though his discussion of the shewbread is less than convincing (*Scrolls and Christian Origins*, 104-11).

sented by the community at Qumran.[82] The cult has been transferred from Jerusalem to the community which itself becomes the 'new temple' and replaces the Jerusalem temple in the ideology of the sect.[83] In this view, the temple becomes a 'spiritual' reality. All the references in the Qumran scrolls available to him are interpreted from this perspective.[84] McKelvey also speaks primarily of the 'spiritualization' of the cultus,[85] whose immediate motive was dissatisfaction with Jerusalem.[86] Fiorenza argues that it is more appropriate to speak of 'transference'.[87] Baumgarten also speaks of how the 'holy spirit' in the Damascus Document "served

[82]. B. Gärtner, *The Temple and the Community in Qumran and the New Testament: A Comparative Study in the Temple Symbolism of the Qumran Texts and the New Testament* (Cambridge: University Press, 1965), p. 16.

[83]. Ibid., 16-22.

[84]. Ibid., 22-46.

[85]. R. J. McKelvey, *The New Temple: The Church in the New Testament* (London: Oxford University Press, 1969), 36-40. The spiritualization theme is a rather common view of Qumran and the temple. Note also H. Ringgren, *The Faith of Qumran* (Philadelphia: Fortress, 1963), 215.

[86]. McKelvey, *Temple*, 46. McKelvey seems to be in that stream of New Testament scholarship which has difficulty finding a positive role for the Law in Judaism: "The one thing more than any other, perhaps, which contributed to the spiritualization of the cultus was the transformation of Israelite religion into a religion of the law"(p. 44).

[87]. E. Fiorenza, "Cultic Language in Qumran and in the NT," *CBQ* 38 (1976) 161.

to compensate for the Temple sacrifices."[88] These claims now require reevaluation because for the most part the texts upon which they are based no longer serve as either the exclusive or even primary evidence for our understanding of the ideology of the sectaries at Qumran. The evidence which these texts do provide now needs to be reinterpreted.[89]

The text of the Qumranic Torah (or Temple Scroll) which has been viewed by Wacholder,[90] Yadin[91] and Milgrom,[92] each in their own way, as the document which is foundational to the sect demonstrates the way in which cult was at the center of communal life. It would appear that the temple and cultic system described in the Qumranic Torah provided the basis for the common life of the sect as described in the Community Rule and the Damascus Docu-

[88]. *Studies*, 46.

[89]. Please note that the following argument is merely presented in outline form. This discussion is not intended to be an exhaustive presentation of the subject. I do hope to develop this argument in a more extensive manner in a future work.

[90]. His work, *Dawn of Qumran*, is an elaboration of that thesis. Note the different views of this document held by Baruch A. Levine, "The Temple Scroll: Aspects of its Historical Provenance and Literary Character," *BASOR* 232 (1978) 5-23 and Lawrence Schiffman, "The *Temple Scroll* in Literary and Philological Perspective," *Approaches to Ancient Judaism: Volume II*, ed. W. S. Green (Chico: Scholars Press, 1980), 143-58.

[91]. Y. Yadin, *Temple Scroll*, 1:393-402.

[92]. J. Milgrom, "The Temple Scroll," *BA* 41 (1978) 119. In public lectures, he has referred to it as the 'constitution' of the sect. See also W. O. McCready, "A second Torah at Qumran?" *SR* 14 (1985) 5-15.

ment.[93] This means that regulations such as those found in CD 9:14, 11:17-18,[94] 11:18-21[95] and 16:13 have a real basis in the cult as it is described in the Qumranic Torah.[96] We can then no longer say with Baumgarten that there is "no mention of such a sanctuary in the Qumran texts" and that "all references to *miqdash* in a literal sense refer to the Temple in Jerusalem."[97] The problem with the Jerusalem temple cult, which is the subject of much of the polemic in CD 1-8, is its refusal to accept as its own ideology the viewpoint advanced in the Qumranic Torah and to recognize

93. Wacholder, *Dawn*, 84-88, 101-35.

94. On the meaning of this disputed passage, see Yadin, *Temple Scroll*, 1:131, 2:128 and Wacholder, *Dawn*, 49-50, 152.

95. See Yadin, *Temple Scroll*, 1:130.

96. At this point the view of L. H. Schiffman, *Sectarian Law*, becomes confusing. In his study of law in the Community Rule he states, "The *Temple Scroll* seeks to define the details of the sacrificial cult and its sanctuary, yet these details were in no way actualized in the life of the sect"(p. 14). However he also argues that the adherents of the sect see themselves as part of a group which understands itself to be a sanctuary, admittedly in exile from Jerusalem (pp. 4, 35, etc.). If 'temple' is so basic to the theology of the sect, why does he place the Qumranic Torah so far away from the center of the life of the sect? In his enlightening discussion of the Sabbath laws in the Damascus Document, we again find that all the laws are discussed with regard to the internal life of the sect until he comes to 11:17-18 which is placed in the context of the relationship of the sect to the temple in Jerusalem: *The Halakhah at Qumran*, SJLA 16 (Leiden: E. J. Brill, 1975), 128-31. See n. 94 above for other discussions of this passage.

97. Baumgarten, "The Essenes and the Temple: A Reappraisal," *Studies*, 61. See also *Studies*, 41, for his earlier statement making a similar point.

the leadership which advocates it.[98] This means that a text like the one named "Florilegium" is rather to be interpreted in the light of the Qumranic Torah, thereby making it a reference to a future rather than to a spiritual temple.[99] In Carol Newsom's outstanding work on the "Songs of the Sabbath Sacrifice," she continually notes the importance of priest and cult for understanding the symbolism of the documents.[100] It would appear that there is some application of the terminology of the temple to the life of the sect in 1QS 9:3-6 and other passages in that text.[101] However this is not a transference from or spiritualization of the temple in Jerusalem. The emphasis on the *beyt qodesh* (house of holiness) and the *qodesh qodeshym* (holy of holies) in these references suggests the kind of purity and sanctity that is characteristic of the Qumranic Torah. These texts are written in the light

98. Wacholder, *Dawn*, 101-35. This is the viewpoint of the sectarian author of the Damascus Document. The validity of any of the charges against the Jerusalem temple hierarchy is not the subject of my discussion.

99. 4Q 174. Y. Yadin, "A Midrash on 2 Sam. vii and Ps. i-ii (4Q Florilegium)," *IEJ* 9 (1959) 95-98; D. Flusser, "Two Notes on the Midrash of 2 Sam. vii," *IEJ* 9 (1959) 99-109; Fiorenza, *CBQ* 38 (1976) 164-68; J. M. Baumgarten, "The Exclusion of 'Netinim' and Proselytes in 4Q Florilegium," *Studies*, 75-87 (originally appeared in *RevQ* 8 [1972] 87-96); A. J. McNicol, "The Eschatological Temple in the Qumran Pesher: 4Q Florilegium," *Ohio Journal of Religious Studies* 5 (1977) 133-41; D. R. Schwartz, "The Three Temples of 4Q Florilegium," *RevQ* 10 (1979) 83-91; Wacholder, *Dawn*, 93-94, 139; Yadin, *Temple Scroll*, 1:185-88.

100. C. Newsom, *Songs of the Sabbath Sacrifice: A Critical Edition*, HSS (Atlanta: Scholars Press, 1985), 1-72. I wonder whether the Qumranic Torah could not be more helpful in interpreting some of the cultic material.

101. 1QS 5:5-6, 8:4-10.

of the vision articulated in that work and represent an attempt to relate it to the life of the sect. The nature of the attempt to live out that 'pure' vision and to make/let it come to pass is a subject which far exceeds the scope of this paper.[102] The major point is not to be forgotten: there was a very concrete vision of the temple and the cult which was the motivation and guide for the sectarian lifestyle.

This vision of the cult found expression in the leadership of the sect. In CD. 4:3-4 we read that "the *beney Ṣadoq* are the chosen of Israel, called by name, who arise in the latter days." In this document as well as in the Community Rule we find these sons of Zadok to be in leading roles in the life of the community.[103] The sons of Zadok are also considered, of course, to be the legitimate and 'true' priests of the temple in the vision of Ezekiel.[104] Elsewhere in the Community Rule and the War Rule as well as other texts we find extensive reference to the role of the priests in all

[102]. One of the ongoing questions concerning the role of the cult at Qumran has been whether the sectaries actually offered sacrifices. In the light of the Qumranic Torah, I would not be at all surprised to learn that at some points in their history they adopted such a practice in an attempt to make their Torah and their temple a reality. Cross, *Ancient Library*, 69, 82, 100-03 has argued that they offered sacrices. Note also Feldman, *Josephus*, LCL 9, pp. 16-17.

[103]. 1QS 3:20,21-22; 5:1-2,8-9; 1QSa 1:1-2,24; 2:2-3; 1QSb 3:22-23; 4Q 174(Florilegium) 1:17. J. Liver, "The 'Sons of Zadok the Priests' in the Dead Sea Sect," *RevQ* 6 (1967) 3-30 or *Eretz - Israel* 8 (1967) 71-81 (Hebrew); J. Baumgarten, "The Heavenly Tribunal and the Personification of *Ṣedeq* in Jewish Apocalyptic," *ANRW* II:19:1: 219-39; Wacholder, *Dawn*, 135-40.

[104]. Ezek. 40:46, 43:19, 44:15, 48:11.

aspects of the life of the sect.[105] In other words, we have here a sect dominated by concerns of purity, led by a group of priests who bore a name that summoned up visions of a faithful, pure core of that institution and which had priests in many of its major roles and activities. Rather than finding no or a rather limited connection between the Essenes and the priesthood, we find in the Qumranic writings a group with cult and priesthood at the very center of its life. Probably it was the institution which provided the central model for the life of the rest of the community. If this is the case, it is very easy to understand how a knowledgeable Greek observer would have used a term reserved for cultic officials in a Greek religion to describe what he saw. With this hypothesis, the problem of the origin of the name *Essēnoi* for the Jewish sectaries in the desert is solved without recourse to a Semitic original. It is rather the application of a known Greek term by a Greek observer to a Palestinian Jewish phenomenon. Why would Josephus have used this Greek name in his writings?

THE NAMES IN PHILO AND JOSEPHUS

When we look at Josephus' reference to the Essenes, we immediately observe, as mentioned above, that he used two names for this group, *Essēnoi* and *Essaioi*. When we examine these references more closely we see that in all those instances in which Josephus is comparing the three 'sects' or 'schools', the term used is *Essēnoi*.[106] Now it has

[105]. See the listing in K. G. Kuhn, *Konkordanz zu den Qumrantexten* (Göttingen: Vandenhoeck & Ruprecht, 1960), 98-99.

[106]. *BJ* 2:119,160; *AJ* 13:171,172,298; 18:11,18; *V* 10. That there is some intermediate step between the record of a Greek observer and the text we find in Josephus is attested by the dif-

frequently been noted that these descriptions of the three sects are somewhat distinctive in Josephus' record as to vocabulary, grammar and style, leading to the possibility that we are here encountering a source used by the Jewish historian.[107] If that source were to be a Greek observer of Jewish affairs such as Nicolaus of Damascus, as has been suggested,[108] the possibility that this deviant but visible group

ferent forms of the term, especially noted in the acc. pl., where the inscriptions employ *essēnas* while in Josephus *essēnous* is found. Josephus himself, not having any contact with the cultic officials at Ephesus, may be responsible for the change. The same phenomenon could be explained if the Greek observer had very limited or second hand contact with the cult in Ephesus.

[107]. A. Bauer, "Essener," PWSup 4:408; R. Marcus, *Josephus*, LCL 7, p. 373, n. d; M. Black, "The Account of the Essenes in Hippolytus and Josephus," *The Background of the New Testament and its Eschatology*, eds. W. D. Davies and D. Daube (Cambridge: University Press, 1956), 172-75; M. Smith, "The Description of the Essenes in Josephus and the Philosophumena," *HUCA* 29 (1958) 273-313; Milik, *Ten Years*, 99, n. 1; Cross, *Ancient Library*, 71-72; Albert I. Baumgarten, "Josephus and Hippolytus on the Pharisees," *HUCA* 55 (1984) 1-25, see pp. 4-5. E. Schürer, *Geschichte*, 2:656, n. 1, suggests that Josephus used Philo in his accounts of the sects. Since Josephus seems to supply more information than Philo, Josephus' use of Philo appears to be a doubtful hypothesis. Commenting on Colson, *Philo*, LCL 9, pp. 514-16, who states that Josephus confirms practically all the points mentioned by Philo but goes into more detail, Feldman, *Josephus and Modern Scholarship*, 593-94, remarks that this confirms their use of a common source. Jones, *Essenes*, 4, assumes the accounts are original with Josephus.

[108]. G. F. Moore, "Fate and Free Will in the Jewish Philosophies According to Josephus," *HTR* 22 (1929) 383-84; Black, *Scrolls and Christian Origins*, 25-26, 173, n. 2; B. Z. Wacholder, *Nicolaus of Damascus*, UCPH 75 (Berkeley/Los Angeles: University of California Press, 1962), 71-72. Moore's thesis that Nicolaus should be creditted with authoring an account that deals with fate is rejected by T. Rajak, *Josephus: The Historian and His Society* (Philadelphia: Fortress, 1984), 37, n. 73, who gives much more

would have been given a Greek name seems quite plausible. In that case, Josephus incorporated within his histories a Greek account of the Jewish sects. In that source they were called *Essēnoi*. What about the other word, *essaioi*?

What seems possible is that the Greek term *essēnoi* would have undergone some change when encountered by the Hebrew or Aramaic tongue. Certainly *Essaioi* fits the pattern established by the Greek form *Pharisaioi* for *Perushym* and *Saddoukaioi* for *Ṣeduqym*. In this case, Josephus used the Greek form when he relied on a Greek source but used the form that reflected Semitic influence at other points. The original author of the account of the sects did consistently use names for the Pharisees and Sadducees which reflected Semitic influence because these terms were well known. Presumably, this was not the same with a deviant sect that lived for the most part in the desert. But what about Philo's use of the term *essaioi*? Shouldn't his usage take precedence over Josephus' text?

credence to Josephus' experience with the sects, a thesis rejected by S. J. D. Cohen, *Josephus in Galilee and Rome: His Vita and Development as a Historian*, CSCT 8 (Leiden: E. J. Brill, 1979), 105-07. For recent discussions of Josephus' use of Nicolaus as a source including bibliography see: M. Stern, "Nicolaus of Damascus as a Source of Jewish History in the Herodian and Hasmonean Age," in *Studies in Bible and Jewish History Dedicated to the Memory of Jacob Liver*, ed. B. Uffenheimer (Tel Aviv: University of Tel Aviv, 1971), 375-89 (Hebrew); id., *Greek and Latin Authors on Jews and Judaism*, v. 1 (Jerusalem: Israel Academy of Sciences and Humanities, 1976), 229-32; *Schürer-Vermes-Millar* 2:383, n.1, and p. 396; Cohen, *Josephus*, 50-58; Daniel R. Schwarz, "Josephus and Nicolaus on the Pharisees," *JSJ* 14 (1983) 157-71; Feldman, *Josephus and Modern Scholarship*, 402-06; H. A. Attridge, "Josephus and His Works," *Jewish Writings of the Second Temple Period: Apocrypha, Pseudepigrapha, Qumran Sectarian Writings, Philo, Josephus*, ed. Michael Stone, *CRINT* 2:2 (Assen: Van Gorcum/Philadelphia: Fortress, 1984), 212-16.

It has already been argued that Josephus' use of this term in the account of the sects was dependent on some other source. A similar case has been suggested for Philo.[109] It has been argued that both of these writers could have been dependent upon that Greek observer of Jewish life in Palestine, Nicolaus of Damascus. Certainly Philo will have rewritten his source more than Josephus will have. It is quite possible that Philo may have used a Hebrew or Aramaic form of a name which he found in the works of Nicolaus. We know that Philo did use Hebrew names and their meanings in his allegorical interpretations.[110] We are not able to establish his level of knowledge of the Hebrew language. However, he need not have had a great deal of linguistic competence to give this group for which he had a great deal of respect a name which would have sounded more like the Hebrew or Aramaic he had heard in his own visit or visits to Judaea.[111] Since we now know the hierocratic nature of life at Qumran as we find it portrayed in the documents connected with that community, we can entertain the idea that a Greek observer could have become knowledgeable about the kind of life lived by the sectaries and given them a name which he knew applied to persons who lived in a similar kind of manner in the famous cult of Artemis at Ephesus. Having dealt with the question of the relationship between

[109]. Black, *Scrolls and Christian Origins*, 25-26; Wacholder, *Nicolaus*, 71-72. See also Bauer, "Essener," PWSup 4, 408 and G. Hoelscher, *Die Quellen des Flavius Josephus für die Zeit vom Exil bis zum jüdischen Krieg* (Leipzig: B. G. Teubner, 1904) 8, 14, 16.

[110]. Samuel Sandmel, *Philo of Alexandria: An Introduction* (New York/Oxford: Oxford University Press, 1979), 27-28, 131.

[111]. Ibid., 34.

the Essenes and the Hasideans, we now turn to that source which includes references to persons called *Ḥasydym.*

V

THE HASIDIM IN TALMUDIC LITERATURE

Our study of 1 and 2 Maccabees has shown that the Hasideans were leading citizens of Israel, scribes who were devoted to the law. These leading religious personalities, called *Ḥasydym* in Hebrew, were one of the groups, according to 1 Maccabees, that supported Mattathias and his sons in their resistance against measures which Antiochus IV took against the Jews of Palestine and the practice of their religion. The company of the Hasideans did later disagree with the Maccabees over the best way to deal with their Greek rulers. It seems that these Jewish scribes had found within the description of the *Ḥasydym* in the Psalms people who faced certain challenges to the Israelite faith. Apparently, the devotion which these scribes saw reflected in this biblical poetry was deemed worthy of emulation in their own time.[1] The adoption of this epithet is also witnessed in sources other than 1 and 2 Maccabees. Throughout talmudic literature this term is applied to certain individuals such as Honi

[1]. D. Berman, "Hasidim in Rabbinic Traditions," *SBLSP* (1979), 2:17-18. See also Chapter 1 above concerning the biblical usage of the term.

and Hillel.[2] The plural use of the word is also found. These talmudic usages pose questions for our study. Are all the uses of this term by the early Rabbis to be viewed in a similar manner, or did they use the word in different ways? Is the use of this term by the Tannaim more closely related to the biblical Psalms than to the group in 1 and 2 Maccabees, or vice versa? We found that 2 Maccabees, while yielding evidence for the existence of the same group as the one portrayed in 1 Maccabees, used them as an example of piety and purity.[3] Do any of the talmudic references reflect that particular viewpoint?

It was formerly assumed that at least some of the persons or groups referred to in the Talmud as *ḥasyd*, whether in its singular or plural form, are to be identified with the *Asidaioi* of 1 and 2 Maccabees.[4] The questions discussed concerned which other groups in Jewish history the Hasidim

[2]. On Honi, see n. 22 below. Concerning Hillel, see A. Büchler, *Types of Jewish-Palestinian Piety from 70 B.C.E. to 70 C.E.: The Ancient Pious Men* (New York: Ktav, 1968-orig., 1922), 7-67. The case for identifying Hillel with the *Ḥasydym* is very weak. For a recent rejection of that claim see Aharon Oppenheimer, *The 'Am ha-Aretz: A Study in the Social History of the Jewish People in the Hellenistic-Roman Period*, trans. I. H. Levine (Leiden: E. J. Brill, 1977), 104. Most scholars would eliminate Hillel from consideration on the basis that there are no miracles attributed to him: Solomon Schechter, *Aspects of Rabbinic Theology: Major Concepts of the Talmud* (New York: Schocken, 1961-orig., 1909), 7; Geza Vermes, *Jesus the Jew: A Historian's Reading of the Gospels* (London: Fontana/Collins, 1973), 93.

[3]. See Chapter 3 above.

[4]. See, e.g., Kohler's article on the Essenes (*JE* 5:224-31) and the bibliography cited there.

were to be identified with, and which individuals were properly to be given this designation. More recently such an equation has been called into question. Louis Jacobs carefully qualified his treatment of the concept of *ḥasyd* by stating that *Ḥasydym Hari'shonym* (the "early" or "first" Hasidim) "may be" the same as the pietistic group of that name in the Maccabean period.[5] Significant, in light of the subsequent studies, is his assertion that the early Hasidim were no longer in existence in the Tannaitic period (usually defined as beginning with the destruction of the Temple in 70 C.E.).[6] With the advent of the Tannaitic period, we find the *ḥasyd* to be a man of special sanctity, the possessor of a special kind of virtue "that is the hallmark of the saint," but no longer does it designate the member of a specific group.[7]

While Jacobs notes that this "saint" represents a divergent tradition from that of the Sages, Safrai makes that point the center of his articles in which he argues that the halakah of the Hasidim is frequently in tension with that of the Sages.[8] In that case, the Hasidim are found to be a distinct

[5]. L. Jacobs, "The Concept of *Ḥasid* in the Biblical and Rabbinic Literatures," *JJS* 8 (1957) 143-53; note pp. 147 and 153.

[6]. Ibid., 149, 153.

[7]. Ibid., 153.

[8]. S. Safrai, "Teaching of Pietists in Mishnaic Literature," *JJS* 16 (1965) 15-33; id., "The Pharisees and the Hasidim," *Sidic* 10 (1977) 12-16. In a recent article he has located them geographically in Galilee, "The Pious (*Ḥassidim*) and the Men of Deeds," *Zion* 50 (1985) 133-54 (Hebrew). That the Hasidim represent a divergent tradition to that of the Sages was also noted by Jacobs, *JJS* 8 (1957) 153.

group; however he dates the 'First Hasidim' much later than Jacobs. Suggesting a parallel to *Zeqenym Hari'shonym* (the first elders), he argues that *Ḥasydym Hari'shonym* were "the first men of the generation transmitting the tradition concerned."[9] The identification of 'first' refers to that group which initially propounded a certain teaching, such as that in *M. Ber.* 5:1 attributed to *Ḥasydym Hari'shonym.* In Safrai's view, this saying is the first of a whole tradition of Hasidic teachings on prayer. Historically, these teachings emanate from "a certain defined group within the society of Pharisees and rabbis" and may be dated to "perhaps as early as the end of the Hasmonean period."[10] However, they designate a later group than the one which gathered around Mattathias and his sons. While he is probably correct in his interpretation of *ri'shon* as 'first', the desire to locate the group at the end of the Hasmonean period appears arbitrary.

More recently, Berman has rejected the notion that a specifically Hasidic legal corpus can be identified.[11] He suggests that *Ḥasydym Hari'shonym* "apparently refers to the pious folks of times past in general, from biblical times up to the destruction of the Temple (end i CE), whose great piety had become legendary."[12] Such a position seems untenable. He cites ARNA 8 as an example of a place where

[9]. *JJS* 16 (1965) 20.

[10]. Ibid., 33.

[11]. *SBLSP* (1979), 2:17, 21, n. 20.

[12]. Ibid., 18.

both Abraham and Hanina ben Dosa are considered to be from 'the early Hasidim', thereby suggesting the impossibility of a specific identification for that group. However, the text rather speaks of *haṣṣaddyqyn hari'shonym* (the early righteous) and says that they are pious. In other words, *ḥasydym* is here being used as a predicate adjective modifying 'the early righteous'. The use of *ḥasyd* as a simple adjective is of course to be expected and can be found elsewhere in Tannaitic literature.[13] Abraham and Hanina ben Dosa are considered in this text to be among those 'early righteous' who are considered to be pious.[14] This is not even a reference to *Ḥasydym Hari'shonym.* Berman also bases his case on instances where an individual biblical personage is referred to in the talmudic literature as *ḥasyd.*[15] While I

[13]. Note Safrai, *JJS* 16 (1965) 18-19. See, e.g., *M. Soṭa* 3:4, *M. Qidd.* 4:14, *M. 'Aḇot* 2:5, 5:10-11, 6:1, *T. Soṭa* 13:3-4, *B. Ber.* 6b, *B. Shabb.* 63a, *B. 'Erub.* 18b, *B. Mo'ed Qat.* 18a, *B. Soṭa* 21b, 48b, *B. B. Meṣ.* 52b, 70a, *B. B. Bat.* 15b, *B. Sanh.* 11a, *B. Nid.* 17a. This is not to mention the use of derivatives such as *ḥasydut* in *T. B. Qam.* 11:14, *ARNA* 8. In other places, it's appearance is due to the presence of comments upon a biblical text in which it appears, e.g., *B. Ber.* 4a, *B. Yoma* 38b, *B. Sukk.* 52b, *B. Rosh. Hash.* 17b, 18b, *B. Ta'an.* 11b, *B. Sanh.* 47a, *B. Aḇod. Zar.* 20b, *Mek. Pisḥa' Bo'* 14 (Horowitz, p. 48; Lauterbach, 1:109).

There are of course the many stories about a *ḥasyd*, often beginning *ma'aśeh beḥasyd*, where the adjective is being used as a substantive such as *T. Ta'an.* 3:1, *B. B. Qam.* 50b, 80a, 103b, *B. B. Bat.* 7b, *B. Ḥul.* 122a, etc. Sometimes these incidents involve more than one pious person such as in *B. Ketub.* 61a, *B. B. Meṣ.* 90b. Admittedly more controversial, it seems to me that *Y. Ter.* 8:10 (46b) should also be grouped with these texts.

[14]. *SBLSP* (1979), 2:26, n. 50. Note that in ARNA 8 *haṣṣaddyqym* has the definite article, making it clear this is not a proper noun.

[15]. Ibid., 26, n. 49.

certainly have not done justice to Berman's development of an ideal type called *ḥasyd* throughout rabbinic literature, I think the weakness of his argument with regard to our subject has become apparent. Not only has he failed to distinguish the texts concerning *Ḥasydym Hari'shonym* from other references, he also has used singular and plural references to *ḥasyd* in this literature without differentiation. While there is some validity to his critique that earlier studies of the Hasidim had rather arbitrarily seized on one or two personages and had used them "as a kind of archetypal hasid" upon which to develop their viewpoint, it seems that he has rather indiscriminately used these references without attempting to make any historical differentiation among them.[16] Safrai also mixes references to individuals called *ḥasyd* with uses of the term in the plural.[17]

The primary interest in this study is to ascertain whether the talmudic literature refers to the group that was called the Hasidim in the time of the Maccabees. While a full analysis of all the references to *ḥasyd* and *ḥasydym* in the talmudic writings demands a full-scale study in its own right, that is not the purpose here. In order to investigate the question of references to this group from the Maccabean period, it is necessary to begin with an analysis of references in the plural to see whether any direct allusions to them can be found. A survey of these citations points up a number of references to *Ḥasydym Hari'shonym* (the 'early' or 'first' Hasidim). Our investigation will center on these citations.

16. Ibid., 17.

17. Note especially *Sidic* 10 (1977) 13-15. The monograph of L. Gulkowitsch also focuses on references to individuals: *Die Bildung des Begriffes Ḥāsīd* (Tartu: K. Mattiesens, 1935).

<u>M</u>. Bera<u>h</u>ot 5:11

The only reference to <u>H</u>asydym Hari'shonym in the
Mishnah reads as follows: אין עומדין להתפלל אלא
מתוך כובד ראש חסידים הראשונים היו שוהים
שעה אחת ומתפללים כדי שיכונו את לבם למקום
(They may only rise to pray with a bowed head. The early
Hasidim used to wait one hour before praying in order that
they might direct their attention toward God.) In the first line
of this mishnah we find a halakah concerning the demeanor
and, by implication, the attitude of the person who rises to
say the tepillah (Eighteen Benedictions). Attached to this
stipulation is an account concerning <u>H</u>asydym Hari'shonym.
It seems that the author of this mishnah is using the practice
attributed to the early Hasidim as an example of a group that
observed the kind of piety he wished to stress.[18] There is no
evidence of a tension between the two statements, as if
<u>H</u>asydym Hari'shonym were advocating a different halakah
than that of the Sages, as would be suggested in the approach of Safrai and others.[19] Neither is there an implication
that these Hasidim advocated this stipulation as a require-

[18]. For an analysis of this passage reaching similar conclusions
see B. M. Bokser, "Hanina ben Dosa and the Lizard: The Treatment of Charismatic Figures in Rabbinic Literature," Eighth World
Congress of Jewish Studies (1982), 3:1-6 and "Wonder-working and
the Rabbinic Tradition: The Case of Hanina ben Dosa," JSJ 16
(1985) 42-92.

[19]. Y. F. Baer, "The Historical Foundations of the Halacha,"
Zion 17 (1952) 1-55 (Hebrew); id., "The Ancient Hassidim in
Philo's Writings and in Hebrew Tradition," Zion 18 (1953) 91-108
(Hebrew); Safrai, JJS 16 (1965) 15-33; Z. Falk, "On the Mishna of
the Pious," Benjamin De Vries Memorial Volume (Jerusalem: Tel
Aviv University, 1968), 62-69 (Hebrew); Safrai, Sidic 10 (1977)
12-16.

ment for all Israel. They are rather being used here as an example.

In *B. Ber.* 32b we do find a halakah attributed to R. Joshua ben Levi in which the person who says the *tepillah* should wait an hour after the prayer in addition to the hour before.[20] Support for this teaching is given using formulas indicating that this is found in a *barayta'*--a statement attributed to one of the Tannaim found in the Palestinian and Babylonian Gemara.[21] When the *barayta'* is cited, we find that the line concerning the early Hasidim is repeated from the Mishnah, however then more information is given:

חסידים הראשונים היו שוהין שעה אחת ומתפללים שעה אחת וחוזרין ושוהין שעה אחת

(The early Hasidim used to wait one hour, pray for one hour, and then again wait for one hour.) Perhaps the *barayta'* records an earlier form of this tradition, more accurately reflecting the practice of the group. The Mishnah passage does seem to be eager to get on to the reason for the hour wait before the prayer, "in order that they might direct their attention toward God."

It is difficult to be certain as to whether its author thought that the remainder of the mishnah under discussion concerned the Hasidim: אפילו המלך שואל בשלומו לא ישיבנו ואפילו נחש כרוך על עקבו לא

[20]. Traditions about prayer continue to be very important in the talmudic references to a person or persons designated as *ḥasyd*, e.g., *B. Ta'an.* 8a.

[21]. *Tanya' nammy haky* (it has likewise been taught thus) and *tanu Rabbanan* (our Rabbis taught); see M. Mielziner, *Introduction to the Talmud*, 5th ed. (New York: Bloch, 1968), 20-21, 220-22, 229.

יפסיק (If the king were to greet him [the person praying], he did not return it [the greeting]. If a snake wound around his heel, he would not interrupt [his prayer].) The talmudic tradition does make a connection between these lines and the traditions about individuals considered to be *ḥasyd*. *B. Ber.* 32b gives an illustration of the first injunction using a *ma'a-śeh beḥasyd* (an incident concerning a pious person). On the following page, the Talmud discusses the second injunction and then records a *barayta'* concerning Ḥanina ben Dosa.[22]

[22]. This account is also related in *T. Ber.* 3:20.

Sean Freyne, "The Charismatic," *Ideal Figures in Ancient Judaism*, eds. George W. E. Nickelsburg and John J. Collins, SBLSCS 12 (Chico: Scholars Press, 1980), 224, n. 5, says he is twice called *ḥasyd*, at *Y. Soṭa* 23b where he claims it is "accidentally added" and ARNA 8. On the latter passage, see the introduction to this chapter.

The Ḥanina traditions have been collected and analyzed by G. Vermes, "Ḥanina den Dosa: A controversial Galilean Saint from the First Century of the Christian Era," *JJS* 23 (1972) 28-50; 24 (1973) 51-64; id., *Jesus the Jew: A Historian's Reading of the Gospels* (London: Fontana/Collins, 1973), 72-82. He assumes that Ḥanina is a *ḥasyd*, even though we do not find him referred to with this epithet in early rabbinic texts. Vermes cites *ARNA* 8 (*JJS* 23 [1972] 46), which we have discussed above. He also mentions *M. Soṭa* 9:15 and parallels where Ḥanina ben Dosa is considered to be one of the *'anshey ma'aśeh* (men of deed) (*JJS* 23 [1972] 38). He seems to assume that *M. Sukk.* 5:4, *T. Sukk.* 4:2, *B. Sukk.* 53a and *B. Sanh.* 97a are referring to the same group when they mention both the *Ḥasydym* and the *'Anshey ma'aśeh*. Since both are named in these texts, it seems much more likely that they are not to be considered identical. See Berman, *SBLSP* (1979), 2:17 and Freyne, *Ideal Figures*, 224. See now also Bokser, *JSJ* 16 (1985) 42-92.

Honi is also used as an example of the Hasidim by Vermes (*Jesus the Jew*, 60-72) as well as G. B. Sarfatti, "Pious Deeds, Men of Deeds, and the Early Prophets," *Tarbiẓ* 26 (1956) 126-48 (Hebrew). His story is found in *M. Ta'an.* 3:8, *T. Ta'an.* 3:1 and *B. Ta'an.* 23a as well as *AJ* 14:22-25. While he is not mentioned by name in the Tosefta text the story is remarkably similar to the one in the Mishnah account. The reference in the Babli becomes the occasion for the inclusion of a number of references to various individuals and groups that do miracles. The identification of Honi

The story about him, much less connected to the point of the mishnah than the *ma'aśeh beḥasyd* just mentioned, may have been included at this point because the talmudic tradition considered him to be a *ḥasyd* or because he is mentioned only a few *mishnayot* later in *M. Ber.* 5:5. I consider the latter the more likely possibility. There is no indication in these texts that the Amoraim considered either the *ḥasyd* in the *ma'aśeh* or Ḥanina ben Dosa to be among those persons called *Ḥasydym Hari'shonym.* For our study, the major point to note is that the Hasidim are again cited in an exemplary fashion.

T. Baba Qammah 2:6

In the midst of a discussion concerning individual responsibility for injuries incurred in the public domain, we find the following line: חסידים הראשונים היו מוציאין אותן לתוך שדות עצמן ומעמיקין להן שלשה טפחים כדי שלא תעכב המחרישה (The early Hasidim used to take them [glass and thorns] out into the middle of their own fields and bury them three handbreadths deep so that the plough would not be caught [on them].)[23] The same account is recorded in *B. B. Qam.* 30a as a *baray-*

with the Hasidim is rejected by William Scott Green, "Palestinian Holy Men: Charismatic Leadership and Rabbinic Tradition," *ANRW* II:19:2:631 and 634, n. 63.

There are many incidents like *T. Ta'an.* 3:1 which are recorded in the anonymous fashion of a *ma'aśeh beḥasyd*, some of which at least contain traditions similar to those attributed to Honi and Ḥanina ben Dosa such as *B. Ber.* 18b.

[23]. See the discussion of this issue by Safrai, *JJS* 16 (1965) 21-22.

ta'. In both cases, the report of this practice of *Ḥasydym Hari'shonym* is placed in the context of a discussion of responsibility for injuries from thorns or glass in the public domain, also a concern in *M. B. Qam.* 3:2. However, it is again clear that the practice attributed to *Ḥasydym Hari'shonym* is not in tension with that of the rabbis. This group is cited here as an example of persons who deal with glass and thorns in such a manner as to make it impossible for them to ever be found in the public domain and injure someone. In both the Tosefta and the Talmud, we then find additional material concerning a *ḥasyd.*

In *T. B. Qam.* 2:13 we find a *ma'aśeh* concerning someone who should have followed the advice a *ḥasyd* gave him. When this same event is recorded in *B. B. Qam.* 50b, it is used to buttress a teaching from the rabbis. The account concerning *Ḥasydym Hari'shonym* in *B. B. Qam.* 30a is followed by a discussion of what one must do to be *ḥasyda'* (pious).[24] The utilization of the example of *Ḥasydym Hari'shonym* again provides the occasion whereby the authors of these works can bring in further cases of persons who are considered to be *ḥasyd,* but nowhere is it suggested that these others are to be taken as members of the early Hasidim.

B. Niddah 38ab

The immediate issue in this text is whether birth is halakically considered to begin on the first day of the ninth month, the 270th day (9 x 30), or whether one must allow

[24]. Note that in the case of disposing of one's fingernails, the one who buries them is a righteous man and the pious man is rather the one who burns them (*B. Mo'ed Qat.* 18a and *B. Nid.* 17a).

one or two days after intercourse for conception to take place, thereby placing childbirth on the 271st, 272nd or 273rd day. In this discussion, Samuel, who argues the latter, cites in a *barayta'* the example of the early Hasidim: חסידים הראשונים לא היו משמשין מטותיהן אלא ברביעי בשבת שלא יבואו נשותיהן לידי חלול שבת (The early Hasidim used to perform their marital duty only on the fourth day of the week so as not to lead their wives into a desecration of the sabbath.)

In this text, as in those discussed above, the early Hasidim are used as an example. In this case, their piety is reflected in their practice of only engaging in intercourse on a Wednesday, so that their wives will not have to defile the Sabbath by giving birth on that day.[25] Since 270 days from Wednesday occurs on a Saturday, it is clear that these early Hasidim believed that childbirth took place on the 271st day or thereafter. However, the question of when a person may engage in intercourse is not the issue in the talmudic passage. Samuel merely uses their example as evidence in support of a different argument that he is pursuing. When Mar Zutra asks *ma'y ṭa'meyyhu deḥasydym hari'shonym* (what is the reason of the early Hasidim?), he is asking, What biblical basis did the early Hasidim have for this

[25]. For another explanation of this injunction, see Safrai, *JJS* 16 (1965) 24, n. 46 and "Religion in Everyday Life," *The Jewish People in the First Century: Historical Geography, Political History, Social, Cultural and Religious Institutions*, eds. S. Safrai and M. Stern, *CRINT* 1:2 (Assen: Van Gorcum/Philadelphia: Fortress Press, 1976), 805. He fails to note that the context of the statement in *B. Nid.* 38a speaks of the length of time required from conception to childbirth.

practice which is not mentioned in the Hebrew Scriptures?[26] They are cited, not because they are halakic authorities, but because they had a reputation for being pious interpreters of Scripture.

We also find a reference to the Sabbath practices of the Hasidim in *B. Shabb.* 121b.[27] In this case, the issue is whether one can kill scorpions or snakes on the Sabbath: "If one kills snakes and scorpions on the Sabbath, the spirit of the Hasidim is displeased with him." The text goes on to say that the spirit of the sages is displeased with those Hasidim. Here we do have evidence of tension between the Hasidim and the Sages. While Weiss maintained that these were the early Hasidim,[28] the notes to the Soncino edition argue that "probably no particular sect is meant."[29] In my opinion, neither of the alternatives suggested is correct. This reference to the *ruaḥ ḥasydym* is to my knowledge unique in the

[26]. Mielziner, *Introduction*, 201-02.

[27]. There are also other stories about the sabbath which come to be attached to the *Ḥasydym*, e.g., *ma'aśeh beḥasyd 'eḥad* in *B. Shabb*. 150b.

[28]. Isaac Hirsch Weiss, Dor Dor weDorshayw, vol. 1 (New York/ Berlin: Platt and Minkus, 1924-orig. 1871), 109.

[29]. H. Freedman, *Shabbatt*, in *The Babylonian Talmud: Translated into English with Notes, Glossary and Indices*, ed. I. Epstein (London: Soncino, 1938), p. 602, n. 3.

Talmud.[30] The use of 'spirit' suggests that the *tanna'* quoted here wishes to say that this activity is what would have been expected of the Hasidim, even though he makes no claim for an explicit record or memory of their having actually done so. In this sense, the Talmud is distinguishing between the actual statements or activities attributed to *Ḥasydym Hari'-shonym* and their spiritual and intellectual legacy. In the opinion of the *tanna'*, as quoted in the Talmud, this would have been the reaction of the Hasidim to this issue, given everything else he knew about these people. In other words, this is a reference to the growth of the tradition concerning the Hasidim in the talmudic literature. Given the attitude of the Hasidim to the issue of sabbath observance expressed in the passage which began this discussion, the *tanna'* is probably correct in his interpretation of their opinion and he may even have been the recipient of some information concerning them, even if the text does not make that claim. While there is evidence of a dispute in this case, the argument between the *Ḥasydym* and the *Ḥakamym* is explicitly described as being over their legacy rather than over their actual practices or teachings. This text, therefore, is not to be used as evidence of a dispute between the early Hasidim and the Sages.[31]

30. See Chaim Josua Kasowski, *'Oṣer Leshon Hattalmud* (Jerusalem: Department of History and Culture-Government of Israel and Jewish Theological Seminary, 1954-82), vol. 14, p. 650.

31. Safrai, *JJS* 16 (1965) 25.

B. *Nedarim 10a*

A more complicated passage concerning the subject of this study is found in *B. Ned.* 10a. In a discussion of the meaning of the phrase *kenidbotam nadar benazir* ("as their freewill offerings," it is binding with a Nazirite vow) in *M. Ned.* 1:1, Rabbi Judah, in a *barayta'* also found in *T. Ned.* 1:1, summons the example of the first Hasidim: חסידים הראשונים היו מתאוין להביא קרבן חטאת לפי שאין הקב"ה מביא תקלה על ידיהם מה היו עושין עומדין ומתנדבין נדירות למקום כדי שיתחייב קרבן חטאת למקום (The early Hasidim used to be desirous of bringing a sin offering because the Holy One Blessed be He did not cause them to commit an offense. What did they do? They arose and freely made nazirite vows to the Lord, in order that a sin-offering to the Lord would be required.) Rabbi Judah says that since the Hasidim never had occasion to bring a sin offering, they would make a nazirite vow, upon the completion of which they were required to bring a sin-offering (Num. 6:14), and thereby they could provide themselves with this opportunity. Rabbi Simeon disagrees. He says these Hasidim did not make Nazirite vows because they did not want to be considered sinners (Num. 6:11). R. Simeon here is allied with Simeon the Just who on the previous page (9b) has refused to partake of a nazirite sacrifice, apparently in reaction against their practice of asceticism. The basic issue in the passage is whether the early Hasidim made Nazirite vows.

A similar dispute concerning the *'asham Ḥasydym* (guilt-offering of the pious) is recorded in *M. Ker.* 6:3 and *T. Ker.* 4:4. Rabbi Eliezer says that a person can bring an *'asham teluy* (suspensive guilt offering) any time one pleases, just in case one has committed a sinful act. He claims that this voluntary guilt offering was called *'asham ḥasydym* (guilt offering of the pious).[32] In this case, a contrary opinion is attributed to the Sages: "They may only bring a suspensive guilt offering for a matter that if committed intentionally is subject to extirpation and if in error to a sin offering." While we find no mention of Nazirites in this passage, the issue is still one of an excessive concern with transgression.[33] The Sages considered that improper, most likely because, as in *B. Ned.* 10a, they related it to asceticism. However this does not mean that the *'asham ḥasydym* should be identified with the sin offering of the early Hasidim. While both are expiatory, the *'asham* and the *ḥaṭa't* were different sacrifices and were not connected with one another in either the biblical or rabbinic traditions.[34]

32. A story possibly related to this passage appears in *T. Pe'a* 3:8 where a *ḥasyd* (pious man) relates to his son the joy experienced in the fulfillment of the commandment concerning the forgotten sheaf found in Deut. 24:19, because this is the one commandment which one cannot set out to perform intentionally (*lo' leda'-tenu*). While this text does not relate to the issue of asceticism discussed below, it rather centers on the joy at the possibility of the fulfillment of one of the commandments, it does provide a glimpse into the perspective of the rabbis concerning the hasidic tradition they knew.

33. Studies of the Nazirites suggest that in the Tannaitic period, the opportunity to make a sacrifice became the most important reason for being a nazirite (A. Rothkopf, "Nazirite," *EJ* 12: 909-10; J. C. Rylaarsdam, "Nazirite," *IDB* 3:527). A. Büchler, when discussing this passage, thinks the only difference between the Pharisees and the Hasidim is their concern about the neccessity for making frequent sacrifices of atonement (*Piety*, 73-78, 114).

34. A. Rainey, "Sacrifice," *EJ* 14:601; T. H. Gaster, "Sacrifices," *IDB* 4:151-52. But note G. B. Gray, *Sacrifice in the Old Testament: Its Theory and Practice* (New York: Ktav, 1971-orig. 1925), 57-60.

What we rather have here are two independent traditions which reflect the rabbinic disdain for asceticism. In *M. Ker.* 6:3 and its Tosefta parallel, the ascetic tradition is related to some people called 'pious', while *B. Ned.* 10a records a dispute concerning whether the early Hasidim did pledge Nazirite vows, i.e., whether they were ascetics. The first passage assumes they were ascetics while in the latter we find both sides trying to cite the example of the first Hasidim to buttress their case. Clearly the talmudic tradition saw the 'pious' to be related to the ascetic movement, probably to the Nazirites. This would seem to be the implication of the reference to the 'early pious' in the later minor tractate, *Śemaḥot.*[35] When we return to the talmudic passage which is the center of this discussion, *B. Ned.* 10a, we first of all note that the same point previously made about these passages concerning the early Hasidim is also relevant here. We do not find that the opinion of this group is cited as an authority. In this case we find a dispute over what their actual practice was. Is this dispute to be regarded as evidence that the Hasidim did originally observe the Nazirite vows?

Of interest is the use of *hitnaddeb* in both this passage and in 1 Macc. 2:42.[36] It is doubtful that the term is used in 1 Maccabees to signify that the Hasideans were Nazirites, since the latter receive mention elsewhere in the work in 3:49. There are similarities between this story and that of the Hasideans in 1 Maccabees 2. In our investigation of that section, we found that the Hasideans were one group named in the midst of a description of the growing power of the

[35]. *B. Śem.* 49a (12:5).

[36]. See the discussion in Chapter 3 above.

Maccabean movement.[37] In 1 Maccabees 3 we find that Antiochus IV has given Lysias an order "to wipe out and destroy" all the residents of Judaea and Jerusalem.[38] Judah and his brothers prepare for this battle by engaging in prayer and fasting at Mizpah.[39] In these religious observances they bring forth the first fruits, the tithes and the garments of the priesthood, and then pour out a lament to God asking what they are to do with all these items that are part of the Temple service. Included in this list of items are the Nazirites who have completed the term which they pledged in a Nazirite vow. At the end of that period, these Nazirites are to offer sacrifices in the temple.[40] This, of course, is impossible while it is under the control of the Greeks. Thus we see that in the cases of both the Hasideans and the Nazirites we find them to be minor figures in the drama of the growth of the Hasmonean resistance forces. It does seem that the Hasmonean historian wants to include as many different groups of Jews as possible in his account of the revolt, implying, of course, that the Maccabees had broadbased support.

It must be noted that the Nazirites in 1 Macc. 3:49 are those who have completed their vows; i.e., we are speaking of persons who made Nazirite vows for a limited period of

37. See Chapter 3.

38. 1 Macc. 3:34-41.

39. 1 Macc. 3:42-60.

40. Num. 6:13-20.

time, and not of lifelong Nazirites.[41] In this passage the people named Nazirites, therefore, could include anyone who was willing to make a Nazirite vow for at least thirty days. This could be any Jew, including the Hasideans. The talmudic evidence does seem to record a tradition that the Hasideans did accept Nazirite vows.

B. Menaḥot 40b-41a

Some clarification of the status of *Ḥasydym Hari'shonym* with regard to the observance and enactment of the halakah is found in *B. Menaḥ.* 40b-41a. In 40b, we find a discussion of the requirements for carrying out the commandment to make *ṣyṣit* (fringes) as found in Num. 15:37-41 and Deut. 22:12. Citing earlier authorities Raba argues that if someone has inserted fringes in a three-sided garment and then adds to it a fourth corner with a fringe, he has not fulfilled the requirements for *ṣyṣit* because Deut. 22:12 says "Thou shalt make," and this does not include using that which is already made, i.e., the fringes in the original three-sided garment. Then the talmudic authorities raise an objection by quoting the following *barayta'*: חסידים הראשונים כיון שארגו בה ג' היו מטילין לה תכלה (The early Hasidim, when they had woven three [fingerbreadths], would insert the blue [fringes].)

On the following page, we find the same *barayta'* cited again, this time with a very interesting phrase attached: שאני חסידים דמחמרי אנפשייהו (it is different [for] the Hasidim imposed heavier obligations upon themsel-

[41]. *M. Nazir* 1:2, *B. Nazir* 4a; cf. Rothkopf, *EJ* 12:909; Rylaarsdam, *IDB* 3:527; M. Black, *The Scrolls and Christian Origins: Studies in the Jewish Background of the New Testament*, BJS 48 (Chico: Scholars Press, 1983-orig. 1961), 15-16.

ves). In this example, there is a dispute, and the talmudic authorities, just before citing the *barayta'*, ask the question, לימא מסייע ליה (Does this *barayta'* support it? [i.e., the opinion of the Amora just cited]). The answer is *sha'ney* (it is different). In other words, the example of the Hasidim cannot be used to settle a halakic discussion because their example is different; they live by different standards. Here we find stated explicitly what has been found to be implicit in the passages examined previously, that the early Hasidim were used as models of pious living and not as halakic authorities.

CONCLUSION

Certain conclusions concerning *Ḥasydym Hari'shonym* have already been suggested in the preceding discussion. The exemplary behavior of the group is held up at appropriate times by talmudic authorities, however they are not used as authorities in talmudic disputes. This casts grave doubt upon Safrai's theory that we find in the Hasidim a divergent halakic tradition. We also found that a talmudic discussion which included the early Hasidim provided the occasion for the insertion of stories about individuals each of whom were considered *ḥasyd* (pious).[42] In these stories, there is no suggestion that these persons were from the first Hasidim. If we take the word *ri'shon* at all seriously, then, as suggested by Safrai and Jacobs, the group with that adjective must precede the other persons who are called *ḥasyd* by the talmudic

42. The reference to the *me'arta' deḥasydey* (grotto of the pious) in *B. Mo'ed Qat.* 17a is probably to be understood in the context of this tradition even though its precise meaning is certainly not clear. In context, it is doubtful that it is a reference to a burial plot for the members of a party or sect who were called *Ḥasydym.*

authorities. In this case, it would seem that Jacobs is as correct in suggesting that these early Hasidim may go back to the group in the time of the Maccabees as Safrai is in his later date.[43] Rather than a divergent halakic tradition, it may be that we are speaking of the way of life of a group prior to the formation of the major halakic traditions.

This analysis of passages alluding to the early Hasidim has suggested that they may go back to the Hasidim of the Maccabean era. It has been demonstrated that other traditions concerning *ḥasyd* and *ḥasydym* were added to these citations in the process of the growth of the talmudic accounts. Clearly, this cursory investigation demonstrates the need for a more extensive study of these references in rabbinic literature. It has shown, however, where such a study could begin.

[43]. This earlier date makes it possible that Jose ben Joezer was one of the Hasidim, for *M. Hag.* 2:7 says that he was *ḥasyd shebakkehunah* (most pious in the priesthood). While in that mishnah he is called Joseph ben Joezer, Albeck (2:394) is surely correct in connecting him with Jose ben Joezer mentioned in *M. Ḥag.* 2:2 as one of the pairs also mentioned in *M. 'Abot* 1:4. This connection is denied by Safrai, *JJS* 16 (1965) 15, n. 8. In his note he fails to mention *M. Ḥag.* 2:2 which undoubtedly is the person referred to in *M. 'Abot* 1:4. Of course, any reference to an individual requires a more complete analysis before it is accepted. On Jose ben Joezer, see Büchler, *Piety*, 34-35.

VI

THE HASIDIM, THE PHARISEES

AND THE MACCABEES

We must now ask the question: How do the tentative conclusions drawn from an analysis of the passages concerning the early Hasidim relate to the major subject of this study, the Hasidim in 1 and 2 Maccabees? To answer this, we must first return briefly to 1 Maccabees. This work is usually thought to have been composed in the latter portion of the reign of John Hyrcanus (134-104 B.C.E.) or during the time of Alexander Jannaeus (103-76 B.C.E.).[1] There is no doubt that it was written from a Hasmonean viewpoint

[1]. J. Goldstein, *I Maccabees: A New Translation with Introduction and Commentary*, AB 41 (Garden City: Doubleday, 1976), 62-64; G. W. E. Nickelsburg, *Jewish Literature Between the Bible and the Mishnah* (Philadelphia: Fortress, 1981), 117; Harold W. Attridge, "Historiography," *Jewish Writings of the Second Temple Period: Apocrypha, Pseudepigrapha, Qumran Sectarian Writings, Philo, Josephus*, ed. Michael E. Stone, *CRINT* 2:2 (Assen: Van Gorcum/Philadelphia: Fortress Press, 1984), 171; id., "Jewish Historiography," *Early Judaism and its Modern Interpreters*, eds. Robert A. Kraft and George W. E. Nickelsburg (Atlanta: Scholars Press, 1986), 317.

and was intended to lend legitimacy and support to that dynasty.[2] This period is very significant for the present investigation.

When we turn to the account of the historian Josephus we find that he records an incident which led John Hyrcanus to switch his allegiance from the Pharisaic party to the Sadducees,[3] while a similar incident is attributed in the rabbinic tradition to Alexander Jannaeus.[4] Such a designation by the rabbis concerning the latter should come as no surprise since the Jewish historian also maintains that the Pharisees were quite strong throughout the reign of Alexander Jannaeus, who opposed them and considered them responsible for some of his difficulties.[5] As indirect substantiation

[2]. Goldstein, *I Maccabees*, 4-26, 64-78; Nickelsburg, *Jewish Literature*, 114-17; Attridge, *CRINT* 2:2:171-76; id., *Early Judaism*, 318.

[3]. *AJ* 13:288-96.

[4]. *B. Qidd.* 66a; *Schürer-Vermes-Millar*, 1:211-15, 221-24. *Schürer-Vermes-Millar*, 1:223, n. 16 suggests that while the story may not be historical, it does fit Hyrcanus better than Jannaeus and is indicative of the relationship during his reign. See also Jacob Neusner, *From Politics to Piety: The Emergence of Pharisaic Judaism* (Englewood Cliffs: Prentice-Hall, 1973), 57-60.

[5]. *BJ* 1:88-98; *AJ* 13: 372-73, 379-83, 401-04. While there is a great deal of recent debate on the nature of the Pharisaic movement during the first century C.E. and some disagreement among persons who attempted to discuss its origins, its political significance during the reign of these Hasmoneans has been widely accepted: Jacob Neusner, *The Rabbinic Traditions About the Pharisees Before 70* (Leiden: E. J. Brill, 1971), 3:304-306; id., *Politics*, 45-66, 146; Ellis Rivkin, *A Hidden Revolution* (Nashville: Abingdon, 1978), 31-

of the important role which they played during the reigns of these two Hasmonean rulers, we find it recorded that the Pharisees were embraced by Salome Alexandra (76-67 B.C.E.) and virtually ran the government during her reign.[6] We do, of course, have to remember that Josephus considered himself a Pharisee and may have overemphasized their influence.[7] What must be noted in this investigation is that the possible dates cited above for the composition of 1 Maccabees coincide with the period for which there is evidence of a considerable rift between the Pharisees and the Hasmoneans. The evidence from the reign of Salome Alexandra demonstrates that the Pharisees were a force to be

50, 211-45; Shaye J. D. Cohen, *From the Maccabees to the Mishnah*, Library of Early Christianity 7 (Philadelphia: Westminster, 1987), 144-46. Cohen (pp. 163-64), in a very brief critical appraisal of the political power of the Pharisees, does conclude that "we have no way of knowing whether it (the picture suggested by Josephus) is correct." In the context of his argument it appears to me that he is more interested in questioning the adequacy of our understanding of the nature of the Pharisaic beliefs at that time than debating the statements which claim that the Pharisees raised problems for some of the Hasmonean rulers. Gary G. Porton lists some of the options concerning Pharisaic origins which have appeared in recent literature: "Diversity in Postbiblical Judaism," *Early Judaism and its Modern Interpreters*, eds. Robert A. Kraft and George W. E. Nickelsburg (Atlanta: Scholars Press, 1986), 71.

[6]. *BJ* 1:110-14; *AJ* 13:405-15, 423. The claim for the influence of the Pharisees during her reign is independent of the debate concerning the relationship of the accounts in *BJ* and *AJ*: Morton Smith, "Palestinian Judaism in the First Century," *Israel: Its Role in Civilization*, ed. Moshe Davis (New York: Harper & Row, 1956), 75-76; Neusner, *Politics to Piety*, 48-65.

[7]. *V* 10-12.

reckoned with during the middle of the Hasmonean era; in other words, a rift with the Pharisees would have been of some consequence. What are the implications of this perception for our view of the Hasidim?

In our earlier discussion of 1 Maccabees, we reached certain conclusions about the Hasidim, as they are presented in that work.[8] We found them to be leading citizens of Israel, scribes who were devoted to the law. While in the early stages of the Maccabean revolt they were to be counted among the supporters of Judah and his brothers, after Alcimus appeared on the scene they naively expected to be able to negotiate with the Greeks because these foreigners had a leading Jewish figure with them. As we learn, that trust was misplaced and sixty of them were slaughtered. The Hasmonean historian was quite simply trying to discount the value of the Hasideans to Israel. They were too important to be ignored; the Hasmonean historian chose to depreciate their significance by portraying them as naive and unrealistic.

Given the history of the relationship sketched above, the Pharisees certainly emerge as the prime candidate for a group which a Hasmonean historian disliked and would have wanted to discredit. The Pharisees apparently did not view very favorably either the adventures in international warfare upon which Alexander Jannaeus embarked or his behavior as high priest, the religious leader of the nation.[9] While Josephus tells us considerably less about the nature of the dispute between the Pharisees and John Hyrcanus, the same

[8]. See Chapter 3 above.

[9]. *Schürer-Vermes-Millar*, 1:221-24.

issues seem to be present. Presumably, these Hasmoneans considered them to be unrealistic with regards to the future of the Jewish state in the turbulent world of the declining Seleucid Empire; certainly the Pharisees were opponents of their policies and power. The perspective which 1 Maccabees reflects concerning the Hasideans could very well be, and I suggest most likely is, that which a Hasmonean supporter would have had, or would have wanted to disseminate, of the Pharisees. There were however also other opinions of this group.[10]

In the earlier discussion of 2 Macc. 14:6 we found that the Hasideans were used in that work to augment the image of Judah as a figure of piety and purity. Its author employed the reputation of this group to enhance the image of the hero of his work, Judah Maccabee. Apparently this author regarded the Hasideans to be well-known, influential people, renowned for their piety and purity during the time of hellenization.[11] He must have considered them among the leading religious personalities of his era. Does this not sound similar to the picture of the early Hasidim found in talmudic literature? Even though we find no apparent link to the Pharisees, the brief glimpse of the Hasidim we get in this work does have some similarities to the picture developed from the First Book of Maccabees. Both works attest to the

[10]. Possibly, as suggested to me by Ben Zion Wacholder, we may also find references to these Hasidim in the liturgy. Examples would be the thirteenth benediction of the *Shemoneh 'eśreh* and the two additional prayers for Hannukah, *'al hannissym* (for the miracles) and *bymey Mattityahu* (in the days of Mattithias). See J. H. Hertz, *The Authorized Daily Prayer Book*, rev. ed. (New York: Bloch, 1948), 144, 150, 152.

[11]. See Chapter 3 above.

prominence and importance of this group's role in the events narrated. The difference between the two is that 2 Maccabees views this group favorably, using them to substantiate the image of Judah Maccabee, while the First Book wishes to negate their influence.

In the previous chapter it was suggested that the period of the early Hasidim may be the same as that of the Hasideans described in 1 and 2 Maccabees. A cursory examination of these literatures might suggest certain conflicts between the accounts. While it has been suggested that there may be a connection between the Hasideans and the Pharisees in 1 Maccabees, our brief analysis of the talmudic record suggested that the early Hasidim were not makers of halaka, as we expect the Pharisees were.[12] We found rather that they were used as models of pious behavior by the talmudic authorities. Their example is cited rather than their argumentation. This means that we cannot speak of these *Ḥasydym Hari'shonym* as representative of a halakic tradition different from that of the Pharisees or the Rabbis.[13] The talmudic literature gives no evidence of points of tension between the early Hasidim and the Rabbis.

Let us recall that nowhere in this study has it been argued that the Pharisees actually date from the time of the Maccabean revolt. It was rather proposed that the Hasmonean author of 1 Maccabees saw a connection between the two at the time he wrote his work. The most likely explanation for such a stance is that he believed the Pharisees arose from the Hasidim. If this is the case, then the spirit of Pharisaism

[12]. Rivkin, *Revolution*, 125-79; *Schürer-Vermes-Millar*, 2:384-403.

[13]. See Chapter 5 above.

would be rooted in the experience of the Hasideans or the early Hasidim, but the particular *halakot* which are distinctive of the Pharisees in rabbinic literature would originate at the time that the group by that name evolved.[14] We must bear in mind, however, that it was also argued earlier in this study that in 1 Maccabees 7 we find evidence linking the Hasideans to the scribes.[15] Clearly both the Pharisees and the early Hasidim are to be found in the scribal circles of early Judaism. This association will be discussed further below.

We have indicated that the rabbinic evidence concerning *Ḥasydym Hari'shonym* probably points back to the same people as those who were called *Asidaioi* in 1 and 2 Maccabees. Our cursory investigation of the talmudic evidence has demonstrated that these people were held up as examples of pious behavior by the Sages. We did not attempt to define more precisely the particular kind of piety which emerges from these passages. More study would be necessary to determine whether that is even possible. We did note that the Rabbis also referred to certain individuals as *ḥasyd* who were connected with the early Hasidim in talmudic literature. For example, in a number of instances we found a *ma'aśeh beḥasyd* (an incident concerning a pious person) which followed a reference to the early Hasidim. Certainly, more investigation of these stories which involve an anonymous

[14]. David Flusser mentions the similarity between the Hasidean and Pharisaic viewpoints, assuming that Pss. Sol. 17:18-20 is a reference to the former: "Psalms, Hymns and Prayers," *Jewish Writings of the Second Temple Period: Apocrypha, Pseudepigrapha, Qumran Sectarian Writings, Philo, Josephus*, ed. Michael Stone, *CRINT* 2:2 (Assen: Van Gorcum/Philadelphia: Fortress, 1984), 573.

[15]. See Chapter 3 above.

ḥasyd as well as of other incidents which concern named individuals who are referred to as *ḥasyd* is necessary to determine whether any of these accounts should be placed together with the passages about the early Hasidim. This would also be necessary for the limited number of places where *ḥasyd* is used in the plural but it is not accompanied by the adjective *ri'shon*. For the most part, such a study would demonstrate the growth of the use of the epithet from the original group which adopted that name. However, such a study would be inadequate if it did not also examine the possibility that later usage of the appellation may shed some light on its earlier significance.

In this study we also recognized that *ḥasyd* is a biblical term and that subsequent usages derive from its use in that literature. We realized that in the biblical texts, primarily in the Psalms, it is used as an adjective to describe people who behave in a certain manner. It is not a proper noun used to name a designated group of persons, as it is in 1 and 2 Maccabees. It was indicated that some persons in the second century B.C.E. or earlier adopted this biblical term as a name for themselves, possibly because they identified with the description of the persons called *ḥasyd* in the Psalms. While the occasion for the insertion of an incident about a *ḥasyd* into the rabbinic texts may be supplied by a citation of the example of the early Hasidim, it seems that the meaning of the term when it is applied to an individual is more closely paralleled by the manner in which it is used in the Hebrew Scriptures. In this case, it should not be considered a proper noun nor should the individual be reckoned a part of the group which existed at the time of the Maccabean revolt. But these passages merit more attention.

The picture of the Hasideans in 2 Maccabees bears some similarity to that of the early Hasidim drawn by the Rabbis. The use of the Hasideans as an example of piety and purity is common to both. It is clear that in both literatures they were viewed as having been an important group whose example bore some weight. An attestation to their importance as a group comes through more clearly in 2 Maccabees than in our study of the rabbinic texts, even though further study may show more clearly that the Rabbis considered them to be a major body in Jewish history and cited their example for that reason. Of course, the clearest attestation to the importance of this 'company' in Jewish society at the time of the Maccabean revolt comes from 1 Maccabees where these scribes are listed as being leading citizens of Israel.

In our study of 1 and 2 Maccabees, we argued that *Asidaioi* as a transliteration of the Hebrew *Ḥasydym* suggests that there was a group by this name in existence in the second century B.C.E. This evidence is not to be explained away as merely a mistake on the part of the translator of the Hebrew text of 1 Maccabees. What we did not deal with is the actual form of the transliteration and its significance. *Asidaioi* appears to reflect more accurately the Aramaic *ḥasydayya'* than the Hebrew *ḥasydym.* This is certainly one more piece of evidence for that argument which denies a direct connection between the Hasideans and Psalm 149 or any other biblical hymn. Does this apparently Aramaic form have other implications for our understanding of Judaism in the second century B.C.E.?

In our examination of the literature on the biblical materials, we accepted the argument of Sakenfeld that *ḥasydym* in the Hebrew Scriptures sometimes refers to all of Israel, sometimes to those upright Israelites who remain faithful to Yahweh and sometimes even to the priests.[16] In

[16]. See Chapter 1 above.

many cases faithfulness here means remaining true to the cult of Yahweh. The Hasmonean author of 1 Maccabees seems to have understood this since he uses terms with cultic associations to describe them in 2:42.[17] The question which arises is, What is the nature of the threat which called for this response of faithfulness and piety? We found that many studies consider the threat to have been the general encroachment of hellenism on Jewish life.[18] Many of these same works consider the Hasideans to encompass the entire Jewish resistance to hellenism or at least to comprise its leadership. We found no evidence to suggest that the Hasideans should be viewed as such a broad movement. The conflicts concerning the Hasideans seem to have a much narrower focus. From the author of 1 Maccabees, we learn that the Hasidim were advocates of *Torah* (law) and *beryt* (covenant) who opposed both the Jews who wanted to remove the marks of circumcision and make a covenant with the Gentiles, and the prohibition of the activities of the temple cult enacted by Antiochus IV. The concerns of the Hasideans in 1 Maccabees focus very particularly on law and covenant with the temple cult having a central spot. The major issue for this group as it is portrayed in 1 Maccabees is the decrees forbidding Jewish religious and temple practices. Is the concern about these prohibitions to be related to a hypothesis concerning the hellenization of the Jews? Assimilation and persecution certainly do not always go hand in hand.

In the discussion of the issue of the Hasideans and hellenization in second century B.C.E. Judaism, we often

[17]. See Chapter 3 above.

[18]. See Chapter 1 above.

find that this group is considered to be the author of a genre of resistance literature labeled apocalyptic. As already mentioned, in our analysis of 1 and 2 Maccabees we found no evidence for that connection. It has also been demonstrated that any identification of the Hasideans with those authors of a particular kind of apocalyptic literature who were known as Essenes is unwarranted. Nowhere have we found evidence which supports bringing the apocalyptic literature into a discussion of the Hasideans. This does not, of course, deny the possibility that the apocalyptic viewpoint is representative of a very specific body of Jews in Palestine prior to the Common Era. This simply means that we should not look to those people called the Hasidim to identify them.

An analysis of the texts in 1 Maccabees strongly suggests an identification of the Hasideans with the scribes. The immediate question which confronts the researcher is whether 'scribe' is too broad a designation to be at all meaningful. Further study of the scribes in third and second century B.C.E. Judaism may aid our understanding at this point. Given the description of the Hasideans in 2:42 which utilizes cultic terminology, it seems that a scribe something like the one described in Ben Sira may be where we should look for more information, since we also find in that work not only a commitment to, but a glorification of, the priesthood. The temple connection of the scribes called Hasideans may also explain their willingness to negotiate with Alcimus in 1 Maccabees. The argument in this study that the Hasideans of 1 Macc. 2:42 were "leading citizens from Israel" would certainly be true of the scribe in Ben Sira.

The identification of the Hasideans as a scribal group bears on the Pharisaic affiliation advanced in this inquiry. Some recent studies have questioned the connection between the scribes, also sometimes called Sages,[19] and the Pharisees.[20] The argument has been that purity and the resulting exclusive table fellowships were more adequate categories for understanding the nature of Pharisaism.[21] These studies, however, are based largely on attempts to describe this movement within the first century C.E. and are not an attempt to describe its origin. The present analysis of the evidence does not permit such a conclusion. While there is some indication of an interest in purity and the priestly connection provides a basis for it, the results of the present investigation also confirm the scribal character of the Pharisees and the significance of that categorization. Our identification of the Hasideans with the scribes raises one more problem for our study.

We find that apocalyptic literature as well as Pharisaism has a great interest in scribal activity. Enoch is referred to as a scribe in a number of instances.[22] The question is whether this negates our earlier denial of a connection be-

[19]. This is assumed by S. Safrai, "Jewish Self-government," *CRINT* 1:1:384 and in *Schürer-Vermes-Millar*, 2:389.

[20]. See the discussion in Michael J. Cook, "Jesus and the Pharisees--The Problem as it Stands Today," *JES* 15 (1978) 448-49.

[21]. Neusner, *Rabbinic Traditions About the Pharisees*, 3:304-06; id., *Politics to Piety*, 73-80, 82-90; Porton, "Diversity in Post-biblical Judaism," *Early Judaism*, 69-72; David L. Balch and John E. Stambaugh, *The New Testament in its Social Environment*, Library of Early Christianity 2 (Philadelphia: Westminster, 1986), 99-101; Cohen, *Maccabees to Mishnah*, 162.

[22]. Enoch 12:3,4; 15:1; Jub. 4:23.

tween the Hasidim and apocalyptic literature. I would suggest that this need not necessarily be the case. As already mentioned, there is certainly a need for a study of the scribe in the various literatures of Judaism from the time prior to the Common Era. I suspect that such an investigation would show differences in the meaning and use of 'scribe' between the various literary traditions. However, there may be one exception to this case. Harrington has aptly suggested that a good example of the scribe described in Ben Sira is Daniel, a pious Jew that observes the law who is also well-educated and influential in important circles.[23] This suggestion certainly merits further investigation. However, such a study may reveal differences between Daniel and other apocalyptic writings such as Enoch rather than result in a proposal which would place the scribe of Ben Sira in the apocalyptic camp. Further study of Daniel may well complement the present work.

Persons involved in the temple cult and in the scribal circles of third and second century B.C.E. Judaism found themselves in a situation where they identified with those persons who had been called *ḥasydym* in the biblical Psalms. These leading religious figures were committed to upholding the law and the covenant. Their outlook would have included an emphasis on the centrality of certain measures such as sabbath and circumcision which were stressed in the restoration after the exile. The centrality of the temple for Jewish life would have also been characteristic of these 'Pious'. The decrees of Antiochus IV would have provoked a strong response from this body of committed Jews; they would have leapt to the defense of their faith. They were also

[23]. Daniel J. Harrington, "The Wisdom of the Scribe According to Ben Sira," *Ideal Figures in Ancient Judaism*, eds. George W. E. Nickelsburg and John J. Collins, SBLSCS 12 (Chico: Scholars Press, 1980), 185.

concerned about the future of their fellow Jews, disagreeing with the Maccabees over the best way to secure a favorable outcome for the people Israel. This disagreement resulted in a less than favorable treatment of them in Hasmonean historiography. Their importance in Jewish society of the time, however, was not to be denied. It may well be that within these scribal circles of the Hasidim we find the origin of that later movement known as Pharisaism.

Bibliography

(Some additional items can be found in the list of abbreviations in the preface to this volume.)

Abel, F.-M. *Les Livres des Maccabées*. Etudes bibliques. Paris: Librairie Lecaffre, J. Gabalda et Cie, 1949.

Abel, F.-M. and J. Starcky. *Les Livres des Maccabées*. Paris: Les editions du Cerf, 1961.

Albeck, C. "Das Buch der Jubiläen und die Halacha." *BHWJ* 47 (1930): 3-60.

---. *Shishshah Sidrey Hammishnah*. 6 vols. Jerusalem: Bialik/Tel Aviv: Devir, 1957.

Attridge, H. W. "Historiography." *CRINT* 2:2:157-84.

---. "Josephus and His Works." *CRINT* 2:2:185-232.

---. *The Interpretation of Biblical History in the Antiquitates Judaicae of Flavius Josephus*. HDR 7. Missoula: Scholars Press, 1976.

Baer, I. F. "The Early Hasidim in the Writings of Philo and in the Hebrew Tradition." *Zion* 18 (1953) 91-108 (Hebrew).

---. "The Historical Foundations of the Halakah." *Zion* 17 (1952) 1-55 (Hebrew).

Balch, David L. and John E. Stambaugh. *The New Testament in its Social Environment*. Library of Early Christianity 2. Philadelphia: Westminster, 1986.

Barish, D. A. "The *Autobiography* of Josephus and the Hypothesis of a Second Edition of his *Antiquities*." *HTR* 71 (1978) 61-75.

Barnett, R. D. "Early Greek and Oriental Ivories." *JHS* 68 (1948) 1-25.

Bartelmus, R. *Heroentum in Israel und seiner Umwelt: eine traditionsgeschichtliche Untersuchung zu Gen. 6:1-4 und verwandten Texten in Alten Testament und der altorientalischen Literatur*. ATANT 65. Zurich: Theologischer Verlag, 1979.

Bauer, A. "Essener." PWSup 4:386-430.

Baumgarten, Albert I. "Josephus and Hippolytus on the Pharisees." *HUCA* 55 (1984) 1-25.

Baumgarten, Joseph M. "The Heavenly Tribunal and the Personification of *Ṣedeq* in Jewish Apocalyptic." *ANRW* II:19:1:219-39.

---. *Studies in Qumran Law*. SJLA 24. Leiden: E. J. Brill, 1977.

Berman, Dennis. "Hasidim in Rabbinic Traditions." *SBLSP* (1979): 2:15-33.

Bickermann, E. J. *Der Gott der Makkabäer: Untersuchungen über Sinn und Ursprung der Makkabäischer Erhebung*. Berlin: Schocken, 1937.

---. *The God of the Maccabees*. Trans. H. J. Moehring. Leiden: E. J. Brill, 1979.

Black, M. "The Account of the Essenes in Hippolytus and Josephus." In *The Background of the New Testament and its Echatology*. Eds. W. D. Davies and D. Daube, 172-75. Cambridge: University Press, 1956.

---. *The Scrolls and Christian Origins: Studies in the Jewish Background of the New Testament*. BJS 48. Chico: Scholars Press, 1983. Orig.-1961.

---, ed. *The Scrolls and Christianity*. London: SPCK, 1969.

---. "The Tradition of Hasidaean-Essene Asceticism: Its Origin and Influence." *Aspects du Judéo-Christianisme*, 19-35. Paris: Presses Universitaires de France, 1965.

Blau, J. *A Grammar of Biblical Hebrew*. Wiesbaden: Otto Harassowitz, 1976.

Blenkinsopp, J. "Interpretation and the Tendency to Sectarianism: An Aspect of Second Temple History." In *Jewish and Christian Self-Definition*. Ed. E. P. Sanders et al., 2:1-26. Philadelphia: Fortress Press, 1981.

Bloch, J. *On the Apocalyptic in Judaism*. Philadelphia: Dropsie College, 1952.

Bokser, Baruch M. "Ḥanina ben Dosa and the Lizard: The Treatment of Charismatic Figures in Rabbinic Literature." *Eighth World Congress of Jewish Studies*, 3:1-7. 1982.

---. "Wonder-working and the Rabbinic Tradition: The Case of Ḥanina ben Dosa." *JSJ* 16 (1985) 42-92.

Boling, R. G. *Judges: Introduction, Translation and Commentary.* AB 6A. Garden City, New York: Doubleday, 1975.

Bowen, B. A. "A Study of *Ḥesed.*" Ph.D. diss., Yale University, 1938.

Bright, J. *A History of Israel.* 2d ed. Philadelphia: Westminster, 1974.

Brownlee, W. H. *The Midrash Pesher of Habakkuk.* SBLMS 24. Missoula: Scholars Press, 1979.

Bruce, F. F. "The Book of Daniel and the Qumran Community." In *Neotestamentica et Semitica: studies in honor of Matthew Black.* Eds. E. E. Ellis and M. Wilcox, 221-35. Edinburgh: T & T Clark, 1969.

Büchler, A. *Types of Jewish Palestinian Piety from 70 B.C.E. to 70 C.E.: The Ancient Pious Men.* London: Jews' College, 1922. Reprint. New York: Ktav, 1968.

Bultmann, R. "*Eleos.*" *TDNT* 2:477-87.

Bunge, J. G. *Untersuchungen zum zweiten Makkabäerbuch: Quellenkritische, literarische, chonologische und historische Untersuchungen zum zweiten Makkabäerbuch als Quelle syrisch-palestinensischer Geschichte im 2. Jh. v. Chr.* Bonn: Rheinischen Friedrich-Wilhelms Universität, 1971.

Burgmann, H. "Ein Schaltmonat nach 24,5 Jahren im Chasidischen Sonnenkalendar?" *RevQ* 8 (1972): 65-73.

Burrows, M. *The Dead Sea Scrolls.* New York: Viking Press, 1955.

---. *More Light on the Dead Sea Scrolls.* New York: Viking Press, 1958.

---. *An Outline of Biblical Theology.* Philadelphia: Westminster, 1946.

Buttenweiser, M. *The Psalms: Chronologically treated with a new Translation.* 1938. Reprint. New York: Ktav, 1969.

Cantineau, J. "Tadmorea." *Syria* 14 (1933) 177.

Charles, R. H. *The Book of Jubilees.* London: A & C Black, 1902.

Cohen, Shaye J. D. *From the Maccabees to the Mishnah.* Library of Early Christianity 7. Philadelphia: Westminster, 1987.

---. *Josephus in Galilee and Rome: His Vita and Development as a Historian.* Leiden: E. J. Brill, 1979.

Collins, John J. *The Apocalyptic Imagination: An Introduction to the Jewish Matrix of Christianity*. New York: Crossroad, 1984.
---. *The Apocalyptic Vision of the Book of Daniel*. HSM 16. Missoula: Scholars Press, 1977.
---. *Daniel, First Maccabees, Second Maccabees: with an excursus on the Apocalyptic Genre*. OTM 15. Wilmington: Michael Glazier, 1981.
Colson, F. H. and G. H. Whitaker. *Philo*. LCL. 10 vols. and 2 suppl. London: William Heinemann/Cambridge: Harvard University Press, 1929-62.
Conzelmann, H. "*Charis*." *TDNT* 9:387-402.
Cook, Michael J. "Jesus and the Pharisees--The Problem as it Stands Today." *JES* 15 (1978) 448-49.
Coppens, J. "Les Psaumes des Hasidim." In *Mélanges bibliques: rédigés en l'honneur de André Robert*, 214-24. Paris: Bloud & Gay, 1955.
Cross, Frank Moore, Jr. *The Ancient Library of Qumran and Modern Biblical Studies*. Rev. ed. Garden City: Doubleday, 1961.
Curtis, E. L. and A. A. Madsen. *The Books of Chronicles*. ICC. New York: Charles Scribner's Sons, 1910.
Dahood, M. *Psalms*. Vol. 3. AB17a. Garden City, New York: Doubleday, 1970.
Dancy, J. C. *A Commentary on I Maccabees*. Oxford: Basil Blackwell, 1954.
Davies, P. "Ḥasidim in the Maccabean Period." *JJS* 28 (1977) 127-40.
Del Medico, H. E. "Une étymologie du nom des Esséniens." *ZRGG* 11 (1959) 269-72.
Derenbourg, J. *Essai sur l'histoire et la géographie de la Palestine d'apres les Thalmuds et les autres sources rabbiniques*. Vol. 1. Paris: Imprimerie Imperiale, 1867.
Dommershausen, W. *1 Makkabäer. 2 Makkabäer*. Die Neue Echter Bibel, Kommentar zum Alten Testament mit der Einheitsübersetzung, v. 12. Würzburg: Echter Verlag, 1985.
Doran, Robert. *Temple Progaganda: The Purpose and Character of 2 Maccabees*. CBQMS 12. Washington: Catholic Biblical Association, 1981.

Duhm, D. B. *Die Psalmen*. KHAT 14. Freiburg: J. C. B. Mohr, 1899.

Dupont-Sommer, A. *The Essene Writings from Qumran*. Trans. G. Vermes. Cleveland: World, 1962.

Eerdmans, B. D. "The Chasidim." *Oudtestamentische Studien*. 1 (1942) 176-257.

Eising, H. "*Ḥayil*." *TDOT* 4:348-55.

Eissfeldt, O. *The Old Testament: An Introduction*. Trans. P. R. Ackroyd. New York: Harper & Row, 1976.

Epstein, I., ed. *The Babylonian Talmud: Translated into English with Notes, Glossary and Indices*. London: Soncino, 1935-52.

Ettelson, H. W. "The Integrity of I Maccabees." *TCAAS* 27 (1925) 249-384.

Ewald, H. *Geschichte des Volkes Israel*. 3d ed. Göttingen: Dieterichschen Buchhandlung, 1864.

Falk, Z. "On the Mishnah of the Pious." In *Benjamin De Vries Memorial Volume*, 62-69 (Hebrew). Jerusalem: Tel Aviv University, 1968.

Farmer, W. R. "Hasideans." *IDB* 2:528.

Farnell, L. R. *The Cults of the Greek States*. New Rochelle: Caratzas Brothers, 1977.

Feldman, L. H. "Hengel's *Judaism and Hellenism* in Retrospect." *JBL* 96 (1977) 371-82.

---. "How Much Hellenism in Jewish Palestine." *HUCA* 57 (1986) 83-111.

---. *Josephus and Modern Scholarship (1937-1980)*. Berlin/New York: Walter de Gruyter, 1984.

Finkelstein, L. "The Book of Jubilees and the Rabbinic Halaka." *HTR* 16 (1923) 39-61.

---. "The Ethics of Anonymity Among the Pharisees." *Conservative Judaism* 12 (1958) 1-12. Also in *Pharisaism in the Making*, 187-98.

---. "The Maxim of the *Anshe Keneset Ha-Gedolah*." *JBL* 59 (1940) 455-69.

---. "The Origin of the Pharisees." *Conservative Judaism* 33 (1969) 25-36. Also in *Pharisaism in the Making*, 175-86.

---. *Pharisaism in the Making: Selected Essays*. New York: Ktav, 1972.

---. *The Pharisees and the Men of the Great Synagogue.* New York: Jewish Theological Seminary, 1950 (Hebrew).
---. *The Pharisees: The Sociological Background of their Faith.* Philadelphia: JPS, 1938.
Fiorenza, E. "Cultic Language in Qumran and in the NT." CBQ 38 (1976) 159-77.
Fitzgerald, A. "*MTNDBYM* in 1QS." *CBQ* 36 (1974) 495-502.
Flight, J. W. "The Nomadic Idea and Ideal in the Old Testament." *JBL* 42 (1923) 158-226.
Flusser, David. "Two Notes on the Midrash of 2 Sam. vii." *IEJ* 9 (1959) 99-109.
Foakes-Jackson, F. J. and K. Lake. *The Beginnings of Christianity.* Vol. 5. London: Macmillan & Co., 1933.
Förster, W. *From the Exile to Christ: a Historical Introduction to Palestinian Judaism.* Trans. G. E. Harris. Philadelphia: Fortress Press, 1964.
---. "Der Ursprung der Pharisäismus." *ZNW* 34 (1935) 35-51.
Frankel, Z. "Die Essäer. Eine Skizze." *ZRIJ* 3 (1846) 441-61.
---. "Die Essäer nach Talmudischen Quellen." *MGWJ* 2 (1853) 30-40, 61-73.
Frend, W. H. C. *Martyrdom and Persecution in the Early Church: A Study of a Conflict from the Maccabees to Donatus.* Oxford: Basil Blackwell, 1965.
Freyne, Sean. "The Charismatic." In *Ideal Figures in Ancient Judaism.* Eds., G. W. E. Nickelsburg and J. J. Collins, 223-58. SBLSCS 12. Chico: Scholars Press, 1980.
Frick, F. S. and E. G. Martin. "Rechabites." *IDBSup* 726-728.
Frick, F. S. "The Rechabites Reconsidered." *JBL* 90 (1971) 279-287.
Gärtner, Bertil. *The Temple and the Community in Qumran and the New Testament: A Comparative Study in the Temple Symbolism of the Qumran Texts and the New Testament.* Cambridge: University Press, 1965
Gaster, T. H. "Sacrifices." *IDB* 4: 151-52.
Geiger, A. "Die Essäer in der halachischen Literatur?" *JZWL* 9 (1871) 49-56.

---. *Urschrift und Übersetzungen der Bibel in ihrer Abhängigkeit von der inneren Entwicklung des Judenthums*. Breslau: J. Hainauer, 1857.

Geiger, Joseph. "The History of Judah Maccabaeus: One Aspect of Hellenistic Historiography." *Zion* 49 (1984) 1-8 (Hebrew).

Glueck, N. *Ḥesed in the Bible*. Trans. A. Gottschalk. Cincinnati: HUC, 1967.

Goldstein, J. A. *I Maccabees: A New Translation with Introduction and Commentary*. AB 41. Garden City, New York: Doubleday, 1976.

---. *II Maccabees: A New Translation with Introduction and Commentary*. AB 41a. Garden City, New York: Doubleday, 1983.

Good, R. M. *The Sheep of his Pasture: A Study of the Hebrew Noun ʻAm(m) and its Semitic Cognates*. HSM 29. Chico: Scholars Press, 1983.

Goranson, S. "'Essenes': Etymology from *ʻaśah*." *RevQ* 11 (1984) 483-98.

Graetz, H. *Geschichte der Juden von den ältesten Zeit bis auf die Gegenwart*. 4th ed. Leipzig: Oskar Leiner, 1888.

Gray, G. B. *Sacrifice in the Old Testament: Its Theory and Practice*. 1925. Reprint. New York: Ktav, 1971.

Green, William S. "Palestinian Holy Men: Charismatic Leadership and Rabbinic Tradition." *ANRW* II:19:2:619-47.

Grimm, C. L. W. *Kurzgefasstes exegetisches Handbuch zu den Apokryphen des Alten Testaments*. Leipzig: S. Hirzel, 1853.

Grintz, I. M. "'אנשי היחד'-איסיים-בית אסין." *Sinai* 32 (1952) 37-44.

Gulkowitsch, L. B. *Die Bildung des Begriffes Ḥāsīd*. Tartu: K. Mattiesens, 1935.

---. *Die Entwicklung des Begriffes Ḥāsīd in Alten Testament*. Tartu: K. Mattiesens, 1934.

Gunkel, Hermann. "Psalm 149." In *Oriental Studies dedicated to Paul Haupt*. Eds. C. Adler and A. Ember, 47-57. Baltimore: John Hopkins/Leipzig: J. C. Hinrichs'sche Buchhandlung, 1926.

---. *The Psalms: A Form-Critical Introduction*. Trans. T. M. Horner. FBBS 19. Philadelphia: Fortress, 1967.

Guthrie, W. K. C. *The Greeks and their Gods*. Boston: Beacon, 1955.

Habicht, C. *2. Makkabäerbuch.* JSHRZ 1:3. Gütersloh: Gerd Mohn, 1976.

Hanhart, R. *Maccabaeorum Liber II.* Septuaginta Vetus Testamentum Graecum. Vol. 9:2. Göttingen: Vandenhoeck & Ruprecht, 1959.

Harrington, D. J. "The Wisdom of the Scribe According to Ben Sira." In *Ideal Figures in Ancient Judaism.* Eds., G. W. E. Nickelsburg and J. J. Collins, 181-88. SBLSCS 12. Chico: Scholars Press, 1980.

Hartman, L. F. and A. A. DiLella. *The Book of Daniel: A New Translation with Introduction and Commentary.* AB 23. Garden City, New York: Doubleday, 1978.

Hauck, F. "*Hekousios.*" *TDNT* 2:470.

Head, B. V. *On the Chronological Sequence of the Coins of Ephesus.* London: Rollin and Feurdent, 1880.

Heaton, E. W. *The Book of Daniel: Introduction and Commentary.* London: SCM Press, 1956.

Hengel, M. *Judaism and Hellenism: Studies in their Encounter in Palestine during the Early Hellenistic Period.* Trans. J. Bowden. 2 vols. Philadelphia: Fortress Press, 1974.

Herberg, W. *Protestant-Catholic-Jew.* Garden City, New York: Doubleday, 1960.

Herr, M. D. "The Problem of War on the Sabbath in the Second Temple and the Talmudic Periods." *Tarbiẓ* 30 (1960-61) 242-56 (Hebrew).

Hertz, J. H. *The Authorized Daily Prayer Book.* Rev. ed. New York: Bloch, 1948.

Hicks, E. L. *The Collection of Ancient Greek Inscriptions in the British Museum.* Part. 3, Section 2, *Ephesos.* Oxford: Clarendon Press, 1890.

Hitzig, F. *Geschichte des Volkes Israel von Anbeginn bis zur Eroberung Masada's im Jahre 72 nach Christus.* Leipzig: S. Hirzel, 1869.

Hoelscher, G. *Die Quellen des Flavius Josephus für die Zeit vom Exil bis zum jüdischen Krieg* (Leipzig: B. G. Teubner, 1904).

Horovitz, H. and I. Rabin. *Mekylta' Derabbi Yshma'e'l.* Jerusalem: Wahrmann Books, 1970.

Jacob, E. *Theology of the Old Testament*. Trans. P. J. Alcock and A. W. Heathcote. New York: Harper & Row, 1958.

Jacobs, L. "The Concept of *Ḥasid* in the Biblical and Rabbinic Literatures." *JJS* 8 (1957) 143-54.

Jeremias, J. *Jerusalem in the time of Jesus: An Investigation into Economic and Social Conditions during the New Testament Period*. Trans. F. H. and C. H. Cave. Philadelphia: Fortress Press, 1975.

Johnson, A. R. "Ḥesed and Ḥâsîd." *Interpretationes ad Vetus Testamentum Pertinentes Sigmundo Mowinckel*. Oslo: Forlaget Land Og Kirke, 1955.

Johnson, B. "On Church and Sect." *ASR* 28 (1963) 539-49.

Jones, Allen H. *Essenes: The Elect of Israel and The Priests of Artemis*. Lanham/London: University Press of America, 1985.

Kahana, A. *Hassep̄arym Hahiṣonym*. 1936-37. Reprint. Jerusalem: Makor, 1970.

Kappler, W. *Maccabaeorum Liber I*. Septuaginta Vetus Testamentum Graecum. 2d ed. Vol. 9:1. Göttingen: Vandenhoeck & Ruprecht, 1967.

Kasowski, Chaim Josua. *'Oṣer Leshon Hattalmud*. 41 vols. Jerusalem: Department of History and Culture-Government of Israel and Jewish Theological Seminary, 1954-82.

Kee, H. C. *Community of the New Age: Studies in Mark's Gospel*. Philadelphia: Westminster, 1977.

Keil, C. F. *Commentar über die Bücher der Makkabäer*. Leipzig: Dörffling and Franck, 1875.

Keil, Joseph. *Forschungen in Ephesos*. Vol. 4:3. Vienna: Österreichischen Archäologischen Institut, 1951.

---. "Vorläufiger Bericht über die Ausgraben in Ephesos." *Jahreshefte des Österreichischen Archäologischen Institutes in Wien (Beiblatt)* 27 (1932) 5-72.

---. "Zur ephesischen *essēnia*." *Jahreshefte des Österreichischen Archäologischen Institutes in Wien (Beiblatt)* 36 (1946) 13-14.

Kohler, K. "Essenes." *JE* 5:225.

---. *The Origins of the Synagogue and the Church*. New York: Macmillan, 1929.

Kosmala, H. "*Gabar*." *TDOT* 2:373-77.

Kraeling, Carl H. *Gerasa: City of the Decapolis.* New Haven: ASOR, 1938.

Kraus, H.-J. *Psalmen.* BKAT 15. Neukirchen: Neukirchener Verlag, 1960.

Kuenen, A. *The Religion of Israel to the Fall of the Jewish State.* Trans. A. H. May. London: Williams and Northgate, 1875.

---. *Volksreligion und Weltreligion.* Berlin: G. Reimer, 1883.

Kuhn, K. G. et al. *Konkordanz zu den Qumrantexten.* Göttingen: Vandenhoeck & Ruprecht, 1960.

Laqueur, R. *Der jüdische Historiker Flavius Josephus: Ein biographischer Versuch auf neuer quellenkritischer Grundlage.* Giesen: Munchow'sche Verlagsbuchhandlung, 1920.

Lauer, M. *Die Essäer und ihr Verhältnis zur Synagogue und Kirche.* Vienna, 1869. Published separately from *Öestterreicher Vierteljahresschrift für katolische Theologie* 7 (1869) 489-562.

Lauterbach, Jacob Z., trans. *Mekilta de-Rabbi Ishmael.* 3 vols. Philadelphia: Jewish Publication Society, 1933.

Lebram, J. C. H. "Apokalyptic und Hellenismus im Buch Daniel." *VT* 20 (1970) 503-524.

Levine, B. A. "The Temple Scroll: Aspects of its Historical Provenance and Literary Character." *BASOR* 232 (Fall, 1978) 5-23.

Lightfoot, J. B. *Dissertations on the Apostolic Age.* London: MacMillan & Co., 1892.

---. *St. Paul's Epistles to the Colossians and Philemon.* Rev. ed. London: Macmillan & Co., 1904.

Lind, M. *Yahweh is a Warrior: The Theology of Warfare in Ancient Israel.* Scottdale: Herald Press, 1980.

Liver, J. "The 'Sons of Zadok the Priests' in the Dead Sea Sect." *RevQ* 6 (1967) 3-30 or *Eretz Israel* 8 (1967) 71-81 (Hebrew).

Lohse, E. *The New Testament Environment.* Trans. J. E. Steely. Nashville: Abingdon, 1976.

Maier, J. *Geschichte der jüdischen Religion: Von der Zeit Alexander des Grossen bis zur Aufklärung mit einem Ausblick auf das 19./20. Jahrhundert.* Berlin/New York: Walter de Gruyter, 1972.

--- and J. Schreiner. *Literatur und Religion des Frühjudentums: Eine Einführung.* Würzburg: Echter Verlag/Gütersloh: Gerd Mohn, 1973.

Mansoor, M. "Essenes." *EJ* 6:899-902.
---. "Hasideans." *EJ* 7:1468-69.
Martola, Nils. *Capture and Liberation: A Study in the Composition of the First Book of Maccabees.* Abo: Abo Akademi, 1984.
McCready, Wayne O. "A second Torah at Qumran?" *SR* 14 (1985) 5-15.
McKelvey, R. J. *The New Temple: The Church in the New Testament.* London: Oxford University Press, 1969.
McNicol, A. J. "The Eschatological Temple in the Qumran Pesher: 4Q Florilegium." *Ohio Journal of Religious Studies* 5 (1977) 133-41
Metzger, B. M. *An Introduction to the Apocrypha.* New York: Oxford, 1957.
Meyer, E. *Ursprung und Anfänge des Christentums.* Vol. 2. Stuttgart/Berlin: J. G. Cotta'sche Buchhandlung Nachfolger, 1921.
Meyer, R. "*Saddoukaios.*" *TDNT* 7:35-54.
---. *Tradition und Neuschöpfung im antiken Judentum: Dargestellt an der Geschichte des Pharisäismus* (Berlin: Akadamie Verlag, 1965.
Mielziner, M. *Introduction to the Talmud.* 5th ed. New York: Bloch, 1968.
Milgrom, Jacob. "The Temple Scroll," *BA* 41 (1978) 105-20.
Milik, J. T. *Ten Years of Discovery in the Wilderness of Judaea.* Trans. J. Strugnell. Naperville: Alec R. Allenson, 1959.
Millar, F. "The Background to the Maccabean Revolution: Reflections on Martins Hengel's 'Judaism and Hellenism'." *JJS* 29 (1978) 1-21.
---. *The Emperor in the Roman World: 31 BC - AD 337.* Ithaca: Cornell University, 1977.
Miltner, Franz. *Ephesos: Stadt der Artemis und des Johannes.* Vienna: Verlag Franz Deuticke, 1958.
Momigliano, A. "The Second Book of Maccabees." *Classical Philology* 70 (1975) 81-88.
Moore, George Foot. "Fate and Free Will in the Jewish Philosophies According to Josephus." *HTR* 22 (1929) 371-89.
Morgenstern, J. "The Hasidim-Who were they?" *HUCA* 38 (1967) 59-73.

Muraoka, Takamitsu. "'Essene' in the Septuagint." *RevQ* 8 (1973) 267-68

Murphy-O'Connor, J. "The Essenes and their History." *RB* 81 (1974) 215-44.

---. "La genése littéraire de la Régle de la Communauté." *RB* 76 (1969) 528-49.

Muth, R. "*Essēn.*" *Anzeiger für Altertumswissenschaft* 5 (1952) 61-64, 123-28.

Neuhaus, G. O. *Studien zu den poetischen Stücken im 1. Makkabäerbuch.* Würzburg: Echter Verlag, 1974.

Neusner, J. *Development of a Legend: Studies on the Traditions Concerning Yochanan ben Zakkai.* Leiden: E. J. Brill, 1970.

---. *From Politics to Piety: The Emergence of Pharisaic Judaism.* Englewood Cliffs: Prentice-Hall, 1973.

---. *The Rabbinic Traditions about the Pharisees before 70.* 3 vols. Leiden: E. J. Brill, 1971.

Newsom, Carol. *Songs of the Sabbath Sacrifice: A Critical Edition.* HSS. Atlanta: Scholars Press, 1985.

Nickelsburg, George W. E. and Robert A. Kraft, eds. *Early Judaism and its Modern Interpreters.* Atlanta: Scholars Press, 1986.

---. "The Epistle of Enoch and Qumran Literature." *JJS* 33 (1982) 333-48.

---. "1 and 2 Maccabees--Same Story, Different Meaning." *CTM* 42 (1971) 515-26.

---. *Jewish Literature Between the Bible and the Mishnah: A Historical and Literary Introduction.* Philadelphia: Fortress Press, 1981.

---. *Resurrection, Immortality and Eternal Life in Intertestamental Judaism.* HTS 26. Cambridge: Harvard University Press, 1972.

---. "Social Aspects of Palestinian Jewish Apocalypticism." In *Die Apocalyptik im Mittelmeerraum und im Vorderen Orient.* Ed. D. Hellholm, 641-54. Tübingen: J. C. B. Mohr/Paul Siebeck, 1983.

Niese, B. *Kritik der beiden Makkabäerbücher: Nebst Beiträgen zur Geschichte der makkabäischen Erhebung.* Berlin: Wiedmannsche Buchhandlung, 1900.

Nilsson, M. P. *Geschichte der griechischen Religion.* 2 vols. 2d ed. Munich: C. H. Beck'sche Verlagsbuchhandlung, 1961.

Noth, M. *The History of Israel.* 2d ed. New York: Harper and Row, 1960.

O'Dell, J. "The Religious Background of the Psalms of Solomon (Re-evaluated in the Light of the Qumran texts)." *RQ* 3 (1961) 241-57.

Oesterley, W. O. E. *The Psalms: Translated with Text-critical and Exegetical Notes.* London: SPCK, 1939.

Oikonomos, G. P. "*Naopoioi kai Essēnes*," *Archaiologikon Deltion* 7 (1921-22) 329-46.

Oppenheimer, Aharon. *The 'Am ha-Aretz: A Study in the Social History of the Jewish People in the Hellenistic-Roman Period.* Trans. I. H. Levine. Leiden: E. J. Brill, 1977.

Orlinsky, H. M. "Maccabees." *IDB* 3:197-201.

Peters, F. E. *The Harvest of Hellenism: A History of the Near East from Alexander the Great to the Triumph of Christianity.* New York: Simon and Schuster, 1970.

Pfeiffer, R. *History of New Testament Times: With an Introduction to the Apocrypha.* New York: Harper & Brothers, 1949.

---. *Religion in the Old Testament: The History of a Spiritual Triumph.* Ed. C. C. Forman. London: Adam & Charles Black, 1961.

Plöger, Otto. *Das Buch Daniel.* KAT 18. Gütersloh: Gütersloher Verlagshaus Gerd Mohn, 1965.

---. *Theocracy and Eschatology.* Trans. S. Rudman. Richmond, Virginia: John Knox Press, 1968.

Pope, M. H. "Rechab." *IDB* 4:14-16.

Porton, Gary G. "Diversity in Postbiblical Judaism." *Early Judaism and its Modern Interpreters.* Eds. Robert A. Kraft and George W. E. Nickelsburg, 57-80. Atlanta: Scholars Press, 1986.

Rabin, C. "Judges 5:2 and the 'Ideology' of Deborah's War." *JJS* 6 (1953) 125-34.

---. *Qumran Studies.* London: Oxford University Press, 1957.

Rabinowitz, L. "The First Essenes." *JSS* 4 (1960) 358-61.

Rainey, A. "Sacrifice." *EJ* 14:601.

Rajak, T. *Josephus: The Historian and His Society.* Philadelphia: Fortress Press, 1983.

Redekop, C. "A New Look at Sect Development." *JSSR* 13 (1974) 345-52.

Reicke, Bo. "Official and Pietistic Elements of Jewish Apocalypticism." *JBL* 79 (1960) 137-50.

---. *The New Testament Era: The World of the Bible from 500 B.C. to A.D. 100*. Trans. David E. Green. Philadelphia: Fortress, 1968.

Reid, S. B. "The Sociological Setting of the Historical Apocalypses of I Enoch and the Book of Daniel." Ph.D. dissertation, Emory University, 1981.

Ringgren, H. *The Faith of Qumran*. Philadelphia: Fortress, 1963.

---. "'*Ab*." *TDOT* 1:8-10.

Rivkin, E. *The Hidden Revolution*. Nashville: Abingdon, 1978.

Robert, J. and L. "Bulletin épigraphique." *REG* 95 (1982) 322-432.

Robert, L. "Bulletin épigraphique." *REG* 66 (1953) 113-212.

Rose, H. J. *Religion in Greece and Rome*. New York/Evanston: Harper & Row, 1959.

Rothkopf, A. "Nazirite." *EJ* 12:909-10.

Russell, D. S. *Apocalyptic: Ancient and Modern*. Philadelphia: Fortress Press, 1978.

---. *The Jews from Alexander to Herod*. London: Oxford, 1967.

---. *The Method and Message of Jewish Apocalyptic: 200 B.C.-A.D. 100*. Philadelphia: Westminster, 1964.

Rylaarsdam, J. C. "Nazirite." *IDB* 3:527.

Safrai, S. and M. Stern, eds. *The Jewish People in the First Century: Historical Geography, Political History, Social, Cultural and Religious Institutions*. *CRINT* 1:1-2. Assen: Van Gorcum/Philadelphia: Fortress Press, 1976.

---. "The Pharisees and the Hasidim." *Sidic* 10 (1977) 12-16.

---. "The Pious (*Hassidim*) and the Men of Deeds." *Zion* 50 (1985) 133-54 (Hebrew).

---. "The Synagogue." *CRINT* 1:2:908-44.

---. "The Synagogue and its Worship." *Society and Religion in the Second Temple Period*. Eds. Michael Avi-Yonah and Zvi Baras, 65-98. WHJP 8 (Jerusalem: Massada, 1977).

---. "Teaching of Pietists in Mishnaic Literature." *JJS* 16 (1965) 15-33.

Sakenfeld, K. D. *The Meaning of Hesed in the Hebrew Bible: A New Inquiry*. HSM 17. Missoula: Scholars Press, 1978.

Sanders, J. A. *The Psalms Scroll of Qumran Cave 11*. DJD 4. London: Oxford University, 1965.

Sandmel, Samuel. *Philo of Alexandria: An Introduction* (NewYork/ Oxford: Oxford University Press, 1979.

Sarfatti, G. B. "Pious Men, Men of Deeds, and the early Prophets." *Tarbiz* 26 (1956) 126-48 (Hebrew).

Schechter, Solomon. *Aspects of Rabbinic Theology: Major Concepts of the Talmud*. New York: Schocken, 1961-orig. 1909.

Schiffman, L. H. *The Halakhah at Qumran*. SJLA 16. Leiden: E. J. Brill, 1975.

---. *Sectarian Law in the Dead Sea Scrolls: Courts, Testimony and the Penal Code*. BJS 28. Chico: Scholars Press, 1983.

---. "The Temple Scroll in Literary and Philological Perspective." *Approaches to Ancient Judaism: Volume II*. Ed. W. S. Green, 143-58. Chico: Scholars Press, 1980.

Schloessinger, M. "Hasideans." *EJ* 6:250-51.

Schreiner, J. "Die Apokalyptische Bewegung." In *Literatur und Religion des Frühjudentums*. Eds. J. Maier and J. Schreiner, 214-53. Würzburg: Echter Verlag/Gütersloh: Gerd Mohn, 1973.

Schubert, K. *The Dead Sea Community--Its Origins and Teachings*. Trans. J. W. Doberstein. New York: Harper, 1959.

---. "A Divided Faith: Jewish Religious Parties and Sects." In *The Crucible of Christianity: Judaism, Hellenism and the Historical Background to the Christian Faith*. Ed. A. Toynbee. Cleveland/New York: World, 1969.

---. *Die jüdischen Religionsparteien in neutestamentlicher Zeit*. Stuttgart: Katholisches Bibelwerk, 1970.

---. "Das Zeitalter der Apokalyptic." *Bibel und zeitgemässer Glaube*, 1:265-85. Klosterneuberg: Klosterneuberger, 1965.

Schunk, K.-D. *1. Makkabäerbuch*. JSHRZ 1:4. Gütersloh: Gerd Mohn, 1980.

---. *Die Quellen des 1. und 2. Makkabäerbuches*. Halle: Veb Niemeyer Verlag, 1954.

Schürer, E. *Geschichte des jüdischen Volkes im Zeitalter Jesu Christi*. 4th ed. 3 vols. Leipzig: J. C. Hinrichs'sche Buchhandlung, 1901-09.

---. *The History of the Jewish People in the Age of Jesus Christ (175 B.C.-A.D. 135).* Rev. and ed. G. Vermes, F. Millar et al. 4 vols. Edinburgh: T & T Clark, 1973-87.

Schwartz, Daniel R. "Josephus and Nicolaus on the Pharisees." *JSJ* 14 (1983) 157-71.

---. "The Three Temples of 4Q Florilegium." *RevQ* 10 (1979) 83-91.

Sharvit, B. "Names of the Judean Desert Sect and its Designations." *Beyt Miqra'* 28 (1982-83) 134-39.

Sievers, J. "The Hasmoneans and their supporters from Mattathias to John Hyrcanus I." Ph.D. dissertation, Columbia, 1981.

Simon, M. *Jewish Sects at the time of Jesus.* Trans. J. H. Farley. Philadelphia: Fortress Press, 1967.

Singer, S. A. *The Hasid in Qumran and in the Talmud.* Wheeling, Ill.: Whitehall, 1974.

Smith, Morton. "The Description of the Essenes in Josephus and the Philosophumena." *HUCA* 29 (1958) 273-313.

---. "Palestinian Judaism in the First Century." *Israel: Its Role in Civilization.* Ed. Moshe Davis, 67-81. New York: Harper & Row, 1956.

Smith, W. F. "A Study of the Zadokite High Priesthood within the Graeco-Roman Age: From Simon the Just to the High Priests appointed by Herod the Great." Ph.D. dissertation, Harvard, 1961.

Sorg, D. R. *Hesed and Hasid in the Psalms.* St. Louis, Missouri: Pio Decima Press, 1953.

Steck, O. H. *Israel und das gewaltsame Geschick der Propheten: Untersuchungen zur Uberlieferung des deuteronomistischen Geschichtsbildes im Alten Testament, Spätjudentum und Urchristentum.* WMANT 23. Neukirchen-Vluyn: Neukirchen, 1967.

---. "Das Problem theologischer Strömmungen in nachexilischer Zeit." *EvT* 28 (1968) 445-58.

Stegemann, H. *Die Entstehung der Qumrangemeinde.* Bonn: Rheinische Friedrich-Wilhelms Universität, 1965.

Stern, Menahem. *Greek and Latin Authors on Jews and Judaism.* 2 vols. Jerusalem: Israel Academy of Sciences and Humanities, 1976-80.

---. "Nicolaus of Damascus as a Source of Jewish History in the Herodian and Hasmonean Age." in *Studies in Bible and Jewish History Dedicated to the Memory of Jacob Liver*. Ed. B. Uffenheimer (Tel Aviv: University of Tel Aviv, 1971), 375-89 (Hebrew).

Stoebe, H. J. "Die Bedeutung des Wortes Häsäd im Alten Testament." *VT* 2 (1952) 244-54.

Stone, M. E. "The Book of Enoch and Judaism in the Third Century B.C.E." *CBQ* 40 (1978) 479-92.

Stone, Michael E., ed. *Jewish Writings of the Second Temple Period: Apocrypha, Pseudepigrapha, Qumran Sectarian Writings, Philo, Josephus. CRINT* 2:2 (Assen: Van Gorcum/Philadelphia: Fortress, 1984).

Talmon, S. "The Desert Motif in the Bible and Qumran Literature." *Biblical Motifs: Origins and Transformation*. Ed. A. Altmann, 31-64. Cambridge: Harvard, 1966.

Tcherikover, V. *Hellenistic Civilization and the Jews*. Trans. S. Applebaum. Philadelphia: JPS, 1959.

Thackeray, H. St. J. *Josephus: The Man and the Historian*. 1929. Reprint. New York: Ktav, 1967.

---, Ralph Marcus, Allen Wikgren and Louis H. Feldman, trans. *Josephus*. LCL. 9 vols. London: William Heinemann/Cambridge: Harvard University Press, 1926-65.

Theissen, G. *Sociology of Early Palestinian Christianity*. Trans. J. Bowden. Philadelphia: Fortress Press, 1979.

Thoma, C. *A Christian Theology of Judaism*. Trans. H. Croner. New York: Paulist Press, 1980.

---. "Der Pharisäismus." In *Literatur und Religion des Frühjudentums: Eine Einführung*. Eds. J. Maier and J. Schreiner, 254-72. Würzburg: Echter Verlag/Gütersloh: Gütersloher Verlagshaus Gerd Mohn, 1973.

Thorion, Y. "Zur Bedeutung von *gibborey ḥayil lemilḥamah* in 11Q T LVII, 9." *RQ* 10 (1981) 597-98.

Troeltsch, E. *The Social Teachings of the Christian Churches*. London: Allen and Unwin, 1931.

Tsevat, M. *A Study of the Language of the Biblical Psalms*. JBLMS 9. Philadelphia: SBL, 1955.

VanderKam, J. C. *Textual and Historical Studies in the Book of Jubilees*. HSM 14. Missoula: Scholars Press, 1977.

Vaux, R. de. *Ancient Israel: Its Life and Institutions*. Trans. J. McHugh. New York: McGraw-Hill, 1961.

Vermes, G. *The Dead Sea Scrolls: Qumran in Perspective*. Philadelphia: Fortress Press, 1978.

---. "Ḥaninah ben Dosa: A Controversial Galilean Saint from the First Century of the Christian Era." *JJS* 23 (1972) 37-64.

---. *Jesus the Jew: A Historian's Reading of the Gospels*. London: Fontana/Collins, 1973.

---. *Post-Biblical Jewish Studies*. SJLA 8. Leiden: E. J. Brill, 1975.

Violette, J.-C. *Les Esséniens de Quomran*. Les portes de l'étrange. Paris: Editions Robert Laffont, 1983.

Wacholder, B. Z. *The Dawn of Qumran: The Sectarian Torah and the Teacher of Righteousness*. Cincinnati: HUC Press, 1983.

---. *Eupolemus: A Study of Judaeo-Greek Literature*. Cincinnati: HUC Press, 1974.

---. "The Letter from Judah Maccabee to Aristobulus: Is 2 Maccabees 1:10b-2:18 Authentic?" *HUCA* 69 (1978) 89-133.

---. *Nicolaus of Damascus*. UCPH 75. Berkeley/Los Angeles: University of California Press, 1962.

Wagner, S. *Die Essener in der wissenschaftlichen Diskussion: Vom Ausgang des 18. bis zum 20. Jahrhunderts--Eine wissenschaftsgeschichtliche Studien*. Berlin: Alfred Töpelmann, 1960.

Weinberg, J. P. "Das Bēit 'ĀB̲ŌT im 6.-4. Jh. v. u. Z." *VT* 23 (1973) 400-14.

Weiss, Isaac Hirsch. Dor Dor weDorshayw. Vol. 1. New York/ Berlin: Platt and Minkus, 1924-orig. 1871

Wellhausen, J. *Die Pharisäer und die Sadducäer: Eine Untersuchung zur inneren jüdischen Geschichte*. Greisswald: Bamberg, 1874.

Whitley, C. F. "The Semantic Range of *Ḥesed*." *Biblica* 62 (1981) 519-26.

Williamson, H. G. M. *1 and 2 Chronicles*. London: Marshall, Morgan & Scott/Grand Rapids: Eerdmans, 1982.

Wood, J. T. *Discoveries at Ephesus: Including the Site and Remains of the Great Temple of Diana.* London: Longmans, Green & Co., 1877.

Yadin, Yigael. "A Midrash on 2 Sam. vii and Ps. i-ii (4Q Florilegium)." *IEJ* 9 (1959) 95-98.

---. *The Temple Scroll.* 3 vols. and suppl. Jerusalem: Israel Exploration Society, 1983.

---. *The Temple Scroll: The Hidden Law of the Dead Sea Sect.* New York: Random House, 1985

Zeitlin, Solomon. "The Essenes and Messianic Expectations: A Historical Study of the Sects and Ideas during the Second Jewish Commonwealth." *JQR* 45 (1954) 83-119.

---. *The Rise and Fall of the Judaean State. A Political, Social and Religious History of the Second Jewish Commonwealth.* 3 vols. Philadelphia: JPS, 1968-78.

--- and Sidney Tedesche. *The First Book of Maccabees.* Jewish Apocryphal Literature, Dropsie College Edition. New York: Harper and Bros., 1950.

--- and ---. *The Second Book of Maccabees.* Jewish Apocryphal Literature, Dropsie College Edition. New York: Harper & Bros., 1954.

Zimmerli, W. "*Ḥesed* im Schrifttum von Qumran," *Hommages a André Dupont-Sommer.* Eds. A. Caquot and M. Philonenko. Paris: Librairie d'Amerique et d'Orient Adrien Maissoneuve, 1971.

---. "*Charis.*" *TDNT* 9: 376-87.